ADVERTISING IN CONTEMPORARY SOCIETY

2d Edition

ADVERTISING IN CONTEMPORARY SOCIETY

Perspectives Toward Understanding

KIM B. ROTZOLL
Head of the Department of Advertising
University of Illinois at Urbana-Champaign

JAMES E. HAEFNER
Associate Professor of Advertising
Director of Graduate Studies in Advertising
University of Illinois at Urbana-Champaign

Consulting Author:
CHARLES H. SANDAGE
Professor Emeritus of Advertising
University of Illinois at Urbana-Champaign

SJ70BA
PUBLISHED BY
SOUTH-WESTERN PUBLISHING CO.
CINCINNATI, OH   WEST CHICAGO, IL   DALLAS, TX   LIVERMORE, CA

Library of Congress Cataloging-in-Publication Data

Rotzoll, Kim B.
    Advertising in contemporary society : perspectives toward
understanding / Kim B. Rotzoll, James E. Haefner ; consulting
author, Charles H. Sandage. — 2nd ed.
       p.   cm.
    Includes index.
    ISBN 0-538-80594-3
    1. Advertising. I. Haefner, James E. II. Sandage, C. H.
(Charles Harold). III. Title.
HF5821.R67 1990
659.1'042—dc20   89-11394
                                            CIP

1 2 3 4 5 6 7 8 9 M 7 6 5 4 3 2 1 0 9

Printed in the United States of America

CONTENTS

◆

FOREWORD

"It appears to me," William Dean Howells said in 1893, "that our enterprising American advertising has about reached its limit."[1] Well, from the perspective of mid-1989, probably not.

Yet, advertising is a paradox. It is with us constantly, sometimes sought out, but generally unloved. It may be tolerated, but is rarely championed. It is the giver of jokes, and the target of them. It displays more about our more selfish, grasping natures than we find comforting to address as often as it relentlessly assures we must. The public's judgments of its ethical standards place it at or near the bottom of virtually any occupational array, while leading academics savage its social and cultural role. There is also no real shelter under the cloak of expertise. For all of us may realize that we couldn't write an acceptable news story, prescribe a drug, examine an optical system, design a house or bridge, or prepare a legal brief, but we're pretty certain *we* could come up with one of those catchy slogans, clever headlines, or arresting jingles.

All of this, of course, sometimes makes it difficult to take advertising seriously. Yet, an article in *The Chronicle of Higher Education* carried the headline, "Scholars sold on the Importance of Studying Advertising's History and Role in Society," with the author discussing six book-length treatments of advertising from communication scholars, historians, and a sociologist.[2] Even more recently, the *New York Times* devoted a half page to a story on "The Big Pitch for Old Ads," with the subheading, "More scholars mine Madison Avenue's past for clues on how the culture has changed."[3] Advertising may be unloved, but it would seem to be at least intriguing.

On a somewhat less lofty plane, T-shirts and everyday discourse attest to the advertising-spawned influences in our popular culture, and the much-publicized Yuppie life style would seem to embrace advertising's siren call with self-centered abandon. As columnist George Will observed, "A country which has the Great Lakes yet spends zillions for French water in little green bottles is probably ready for designer anti-freeze. Are you paying attention, Bill Blass?"

Well over a decade has passed since the first edition of our work with this title. And, as the brief sampling of diversities above suggests, advertising in contemporary society is still a crossroad where many interests meet, and, not infrequently, collide. Then, as now, we attempt to offer readers:

1. A basically *deductive approach* to the subject matter.
2. A source that attempts to raise provocative *questions* in a context that hopefully offers some overall understanding of their implications.
3. A basic *format* for the organization of a college-level or university-level course in the subject area.

When approaching this subject area, there is a great temptation to fill academic hours with yeasty discussions of timely topics likely to spur immediate student interest. Such potentially provocative subjects might include children and advertising; cigarettes, beer, sex and advertising (perennial favorites); and the elusive, advertising and the "quality of life."

For better or worse, we have avoided this *ad hoc* avenue of study. We first offer basic perspectives (Part I) that may be fruitfully brought to bear in an attempt to understand advertising, and only then turn our attention to issues of consequence (Part II) that seem likely to endure as long as the institution itself.

If there is a prevailing theme to the book, it is simply that how we as individuals think about things has a great deal to do with how we perceive them; how we act toward them; the kinds of "problems" that we define; and what we may consider appropriate "solutions."

Our former colleague Richard Nielsen once offered the tale of the three scholars shipwrecked on a desolate island with but a single can of beans. The chemist suggested, "We can build a fire, place the can in it, and the ensuing molecular activity will cause the can to rupture, thus freeing the contents." The engineer added, "If we constructed an enclosure from indigenous materials, we could contain the contents of the ruptured vessel." Their eyes turned to the economist, who said, "Assume we have a can opener. . . ."

Basically, the "assumptions" we make about what advertising *is* doing in society, as well as what it *ought* to be doing, are, we believe, crucial to understanding much about the defenses raised, charges aired, and practices endorsed or condemned.

This new edition maintains the thrust of its predecessor but is, we feel, conceptually richer and more ambitious in its sweep. Every word has been examined anew, and thousands have been altered or added. Specifically, there is a reconceptualization of "neo-liberalism" in Chapter 3. There is a considerably expanded discussion of the dimensions of the neo-liberal critique in both Chapter 3 and, with the addition of an examination of the "mirror" controversy via Richard Pollay and Morris Holbrook, in Chapter 4.

In Part 2, the chapter on advertising's economic dimensions is updated, with new studies brought to the discussion. Chapter 6, on audiences, offers new hierarchy models and many new references. Advertising and the media as a topic has added a mass communication theory dimension to its existing strengths in critical areas such as concentration and diversity. Chapter 8, on regulation is extensively updated, particularly in the areas of the FTC and deception, as well as the evolving activities of the National Advertising Review Board system. Advertising and its ethical dimension has been completely reconceptualized to reflect new thinking in this increasingly popular topic area.

We are, of course, indebted to many. Vince Norris first exposed Rotzoll to advertising's larger picture during provocative years at Penn State, and he has continued to serve as one of advertising's and advertising education's most arresting gadflies. Arnold Barban, now of Alabama, suggested the idea of a book, based on the structure of the University of Illinois' course by the same name.

Our colleague Charles Sandage has been elected to the Advertising Hall of Fame, the only modern-day educator so honored. It was clearly Sandy's farsighted principles-first approach to advertising education in general, and his Socratic probings with this subject area during his prolific teaching years at Illinois, that provided the true inspiration for this work. His insights, at 86, continue to work their way.

And a word of appreciation to countless colleagues who have, over the years, provided us with insights through their conversations, letters, and general probings in these interesting waters. Particular thanks here to Richard Pollay of the University of British Columbia and Gordon Miracle of Michigan State. Both offered valuable suggestions on the last edition which, we hope, they will find reflected in this work.

Since the earliest years of this endeavor the word processor may have replaced the typewriter, but the effort is still intense. Our thanks to Kathy Abbott and Mary Lowrey for that intensity and for their unflagging good spirits when other options might have seemed more apt.

Finally, Rotzoll has had the pleasure of teaching Advertising in Contemporary Society at Illinois for the last 18 years. To all the students from whom I have learned so much, my thanks. The torch is passed.

Urbana, Illinois
March 1989

ENDNOTES

1. Stephen Fox, *The Mirror Makers* (New York: Vintage Books, 1984), p. 39.
2. "Scholars Sold on the Importance of Studying Advertising's History and Role in Society," *Chronicle of Higher Education,* October 3, 1984.
3. Randall Rothenberg, *The New York Times,* October 9, 1988.

PART 1

◆

BASIC
PERSPECTIVES

1
INTRODUCTION: TOOLS TO "CLEAR THE DEADWOOD"

The late Howard Gossage, a member of the Copywriters Hall of Fame and resident critic of the business, once served a stint as a Visiting Professor of Advertising at Penn State. Reflecting on the experience, he observed:

> In my lecturing I find I must spend about half my time clearing away the deadwood before I can begin to talk constructively about advertising and what it can do and occasionally does do.[1]

Students and teachers of advertising can probably be sympathetic. Simply, advertising in America comes with a great deal of baggage, which often gets in the way of any reasonably dispassionate attempt to understand the subject. As we will attempt to make clear, some of this baggage comes with each of us—i.e., we each "see with our ideas as well as our eyes," to borrow Walton Hamilton's wonderful phrase[2]—while some baggage is simply inherent in the complexity of the business and its processes.

We all know advertising very well—often *too* well—in part because we are exposed to so much of it and also because its simpleminded content gives us a feeling of understanding (and superiority). As a result, we find it easy to generalize. Thus, it is tempting to fall into statements such as "Advertising does . . ." and "All ads are. . . ." (For example, a recent article in *TV Guide* warned, "Madison Avenue Has a New Bag of Tricks to Keep Viewers from Turning Off its Ads"; while, a seasoned advertising executive stated baldly, "Advertising follows, it doesn't lead.") So much for caution in murky waters. Such thinking deadens analysis, cheapening the subject and the observer alike.

The purpose of this chapter then, is to share with you four premises that we have found quite useful in preparing this fascinating topic for meaningful discussion. Simply, if we keep these four ideas in mind from the outset, advertising in contemporary society is more likely to be illuminated by the light of analysis rather than the fires of rhetoric. These premises are:

2

1. Advertising must be considered in light of cultural expectations.
2. The advertising process has varied intents and effects.
3. Advertising's actual effects are usually not clearly known.
4. Because of its cultural boundness, its complexity of forms and functions, and the difficulty in ascertaining its outcome, advertising is highly prone to disparate interpretations.

ADVERTISING MUST BE CONSIDERED IN LIGHT OF CULTURAL EXPECTATIONS

Advertising Age recently reported that in 1986 the United States spent more money on advertising than 66 other nations combined, including Japan, the U.K., West Germany, Canada, and France.[3] One might pause to wonder why our young nation should assume such leadership and why first-time visitors to this country are often stunned by the sheer presence of advertising in virtually every facet of our lives—a presence many of us accept as simply "world taken for granted."

Two authors of important books on American advertising—one an historian, the other a sociologist—offer us clues, with these observations about the wellsprings of advertising in America:

Stephen Fox:

One may build a compelling case that American culture is—beyond redemption—money mad, hedonistic, superficial, rushing heedlessly down a railroad track called Progress. De Tocqueville and other observers of the young republic describe America in these terms in the early 1800s, decades before the development of national advertising.[4]

And Michael Schudson:

We live and shall live, barring nuclear or other disaster, in what has been called a "promotional culture." America has long been a nation of salesmen and the "shoeshine and a smile" that were Willy Loman's stock-in-trade are now the tools of politicians and religious evangelists and hospital administrators as much as of advertising agents and public-relations directors. The promotional culture has worked its way into what we read, what we care about, the ways we raise our children, our ideas of right and wrong conduct, our attribution of significance to "image" in both public and private life. The promotional culture has been celebrated and indulged in. It has been ridiculed and reviled. It still needs to be understood.[5]

Given these deeply rooted values in our society, it is not difficult to understand how advertising could seem so "natural" to us. It would seem, then, that an important first step to be taken in coming to grips with advertising in contemporary society is to grasp what, generally, the society expects of it; or, as Walton Hamilton puts it, "that body of ideas taken for granted which is called common sense."[6]

In this society, these ideas have generally included at least a toleration (and sometimes admiration) of *persuasion,* based on such well-worn assumptions as self-interest as a driving force of human action, the ability of the individual to be "deliberate and calculating" in pursuit of that self-interest, and the implicit expectation that the self-interested actions of individuals will ultimately work themselves out for the good of the whole. (Contrast this, for example, with the cultural expectations in many socialist countries, where government policy specifically holds that the purpose of advertising is first to serve the good of the *society,* not the individual advertiser.)

Now, most Americans feel quite at home with these notions of self-interest and the assumed rationality of the consumer. And these "understandings" that we carry with us have strong influence on our perceptions of the world around us, often without conscious thought. Consider, for example, how easily we accept not only the enormous presence of advertising in our mass media, but also in/around/above our athletic stadiums, on our clothing, beside our roadways, in our motion picture theatres, and so forth. Somehow, it all seems "natural," and it is important that we keep in mind this relationship between expectations and reality.

For much of advertising in contemporary society can be understood with greater clarity if we realize that, as Carey expressed it, "institutions are the embodiment of ideas."[7] And from the beginning, we need to understand what these ideas, these expectations, are. Certainly they differ from culture to culture and even, as we shall see, *within* a culture. Now, what else do we need to keep in mind to "clear the deadwood"?

THE ADVERTISING PROCESS HAS VARIED INTENTS AND EFFECTS

In addition to understanding the ideas with which we "see" advertising, we next have to keep in mind that the advertising that we normally experience is only a fraction of all the advertising going on. And, all too frequently, we tend to generalize from our relatively limited experience to the whole. Consider, for example, that while you read these pages, *at least* the following advertising activities are under way:

◆   *Producers* (singly or in association, national or regional) of consumer goods and/or services are advertising to reach individual consumers through radio, television, magazines, newspapers, billboards, direct mail, transit, and other media to encourage sales of a branded product or service. (An ad for a soft drink on network television is an example.)

◆ *Producers* (singly or in association, national or regional) of consumer goods and/or services for *resale* are advertising to reach retailers and wholesalers through trade magazines, newsletters, and direct mail to encourage retailers and wholesalers to stock and/or promote the product or service to their customers. (An ad for a brand of flea collar in *Pet Store Owner* is an example.)

◆ *Producers* (singly or in association, national or regional) of consumer and/or business goods and/or services are advertising to reach individual consumers, government, social institutions, groups, and their own employees through consumer and business print and broadcast media to influence favorable thinking and possible action among key publics concerning *public relations*. (An oil company advertising in the *New York Times* to boast of their conservation efforts is an example.)

◆ *Producers* (singly or in association) of consumer and/or business goods and/or services are advertising to reach other producers, retailers and wholesalers, government, social institutions, and groups through business magazines and newsletters, direct mail, and some consumer media to encourage sales for a particular *business* product and/or service for use and/or recommendation. (A manufacturer of oil drilling bits advertising in *Oil and Gas Journal* is an example.)

◆ *Producers* (singly or in association) of consumer and/or business goods and/or services in *international* distribution are advertising to reach individual consumers, retailers, other businesses, governments, social institutions, and groups through consumer and business media in other countries to encourage specific purchase, to influence key publics, and to foster retail distribution. (An American fast-food franchise advertising in German newspapers and a Russian vodka company advertising in American magazines are examples.)

◆ *Retailers* (singly or in association) of goods and/or services are advertising to reach individual consumers through local newspapers, radio, television, magazines, billboards, transit, and direct mail to encourage purchase of particular items and/or services. (A supermarket ad is an example.)

◆ *Individual citizens* are advertising to reach other individuals, primarily through local newspapers (classified), posters, and CATV to encourage purchase of a particular item(s) and/or services. (A student advertising to sell a bike in the campus newspaper is an example.)

◆ *Governments, social institutions, and groups* are advertising to reach individual consumers, government bodies, groups, and associations through consumer and specialized media to encourage belief in particular practices, to alter behavior in socially desirable ways, and to seek political ends, as well as to "sell." (The Save the Children Foundation seeking donations in a magazine ad is an example.)

There is much to be learned from these numerous advertising activities, particularly in the clearing-the-deadwood sense. Simply, when we begin to discuss advertising with others, there is a strong pull to have the common denominator become *television* advertising, and that in a rather generic sense. Yet, as we all know, and the above listing clarifies, there is much more under the advertising banner. Are critics, for example, as concerned about the advertising of the "Great Book Series" in the *New Yorker* as the 30-second minidrama concerning sanitary napkins in late prime time? Are supporters of advertising as willing to defend advertising as the consumer's best friend when confronted with a simpleminded jingle for toothpaste rather than a supermarket's weekly shopping agenda, or a fact-laden message on business equipment?

And do all advertisers use advertising with identical expectations? Most, of course, are ultimately interested in altering behavior in some way—for instance, selling more of a product—but even here advertisers may have different communication aspirations in terms of establishing awareness, or communicating new selling information, or reinforcing or attempting to alter attitudes.

Then, there are the factors relating advertising to other tools of marketing. Clearly, for example, the expected contribution of Avon's advertising (to reinforce personal selling efforts) is quite different than that of Revlon's (to presell for sales in traditional retail outlets). Not infrequently, there are also intents that are anything but obvious to the outside observer. For example, a marketing manager of a large urban hospital recently confided, "I'm certain that at least two important groups read our ads—our employees and our competitors. If the ads do nothing more than influence them they'll have paid their way." Yet, if we were asked to assess whether this hospital's advertisements were "effective," we would probably have assumed they were directed to potential patients and make our judgments accordingly.

Thus, to evaluate an advertisement, it would seem prudent to at least attempt to understand the advertiser's intent. Due to the presence of myriad agendas—some more apparent than others—even that may not be as simple as we might expect.

Nor, of course, is the *individual's* response. A headline for a recent advertisement from the American Association of Advertising Agencies stated, "Isn't it Funny How Stereo Ads are Boring Until You Want a Stereo?" A reasonable point, although far more applicable to media to which we control exposure (magazines, newspapers) than others (television, billboards). We do, of course, selectively perceive advertisements, as we do other items in our environment. Howard Gossage frequently observed that, "Nobody reads ads *per se*. People read what interests them, and sometimes it's an ad."[8] One could, then, assume that as media become more specialized the irritation factor of advertising will diminish. Thus, an individual watching a cable sports channel or another reading *Modern Maturity* magazine may be more likely to find the respective advertisements of interest than the same persons watching the unpredictable commercial mix on prime-time network television.

We all know, of course, that much of the time advertising seeks *us* rather than the other way around. And our responses to these often unintended encounters can range from surprise, amusement, and interest, to irritation, disgust, and apathy.

There are, then, many different advertisers using advertising for many different purposes with many different possible reactions from those exposed, much less those missed. All of which would seem to reinforce the folly of "Advertising does . . ." thinking.

ADVERTISING'S ACTUAL EFFECTS ARE USUALLY NOT CLEARLY KNOWN

Commenting on advertising's presumed cultural impact, historian Stephen Fox observed:

> Outsiders see only the smooth, expertly contrived finished product, often better crafted than the programming and editorial material it interrupts. Insiders know the messy process of creating an ad, the false starts, rejected ideas, midnight despair, the failures and account losses and creative angst behind any ad that finally appears.[9]

If one were to harbor any illusions about the omnipotence of the advertising process in the hands of steely eyed technicians of communication, Fox's observation should give us pause. Then, television critic Michael Arlen's engrossing account of the creative odyssey of a single AT&T advertisement, *Thirty Seconds,*[10] and John Pfeiffer's disbelieving description of the creation of two Rolaids commercials,[11] should turn us into card-carrying skeptics.

Simply, advertising is still far more art than science, and advertisers are not nearly as powerful as they would like to be. There are, we believe, two central reasons:

1. *It is difficult to determine advertising's effect in relation to other possible influences on the same outcome.*

    Most advertisers, most of the time, are interested in affecting behavior with their messages. But they are also interested in affecting behavior with their pricing strategy, sales promotional efforts, sales force deployment, packaging, and so on. (In his 1984 work, Schudson reported that, on the average, advertising through the mass media represents only about 20 percent of all selling costs—the rest going to sales promotion and personal selling.[12] Four years later, *Advertising Age* columnist Sidney Bernstein commented, "[advertising] is now falling into its place on the marketing team, sometimes leading the parade but sometimes playing only a supporting role."[13]) It is, of course, difficult to determine which part (if any) of the behavior change (if any) belongs to advertising, and which to all of these other factors controlled by the advertiser attempting to achieve the same end.

Then there are those factors the advertiser *cannot* control. Start with the fickle fads and fancies of the public, currently embracing such socio-pop phenomena as wellness, cocooning, grazing, "safe" sex, and a generalized return to tradition. Add the often vexing unknowns of the weather, for example, or the competition. Or consider the impact of the state of the economy, the regulatory/antiregulatory mood in Washington or in the state capitols, breakthroughs in technology, and on and on. These and many other such factors influence the outcome, and are the "givens" that firms may attempt to alter but must inevitably accommodate. With the notable exception of direct-response advertising, and a few other forms with an extremely tight advertising-action loop, advertising's workings with and against these forces are often more acts of faith than the workings of any marketing science. (Commenting on the enormously expensive Pepsi campaign featuring megastar Michael Jackson, a veteran advertising columnist stated off-handedly, "There's no way of saying precisely what all this means to Pepsi-Cola."[14])

2. *It is difficult to determine advertising's actual effects because of the quixotic nature of human thought and behavior.*

It is entirely possible, of course, to have behavior (sales) without advertising. Without scratching the surface, Schudson mentions marijuana and cocaine, scholarly books, racehorses, sailboats, historical romance paperbacks, and even the early years of the Volkswagen bug. On the advertising-without-sales docket, Schudson finds that perennial favorite the Edsel, Lady Gillette, the still struggling Pringle's, men's hats, (let's add the IBM PC Jr.), all played against oft-quoted statistics of the percentage of new product failures ranging from 23 to 80%.[15]

Human beings are, to quote one practitioner, "no damned good" when it comes to always behaving according to plan. A creative chief at an enormously sophisticated advertising agency recently admitted with a shrug that a two-year multimillion-dollar campaign for a popular soft drink was simply "wrong," even though they had every reason to believe they were "right on target" going in.

Advertising's elusive target is, of course, the individual. And since most of us are not certain of our own behavioral intentions from one moment to the next, the chances of an outside observer being able to figure us out in advance are, to be charitable, problematic. Now, if we conceive of the forces at work to influence an individual's observed behavior at any given moment as constituting a "frame of reference," we must realize that the interaction of factors outside of ourselves (e.g., the presence or absence of other people, the physical environment, etc.) and those inside ourselves (e.g., our moods, past experiences, current knowledge, physiological state, etc.) *changes from moment to moment.*[16] To return to the earlier example, we may not be interested in that stereo ad at the moment, but tomorrow, or even later in the day . . . .

Given this backcloth of uncertainty, then, much can be understood about advertising thought and practice—some trivial, some of considerable consequence.

◆ For example, the longevity of the commission system of agency remuneration. Given any adequate measure of performance in the marketplace, advertisers would compensate their agencies on the basis of their proven successes on the advertiser's behalf. Lacking that, they frequently rely on a system that rewards the agency not for how well its products (ads) perform, but for how much of the advertiser's money it spends. ("You show me a business," Gossage commented, "where one's income is dependent on the amount of money spent rather than on the amount of money that comes in and I will show you a business that is doomed, even with the very best of intentions, to mutual distrust and enormous psychological barriers.")[17]

◆ For example, the "me-too" nature of much advertising content. If practitioners are frequently uncertain what will "work" with their ads, they may be inclined to imitate those that presumably do. Just think of the countless imitators of the "MTV style," or the use of the hand-held camera with quick/jumpy cuts, or the use of nighttime urban settings—frequently with rain-dampened, reflective streets—or the many imitators of the Apple advertising with its blend of simplicity and starkness, or . . . fill in your own examples.

◆ For example, the lack of true "professionalism" in the business. Here the wife of the vice president scuttles an advertising campaign because she doesn't like the "look" of the female model. There an account executive is browbeaten by an advertising manager about the failure of the agency to come up with some "new, creative ideas." Or witness the pomp and circumstance of the "Clio" awards midst black ties and Lincoln Center with giant screens for the embellishment of thirty-second color commercials, now transformed from uncertain exercises in persuasive communication to art forms. (The J. Walter Thompson agency, having lost the giant Burger King account, ran a farewell ad in *Advertising Age* with a graph showing that Burger King's sales had increased 145% since coming with the agency. *Sic transit gloria.*)[18]

If we are to begin to understand advertising in contemporary society, then, it is essential that we constantly keep in mind the frequent uncertainty of the process—and the far-reaching consequences.

BECAUSE OF ITS CULTURAL BOUNDNESS, ITS COMPLEXITY OF FORMS AND FUNCTIONS, AND THE DIFFICULTY IN ASCERTAINING ITS OUTCOME, ADVERTISING IS HIGHLY PRONE TO DISPARATE INTERPRETATIONS

Psychologists tell us that ongoing psychological activity tends toward *patterning* of experience—i.e., looking for patterns rather than being satisfied with randomness. Now, sometimes the pattern is found in the subject itself—e.g., a picture of a cube—and requires little additional structuring from our own experiences. But when the external phenomenon is fluid, ambiguous, lacking in clear definition—e.g., an inkblot—we often supply the patterning. This is, of course, the basis for a great deal of psychological testing. Ask people what they "see" in a Picasso painting, and there will probably be as many different interpretations as there are people; ask the same people what they "see" in one of Rembrandt's masterworks, and there will be general agreement that it's a "man in a gold helmet."

Now, given the complexity and unpredictability of advertising asserted in the three preceding premises, it can be contended that advertising in contemporary society is highly susceptible to differing interpretations because of its complexity, fluidity, lack of clear outcome, etc. That is, it's much more like an inkblot than a cube, more a Picasso than a Rembrandt. To follow this reasoning, then, *much of what is seen in advertising depends on who's looking and where.*

To note the obvious, critics "see" advertising very differently than do supporters. For them, the reality is very clearly patterned as exploitation of a frequently hapless (and possibly helpless) public by advertisements that intrude, debase the language and our symbolic life, and appeal to our worst rather than best characteristics. Supporters, observing the same spectrum, "see" advertising joining the self-interests of sellers with the self-interests of savvy customers to their mutual satisfactions with advertisements that faithfully mirror the totality (rational *and* emotional) of the human condition. These strikingly different perceptions can be explained in part by the past experiences, values, and current aspirations of the observers. Argue though they may, they're simply not likely to "see" advertising the same way.

There is also the very real possibility that discussants may simply be observing *different parts of the whole.* As we know, business-to-business advertising, for example, is quite different in purpose, content, and media form than most "consumer" advertising directed to individuals. Even within a type (say, retail advertising), one can come to quite different conclusions because all retailers do not have similar intents with their advertising, nor are they likely to have similar effects. So if we are using a particular type of advertising as our reference point, we may come to very different conclusions, regardless of our predispositions, than if we were looking elsewhere.

So, to begin to clear away the deadwood in any discussion of advertising, it would seem prudent to *at least* determine what the culture expects of advertising and to recognize that it presents itself in many different forms for many different purposes. Further, we need to recognize that the determination of the success of those efforts is, under the best of conditions, obscure; and finally, because of all these conditions, we need to be clear about who's looking (what his or her assumptions are) and where (at what form or forms).

SUMMARY

"Advertisements" are bits and pieces of reality. "Advertising" is an abstraction from these elements, and much more. At the outset of our approach to advertising in contemporary society we suggest four premises to begin a serious look at advertising. They are:

1. *Advertising must be considered in light of cultural expectations.* Advertising can play different roles in different societies, depending on the set of assumptions held about such fundamental matters as the relationship between individual and societal interests.
2. *The advertising process has varied intents and effects.* There are many different types of advertisers using advertising for a variety of different purposes, arguing against the common tendency to generalize to the "All advertising . . ." level.
3. *Advertising's actual effects are usually not clearly known.* Most advertisers are interested in affecting behavior—usually sales. But because advertising is affected by societal forces and is only one factor in the firm's marketing options, and because individuals' reactions to advertisements are inherently complex and unpredictable, simple cause-and-effect conclusions are elusive.
4. *Because of its cultural boundness, its complexity of forms and functions, and the difficulty in ascertaining its outcome, advertising is highly prone to disparate interpretations.* Advertising can be loosely compared to the inkblot, with patterning through perceptions affected by who is doing the observing and where in its complex overall structure one chooses to look.

These are, we feel, necessary reference points as we begin to probe this fascinating subject—advertising and advertisements—which Daniel Boorstin has called "the characteristic rhetoric of democracy."[19]

ENDNOTES

1. Howard Luck Gossage, *Is There Any Hope for Advertising?* Kim Rotzoll, Jarlath Graham, and Barrows Mussey, eds. (Urbana, IL: University of Illinois, 1986), p. 18.
2. Walton Hamilton, "Institution," *The Encyclopedia of the Social Sciences,* vol. VIII (New York: Macmillan, 1932), p. 88.
3. Lena Vanier, "U.S. Ad Spending Doubles All Other Nations Combined," *Advertising Age,* May 16, 1988, p. 36.
4. Stephen Fox, *The Mirror Makers* (New York: William Morrow and Company, 1984), p. 381.

5. Michael Schudson, *Advertising, The Uneasy Persuasion* (New York: Basic Books, 1984), p. 13.
6. Hamilton, *op. cit.,* p. 85.
7. James W. Carey, "Advertising: An Institutional Approach," in C. H. Sandage and V. Fryburger, eds., *The Role of Advertising* (Homewood, IL: Richard D. Irwin, Inc., 1960), p. 4.
8. Gossage, *op. cit.,* p. 19.
9. Fox, *op. cit.,* p. 380.
10. Michael G. Arlen, *Thirty Seconds* (New York: Penguin Books, 1980).
11. John Pfeiffer, "Six Months and Half a Million Dollars, All for 15 Seconds," *Smithsonian,* October 1987, pp. 134-145.
12. Schudson, *op. cit.,* pp. 20-21.
13. Sid Bernstein, "Advertising Losing Lead," *Advertising Age,* June 27, 1988, p. 16.
14. Bob Garfield, "Ad Review," *Advertising Age,* November 2, 1987, p. 103.
15. Schudson, *op. cit.,* pp. 32-43.
16. C. H. Sandage, Vernon Fryburger, and Kim Rotzoll, *Advertising Theory and Practice* (New York: Longman, 1989), ch. 8.
17. Gossage, *op. cit.,* p. 9.
18. *Advertising Age,* October 12, 1987.
19. Daniel G. Boorstin, "Advertising and American Civilization" in Yale Brozen, ed., *Advertising and Society* (New York: New York University Press, 1974), pp. 11-12.

2
IDEA SYSTEMS ——>INSTITUTIONS ADVERTISING AND CLASSICAL LIBERALISM

In the first chapter, we suggested that it's important to keep in mind that advertising can be better understood by examining it in light of cultural expectations. And since the sets of assumptions that cultures hold are commonly expressed as institutions, it would seem appropriate to begin with an attempt to explore the relationship between ideas and institutions. For, as Carey contends:

> An understanding of advertising rests on an understanding of the nature of ideas and institutions in which advertising found a fertile seedbed to grow. Consequently, much of the modern controversy surrounding advertising is meaningless unless the listener is aware of the implicit assumptions carried by the protagonists about the nature of man, of society, of the economic and political order.[1]

Institutions, Hamilton informs us, "fix the confines of and impose form upon the activities of human beings,"[2] or, as Norris puts it, institutions "are the 'rules' according to which social life is carried on."[3] We will later explore in considerable depth why advertising in the United States can be considered one of these powerful phenomena. Let's begin, however, with the *ideas,* the "implicit assumptions" as Carey calls them, that are shared in some fundamental way by the members of a society; and, hence, shape its institutions.

THREE POWERFUL IDEA SYSTEMS

Any attempt to classify the incredible diversity of human societies risks ridicule. Yet a great deal can, we feel, be illuminated by asserting with Heilbroner[4] that at least three powerful idea systems (or "world views" or *Weltanschauungs*) have characterized many of our societies; and, consequently, have shaped the institutions that arise to deal with ongoing societal problems. They are: (1) Tradition, (2) Authority, and (3) Classical Liberalism. Some, as we shall see, are far more likely to produce Carey's "fertile seedbed" for advertising than others.

Tradition

Briefly, a society embracing ideas of tradition places a heavy investment in the status quo, often for religious reasons. Things are thought to be as they are for a reason, perhaps known only to God or the fates. It is frequently assumed that individuals are performing roles in a drama staged by a strong-willed deity or, at least, stern ancestors. Thus, economic tasks are handed down from father to son, mother to daughter, with "life chances" virtually set at birth. Any deviation would be considered an affront to those keepers of the tradition, both seen and unseen.

Now, *all* societies have traditional *elements* (e.g., our own family "traditions" about holidays, birthdays, etc.), and given the spread of worldwide communications, current examples of entire *societies* based solely on idea systems of tradition do not readily leap to mind. But we need to expand our vision; for, this idea system, along with authority, has dominated the activities of millions throughout history.

To get a better grasp of the trappings of a traditional society, remember the musical *Fiddler on the Roof*. From the opening song ("You ask me why we do these things, and I'll tell you . . . I don't know. It's *tradition!*") and throughout the play, Tevye, the milkman, confronts the pain of the shattering of tradition as his daughters break from the institution of the matchmaker and his village and its population are uprooted, along with the heavy investment in the past they embody. A recent example is found in the film *Witness* with actor Harrison Ford's detective character intervening in the subculture of the Amish and producing a predictable clash of values and actions ("It's not *our way!*"). On the grand scale of history, virtually every facet of life in the Middle Ages can be illuminated by understanding the implicit assumptions of the traditional world view, with the ensuing dominance of the medieval church.

Now, if Idea Systems——>Institutions, would we expect advertising to arise as an institution under an idea system based on tradition? It would seem unlikely. Certainly, a compelling case can be made that one of advertising's primal messages is a call for *change*. Change your hair, your toothpaste, your life style. Aspire to be more. Indulge yourself. Be "all that you can be." These and other siren calls are familiar to us, but they would seem both alien and threatening when perceived from a world view of tradition.

This is not to say that the modern world cannot produce some striking accommodations of presumably conflicting idea systems. In a recent trip to Bahrain, a country of the Middle East, one of the authors led a seminar on advertising practices during which one of the participants used the coffee break to face Mecca and pray. At a nearby shopping center, Arabic women in traditional dress could be seen wearing fashionable footwear and shopping with apparent ease among a plethora of stores offering luxurious Western products.

Still, a society dominated by ideas of tradition generally would not seem likely to have advertising seen as a "natural" practice.

Authority

If the idea system of tradition relies on direction from the past, authority asserts it in the present and from the top. Basically, it contends that actions in a society are better determined by a few rather than the many. These few may be presumed to have special connections to God, be proven in combat, hold particular expertise, have been blessed with a high level of intelligence, or possess that elusive element, wisdom. They may be annointed, elected, or affirmed by raw power; and they may be one, a few, or a body. Whatever the rationale and structure for authority, it is assumed that some will direct while others will follow.

Throughout history more civilizations have shared this idea system than any other, with variations ranging from the iron rule of the dictator to the presumed enlightened leadership of a popular revolutionary leader or to the presumed representativeness of an elected legislature. Here, we find the seedbeds for institutions as diverse as planning boards, concentration camps, five-year plans, and "cultural revolutions."

And what of advertising's presence? On the surface, it would seem that a society choosing, to one degree or another, to have many decisions made from the top down would have no compelling reason to call on such a pervasive form of paid persuasion to attempt to influence the decision making of individuals. Certainly, Hitler had little need for advertising as we know it. Yet even in highly structured societies, there are apparently reasons to attempt to reinforce individual thinking and action, if not change it, and advertising has been called on to play a role. Thus, we have seen advertising in Russia—to serve to inspire in pursuit of national goals; to attempt to encourage particular consumption patterns (e.g., buy margarine rather than butter)—and are likely to see more with intents dealing with personal consumption as *Perestroika* becomes more evident in the day-to-day workings of Soviet life. For, as planning and decision making become more decentralized, advertising would predictably seem more compatible—e.g., advertising is a greater presence in Yugoslavia and Hungary than Russia and Poland, and it is becoming more important in China as the economic transformation to a more decentralized society continues in that enormous "people's republic." In the United States, the federal government is frequently listed among the country's top 25 advertisers, with the tasks ranging from attempts to sell in stiff competition (e.g., join the armed forces rather than take a traditional job) to the promotion of primary demand for primarily monopoly services (e.g., the post office, Amtrak).

Basically, then, societies relying heavily on an idea system of authority make many of the decisions *for* the citizens. Yet, advertising may still be a presence to reinforce decisions that have already been made—e.g., practice family planning in line with government policy—or, as decentralization of authority allows, to offer individuals real choices of alternatives—e.g., government brands competing against imported brands.

Now, as it becomes clear that advertising is more likely to flourish where decision making is decentralized rather than concentrated, we logically move to the most fertile of advertising seedbeds.

Classical Liberalism

Classical liberalism, Girvetz informs us, was crucial to the "epic transition of the Western world from an agrarian, handicraft society to the urban mechanized civilization of the present century."[5] (It is not, of course, liberalism as we think of it today; and, indeed, staunch believers in the tenets of *classical* liberalism today would tend to be labeled as arch conservatives.) Classical liberalism's ascendance in the 17th and 18th centuries was made possible, in part, by such enormous social convulsions as the Protestant Reformation, the Scientific Revolution, and the Renaissance. Based on these and other major societal forces, this startling idea system presented both an attack on the feudal order and an assertion of basic concepts about man and society that we still find engraved on public buildings, enshrined in the Constitution and Declaration of Independence, and falling easily off the tongues of politicians at many points on the political continuum. It is simply impossible to overstate the significance of this body of related ideas about human nature and the relationship of the individual to the whole in a quest for understanding virtually every facet of American society.

These ideas, breaking with the sway of tradition and authority that had dominated Europe for centuries, centered on the sovereign individual. The starting point was *EGOISM*. Apparently the ideas of Thomas Hobbes (psychological egoism) and Jeremy Bentham (psychological hedonism) found the time (roughly the seventeenth and eighteenth centuries) a fertile one. Basically, the egoistic interpretations of "human nature" held that the individual was, by nature, self-seeking. Thus, *all* of an individual's actions—even compassion—could be interpreted as being motivated by self-interest. It is important to realize that there was *no moral judgment* to be applied to the actions. In this context, Girvetz suggests an interpretation of particular relevance to activities of the economic system:

> Passion is no less noble than compassion. And, more significantly in the rough youth of capitalism, the callousness and venality of the most aggressive businessman are morally indistinguishable from the humanity and generosity of the dedicated idealist: each has exercised his preference and, while anyone may err in what best satisfies his preference, here error halts. (p. 10)

Even by today's decidedly selfish *zeitgeist*, these sentiments may seem shockingly stark. Yet, consider how frequently we ascribe the motives of others to naked self-interest—"She's (or he's) only out for number one." Or, how regrettably common it is to see the misdeeds of public officials attributed to unvarnished greed. Of course, somewhat closer to home, who would expect to find a text on advertising copywriting without the directive of appeal to the consumer's self-interest woven throughout its chapters?

Individuals, the classical liberals held, are self-interested animals. But there were other dimensions of the classical liberal idea system that served to lift us from the jungle.

The most important of these was *INTELLECTUALISM.* It held that the individual was "rational," to use that much abused word. Unlike the instinct-driven brutes of the animal world, an individual's behavior was thought to be deliberate and calculating.

> Reason looks to the consequences, carefully balances one promised pleasure or pain against another, and then, solely by reference to the quantity of pleasure or pain involved, delivers the verdict. The verdict having been rendered, conduct follows automatically. If the verdict should prove to be wrong, this will be because of imperfect education or inadequate information. (p. 15)

Herein, we find the skeletal structure of "economic man," the basic rationale for public education, and, lo, one of the more persistent arguments behind the consumerist's call for more "informative" advertising content, more functional package labeling, and so forth.

Dwell on this. After centuries of individuals being controlled by the cake of custom or the pressure of authority, the individual is now seen as capable of discovering the laws of his/her world (the Scientific Revolution), of communing directly with God (the Protestant Reformation), and of being celebrated in art, architecture, and literature (the Renaissance). As John Stuart Mill professed in his classic essay *On Liberty,* "Over himself, over his own mind and body, the individual is sovereign."[6] And lest you think this has little bearing on a subject like advertising in *contemporary* society, think of the defenses that cigarette advertisers are, *at this moment,* using to fend off proposed government regulation of their advertising activities. "Let the individual," they assert, "make up his or her own mind." Intellectualism—a powerful idea—was embraced, as we shall see, by both supporters and critics of advertising thought and practice.

It is the proposition of *QUIETISM* that adds a necessary dimension to the idea of a self-seeking, calculating individual. For if, as was assumed, effort is painful, it must follow that a person will expend energy only when there is some definite promise of reward, such that effort is worthwhile. The implication, then, is that an individual pursues various activities—backpacking, cooking, reading—not because the activity is desired for itself, but rather as a means to the end of pleasure. Thus, in the absence of an acceptable stimulus to self-interest, the individual will remain "quiet," apathetic, disinterested.

Certainly the recruiters who visit college campuses still operate—in addition to the more tentative flirtations with the "quality of the work experience"—under the assumption that work itself is not sufficiently appealing and that blandishments of salary, bonuses, and employee benefit programs ʾre not required. The importance of the assumption of quietism to advertising ͜ perhaps best captured in these oft-quoted lines from Winston Churchill:

> Advertising nourishes the consuming power of men. It creates wants for a better standard of living. It sets up before a man the goal of a better home, better clothing, better food for himself and his family. It spurs individual exertion and greater production. It brings together in fertile union those things which otherwise would never have met.[7]

Today, it is still an article of faith among many advertising practitioners that without the strong and continuing presence of advertising, the economy would falter. Thus, they express their implicit assumption that individuals are in need of constant stimulation to enter the market as buyers. Without that belief, one of the stronger rationales for the existence of advertising would be removed.

Now, thus far in the classical liberal vision we have self-seeking individuals pursuing their self-interests in deliberate and calculating manners after concluding that the reward is worth the effort. But what prevents this clash of self-interests from resulting in chaos? That is the province of *ATOMISM*.

Notice the root of the word. The classical liberals had drunk deeply of the elixir of "natural laws" as formulated by Newton and other giants of the time. And if, as the physical sciences suggested, the atom was the fundamental building block of all matter, then the individual could be assumed to be the essential element in society. The whole (society) was thus perceived as nothing more than the sum of its parts (sovereign individuals) in the same manner that a chair was nothing more than the sum of its individual atoms.

Now, from this perspective, it is simply absurd to believe that individuals can be "manipulated" by institutions of any form—e.g., government, the mass media, religion, advertising. For:

> ... social institutions are created by the fiat of self-contained individuals, they are instruments, even expedients, which the individual can employ or discard without fundamentally altering his own nature. (Girvetz, p. 23)

So the picture completes itself. *The sovereign self-seeking individual is the key.* She or he acts in a calculating manner to obtain self-interest after it has been aroused by a sufficient promise of reward. He or she creates institutions to further reasoned self-interests and can discard them as they prove unproductive to achieving that end.

Egoism, Intellectualism, Quietism, Atomism—the Psychological Crucible of the Classical Liberal Idea System.   One emerges with a pattern of ideas which, even though no individual nor generation has entertained in its entirety, has profoundly influenced the intellectual climate of this country (p. 27).

It is, we believe, simply impossible to understand the American society and its institutions without first understanding the power of classical liberal thought. For, from this body of ideas emerges our institutions of religion, speech, press, justice, government, and countless others that touch the fabric of our daily lives. Commenting on one of these, *Time* magazine observed:

> . . . trial by jury realizes an essential democratic ideal: that the citizen's security is best protected not by any institutional or intellectual elite, but by the common sense of his fellow citizens; and that the jury system was quite properly designed, not to be efficient, but to be just.[8]

Thus, the institution of the jury system is a "natural" outgrowth of classical liberal roots. And it is in classical liberalism's dominant economic institution where we will find the most fertile of seedbeds for our subject. To understand advertising in contemporary society, we must first understand classical liberalism and then come to understand one of its most important institutional progeny: the remarkable market system.

THE CLASSICAL LIBERAL MARKET

Markets, as exchanges between buyers and sellers occurring at particular times in particular places, have existed through much of recorded history. (Think of today's farmer's market or flea market as an approximation.) But the *market system,* as a means of allocating resources of an entire society, is really quite new, a creature of classical liberalism scarcely more than 200 years old. The market system has been so much a part of this country that it is difficult to realize what a revolutionary idea it was. Ask the typical college student about the market system, and he or she will probably offer something about the interplay of supply and demand, but little more. Yet, here was a system that, as classical liberalism itself, "staked it all" on the *individual.* What an astounding contrast to the institutions based on tradition and authority that preceded it and that coexist to this day.

Consider that under an economic system whose institutions are creatures of an idea system based on *tradition,* economic roles established by custom are perpetuated from generation to generation. The goods of the society that are not provided within the self-sustaining household are usually distributed in accordance with status hierarchies—more for the feudal lord, less for the serfs, and so on.

Under *authority,* on the other hand, economic priorities and the life chances of the workers in the society can change dramatically, depending on the whim of the authority structure—planning board, dictator, etc. If the space program is considered more important than consumer goods, human and natural resources will be channeled accordingly.

But consider the *market.* As an institution arising from the classical liberal world view, it holds that the priorities of the society should be determined not by the cake of custom or the directives of the few, but rather by the aggregate of *individual decisions—all* individuals, not simply the elect or select.

The market emerged in part *inductively*, with pressures from the growing activities of the practitioners of commerce in seventeenth and eighteenth century Europe and England. These aspiring entrepreneurs sought change and agitated government to permit their profit-seeking activities to be carried on without undue restraint. And, as we have seen, the market as an articulated system also emerged *deductively*; with the supporting ideas of egoism, intellectualism, quietism, and atomism that culminated in the "world view" of classical liberalism.

If the writings of John Locke still influence our governmental system, there can be little doubt that Adam Smith and his masterpiece *An Inquiry into the Nature and Causes of the Wealth of Nations* (1776) still shape the ideology of much of our economic system. (There are no value judgments intended here—merely the observation that the rationale for the classical liberal market remains very much a part of the "conventional wisdom" of much of American economic life in spite of often glaring discrepancies between idea and reality.)

Smith, Heilbroner informs us,[9] was living in a time (the eighteenth century) and place (England) when the division of labor was becoming a dominant economic fact. Thus, the decline of self-sufficiency was a major current in his work, as, apparently, was the thinking of 17th and 18th century British clergymen, particularly the Puritans, with their belief in a rational, mechanistic universe.[10] But how was this supposed to relate to a system of resource allocation with the sovereign individual as its master?

First, Smith assumed that individuals were self-seeking by nature (egoism). "It is not from the benevolence of the butcher, the brewer or the baker that we expect our dinner," Smith reminded us, "but from their regard to their own interest."[11] Likewise, someone buying goods would attempt to acquire those that brought the greatest pleasure at the *lowest* price and, while in the labor market, would strive to perform as *little* work as possible for as *much* money as he or she could secure. The producer, of course, would attempt to sell the *lowest* quality merchandise at the *highest* possible price, and hire the *cheapest* labor to perform as *much* work as possible. It seemed a sure formula for chaos.

But, it was reasoned, the self-seeking individual would inevitably collide with others (atomism) seeking the same end. What then? Violence? Not if it is also assumed that the individual is by nature deliberate and calculating (intellectualism). For the self-seeking individual, stimulated from apathy (quietism) by an appeal to gain (egoism), will quickly realize that the reward for which he or she has exerted effort will not be achieved unless behavior is modified to some minimal degree. Thus, the producer who wishes to sell a poor quality good at a high price will have to face the realization that the deliberate and calculating individuals will not purchase the offerings if more "rational" choices are available. And the individual entering the labor market may shortly find herself/himself without work if she/he encounters others willing to toil slightly longer for the same wages.

But all of this hinges on the assumption that economic power will be fragmented among *many* buyers and sellers (atomism). With many suppliers, it is assumed that some will attempt to seek their self-interests by offering a better economic and/or qualitative value than their competitors. With many potential self-seeking laborers, it is certain that some will work longer hours for less money, and so on. If this fragmentation did not exist, it is easy to predict (according to the classical liberal world view) that those with some degree of power would pursue their self-interests by the exploitation of others.

Thus, in order for the market mechanism to perform its task of resource allocation with greatest efficiency, individuals *must* be stimulated to put forth effort in pursuit of self-interest, they *must* be deliberate and calculating in that pursuit, and there *must* be a sufficient number of buyers and sellers so that no one or few can influence the process.

And on whom does the market shower its favors? On the *efficient*. It is the efficient individual who stretches his/her earnings by buying the best quality at the lowest price. It is the efficient wage earner who expends appropriate effort to maximize his/her return. And it is the efficient producer who can offer the highest-quality goods at the lowest possible cost, and hence be rewarded with the patronage of the efficient consumer.

With this background, let us examine three pressing economic questions common to *all* societies, which, until the evolution of the market, had been answered only by tradition or authority.

What Will Be Produced?

What will be produced will, simply, be determined by what sovereign individuals, in their self-interests, wish to buy. Thus, as Heilbroner observes, the market "has no goal orientation, save to existing demand."[12] If there is a considerable demand for shoes, the fact that shoe supply lags behind existing demand means that shoe prices will rise, along with the profits of the current producers. But the abnormally high profits will soon attract producers from other fields (say, hats) who have fallen upon hard times with potential supply exceeding existing demand, thus leading to subnormal return. As hat producers become shoe producers, shoe supply increases until demand is met. Thus, in the long run, aggregate demand determines the types and qualities of what is to be produced. (To use a contemporary example, a demand for pornographic films, particularly for the home-video market, has led to a sizable allocation of human and material resources to meet that demand. It was not decreed by authority that this should be so, nor was it determined by custom—at least not in this country—but rather by a sufficient number of individuals willing to part with a certain portion of their earnings for the opportunity to view these epics. If demand slackens, many of the current participants will presumably seek other opportunities for profit and employment.)

To Whom Will It Be Distributed?

The output of the market system will be distributed to whomever has money to pay for its offerings. There is no welfare built into the pure ideology or its mechanism. Social Darwinism is a reasonable approximation of the humanitarian dimension of the market in its pure classical liberal form. Those having "marketable" skills who are willing to sell their services in the labor market will be compensated. They may then, in turn, partake of the output of the production sector that is theoretically responding to their demands and those of other sovereign individuals like them. Yet, if the lure of gain is not sufficient to overcome their quietistic nature, the market will offer no rewards. (Certainly the still heard call that disenfranchised individuals should "pull themselves up by their bootstraps" comes from this credo, as does the resistance some still express to the idea of "welfare.")

How Will the Work of Society Get Done?

Since the market visionaries assumed a geographically mobile labor force (a crucial condition), self-interested individuals will seek employment wherever wages are highest. As we have already seen, it is in production areas of high demand and short supply (to use our earlier example—shoes) where wages are likely to rise. Thus, workers are attracted to those areas of production that are currently high on the economy's list of priorities. Always assuming the lure of gain and the deliberate and calculating path to self-interest, it is assured that, at least in the long run, those tasks that society deems important will be undertaken. (Today, we see reference to "pockets of poverty," while other sections of the country are experiencing "boom times" with a presumably desirable market for labor. Classical market theorists would assume that rational individuals would go where the jobs are. Obviously, today, we consider the matter more complex.)

Now, it is important to keep in mind that the market was seen as a system harmonious with the *natural laws* of society as articulated by the classical liberals. If supply should fall short of demand, the "laws" of the market would naturally be set into motion to correct the deficiency. Being in tune with "natural" order, it was, of course, self-correcting. It follows that the market, as a self-contained, self-repairing, complex mechanism, must be left alone (*lassiez-faire*) to follow its natural course. Its greatest enemy, then, was predictably, *any* concentration of power that could disrupt the atomistic nature of the market and hence the natural processes of the system. (It is often assumed that government was considered the greatest potential villain in the saga. Not so. Equally calamitous effects could be expected to result from concentration of undue—i.e., "unnatural"—power by big business, big labor or even consumer co-ops. *Any form of action that superceded individual decision making was considered a threat to the system.*)

The self-corrective powers of the market could thus be impaired by any deviation from its fundamental assumptions. For example, the development of a producer monopoly (affecting atomism) would enable the supplier to with-hold output, leading to higher prices. Thus, wages and prices would be distorted, and the deliberating and calculating consumer would be thwarted.

"The great flaw in the market," one may hear from some sectors, "is that it provides no incentive for social responsibility on the part of the participants." Precisely. Under the assumption of the pure atomistic market, it was assumed that the participants would follow only one overriding law—do what is best for their own monetary interests. The atomistic force of competition (producers, laborers, buyers) would take care of the rest. For, in the process of "naturally" seeking his or her own self-interest, the individual contributes to the good of the whole (society) "as if by an invisible hand."[13] Indeed, always assuming that the other factors are operative, *the individual who did not seek monetarily selfish ends would be doing a disservice to himself or herself, and society.*

There is yet another point deserving of emphasis. The ghost of Adam Smith is far more likely to be called forth at a meeting of the Association of National Advertisers than the Consumer Federation of America. Yet, Smith must certainly be considered a "Consumerist," who regarded the end of all production as consumption and held no lofty illusions of the motives of businessmen. As he stated:

> People of the same trade seldom meet together, even for merriment
> and diversion, but the conversation ends in a conspiracy against the
> public, or in some contrivance to raise prices.[14]

To counter this, Smith looked to the fragmentation of power through competition and relied upon the individual's presumed deliberate and calculating nature.

So the *sovereign individual*—particularly the industrious and efficient—would be the beneficiary in the market. As production increased, so would the division of labor and the varieties of goods and services offered in response to aggregate demand. All who would diligently and intelligently participate would benefit. The lure of gain, the directive of reason, and the discipline of competition . . .

> The market thus determines how society shall invest its resources,
> human and material. It decrees when, where, and how men shall
> labor. It determines the disposition of capital. The market be-
> comes the regulator of what shall be produced, its quality, quantity,
> and price. The market is truly called sovereign. (Girvetz, p. 117)

A remarkable vision and an essential reference point for understanding advertising in contemporary society.

A "FERTILE SEEDBED" FOR ADVERTISING

After examining the relationship between idea systems and institutions, it seems clear that the perspective of *tradition* provides the least compatible idea environment for advertising. The idea system centered around assumptions that *authority* could provide some promise, dependent upon the degree of individual decision making allowed. But it is clearly in the ideas of *classical liberalism* that we find the most promising basis for the emergence and proliferation of advertising as "world taken for granted."

Understanding Advertising's Classical Liberal Roots

In a 1987 statement on advertising and the Federal Trade Commission, newly appointed chairman Dan Oliver asserted:

> Advertising is one of the basic mechanisms through which the marketplace acts to ensure consumer sovereignty. It contributes to the achievement of an efficient allocation of resources and benefits consumers in several different ways. . . .
>
> First, advertising provides information about product characteristics and enables consumers to make informed choices among competing goods. . . .
>
> Second, economic theory and empirical studies indicate that advertising generally increases new entry and price competition and hence reduces market power and prices.[15]

Note the key symbols: "consumer sovereignty"; "efficient allocation of resources"; "informed choices"; "new entry"; and "price competition." The roots are clear. From "egoism" comes the assumption that advertisers can feel free to seek their self-interests through various forms of business activities, including advertising. So are potential buyers seeking *their* self-interests, assuming they are aroused from their natural "quietistic" state by appeal to their self-interests, perhaps through advertising messages. Advertisers can, of course, attempt to persuade as robustly as they wish, safe in the assumption that the "deliberate and calculating" individual will not be manipulated. Potential buyers can, of course, sort through the wealth of competing messages caused by the "atomism" of the competitive structure and arrive at a reasoned choice. And, who, presumably, is in charge of this directionless, self-correcting system? With this set of assumptions at least, the *individual* who can accept, reject, or ignore, directs the flow of societal resources through the full meaning of *consumer sovereignty*.

The seeds of conflict should also be apparent. As Leiss, Kline, and Ghally observe in their investigation of *Social Communication in Advertising,* the starting point of advertising supporters . . .

> is not the "bewildered" but the "rational" consumer who uses the goods of the capitalist marketplace and the information provided by advertising to satisfy his or her needs. This concept of how things *should* work, rooted in classical liberal economic theory, is some-

thing many defenders and critics of advertising share, but while the defenders claim that with the help of advertising, the market actually operates in this way to match peoples needs with suitable products, many of the critics think that advertising actually destroys the competitive and rational nature of the free market.[16]

An interesting insight into this clash of visions is provided by a series of print advertisements prepared by the American Association of Advertising Agencies to attempt to counter some of the common criticisms of advertising. They hoped to raise advertising's standing in public opinion polls, while attempting to make advertising's case among such key ''publics'' as government officials, academics, and so forth. Here are some of the headlines from the series:

◆ "Isn't It Funny How Stereo Ads Are Boring Until You Want a Stereo?" (Advertising as a guide to the rational consumer.)
◆ ''Without Advertising Even the Best Ideas Take Ages to Catch On'' (Advertising quickly joins the self-interest of sellers and buyers for the benefit of both.)
◆ ''Is Advertising a Reflection of Society or is Society a Reflection of Advertising?'' (Advertising is a mirror, not a shaper.)

You get the idea. As a particularly telling example of the ideas behind this defensive posture of advertising supporters, examine another ad in the series, shown in Figure 2-1. Notice the reasoning behind the refutation of each of the ''lies'':

◆ ''Advertising makes you buy things you don't want.'' (No one, short of actual force, can do that. You're too smart, and there are too many other choices open to you.)
◆ ''Advertising makes things cost more.'' (Competition, spurred by advertising, makes possible the efficiencies of mass production as advertising introduces individuals to products suited to their self-interests.)
◆ ''Advertising helps bad products sell.'' (Once consumers have tried a product, they decide, in some self-interested manner, whether it is of value to them. If it isn't, future advertising efforts are wasted.)
◆ ''Advertising is a waste of money.'' (Advertising is a friend of the market because it provides information and fosters competition. We *all* benefit.)

And finally the slogan for the entire campaign, encompassing strong classical liberal themes—"Advertising. Another word for freedom of choice.''

(There are some interesting asides. Note, for example in Figure 2-1, that it is asserted that it is a ''lie'' that advertising *makes* you buy things you don't want. Yet advertising is given credit for ''creating'' a mass market for calculators. If it needed to be created, was it wanted in the first place? Etc. The tone of the entire message, however, is clearly set on a classical liberal foundation.)

FIGURE 2-1

THIS AD IS FULL OF LIES.

LIE #1: ADVERTISING MAKES YOU BUY THINGS YOU DON'T WANT.

Advertising is often accused of inducing people to buy things against their will.

But when was the last time you returned home from the local shopping mall with a bag full of things you had absolutely no use for? The truth is, nothing short of a pointed gun can get *anybody* to spend money on something he or she doesn't want.

No matter how effective an ad is, you and millions of other American consumers make your own decisions. If you don't believe it, ask someone who knows firsthand about the limits of advertising. Like your local Edsel dealer.

LIE #2: ADVERTISING MAKES THINGS COST MORE. Since advertising

costs money, it's natural to assume it costs *you* money. But the truth is that advertising often brings prices down.

Consider the electronic calculator, for example. In the late 1960s, advertising created a mass market for calculators. That meant more of them needed to be produced, which brought the price of producing each calculator down. Competition spurred by advertising brought the price down still further.

As a result, the same product that used to cost hundreds of dollars now costs as little as five dollars.

LIE #3: ADVERTISING HELPS BAD PRODUCTS SELL.

Some people worry that good advertising sometimes covers up for bad products.

But nothing can make you like a bad product. So, while advertising can help convince you to try something once, it can't make you buy it twice. If you don't like what you've bought, you won't buy it again. And if enough people feel the same way, the product dies on the shelf.

In other words, the only thing advertising can do for a bad product is help you find out it's a bad product. And you take it from there.

LIE #4: ADVERTISING IS A WASTE OF MONEY. Some people wonder why

we don't just put all the money spent on advertising directly into our national economy.

The answer is, we already do.

Advertising helps products sell, which holds down prices, which helps sales even more. It creates jobs. It informs you about all the products available and helps you compare them. And it stimulates the competition that produces new and better products at reasonable prices.

If all that doesn't convince you that advertising is important to our economy, you might as well stop reading.

Because on top of everything else, advertising has paid for a large part of the magazine you're now holding.

And that's the truth.

ADVERTISING.
ANOTHER WORD FOR FREEDOM OF CHOICE.
American Association of Advertising Agencies

Reprinted with permission of the American Association of Advertising Agencies.

In a similar mode, Professor Jerry Kirkpatrick provides a "Philosophical Defense of Advertising," relying heavily on the thinking of economist Ayn Rand. Confronting several of the common criticisms of advertising's social role (e.g., "Advertising Changes Tastes," "Advertising Offends Tastes") he asserts:

> The moral justification of advertising is that it represents the implementation of an ethics of egoism—the communication of one rational being to another rational being for the egoistic benefit of both.[17]

He summarizes, "The relationship between advertisers and consumers is strictly voluntary" (p. 48).

If we return to the working premise IDEAS SYSTEMS ——> INSTITUTIONS then, it seems apparent that advertising's roots (its "fertile seedbed"), as well as much of its current rationale and defense, can be found in the idea system of classical liberalism and its major economic institution, the market system.

To begin to understand advertising in contemporary society then, we must begin here. For, as suggested in the preceding chapter, much about the controversies of advertising can be illuminated by realizing "Who's looking and where." And those asserting advertising's case generally believe:

> Advertising is part and parcel of a highly industrialized, market-oriented society. Information and persuasion from uncounted sources swirl around all the individuals who live, work, and shop in this setting. Both informative and persuasive communications are vital and indeed necessary ingredients of decision-making processes in politics, in social relations, and in the marketplace. (Leiss, *et al.,* p. 42)

Now, in the next chapter we continue to explore this IDEA SYSTEMS ——>INSTITUTIONS relationship by examining how well the classical liberal assumptions have fared in the late 20th century. For, if our idea systems differ, so, logically, will our perceptions and expectations of the resulting institutions.

◆

SUMMARY

In examining the relationship between fundamental societal idea systems and institutions, we began a search for the "fertile seedbed" of ideas that provides an appropriate growth medium for advertising as an institution.

It is clearly not in TRADITION, the set of assumptions placing heavy emphasis on the status quo, based on a well-understood societal plan provided by the Gods, ancestors, or both.

It may, in part, be in AUTHORITY, with its assumptions of the wisdom of the few directing the many. But much depends upon the degree of individual decision making allowed.

The fit seems tightest with CLASSICAL LIBERALISM, with its assumptions of self-interest (egoism), rationality (intellectualism), apathy (quietism), and the whole being no greater than the sum of the parts (atomism).

Still more understanding is added by examining the *market* as a resource allocation mechanism. Based on classical liberalism, it is assumed to be self-perpetuating and self-correcting, with the good of the whole ensuing from self-centered actions of individuals—"as if by an invisible hand."

Much assertion and defense of advertising's thought and action can be seen in these ideas. Shopworn and controversial as they may be in the last years of the 20th century, they still provide much comfort for supporters of advertising in contemporary society, and useful analytic perspectives for those seeking to understand its dimensions.

ENDNOTES

1. James W. Carey, "Advertising: An Institutional Approach," in C. H. Sandage and V. Fryburger, *The Role of Advertising* (Homewood, IL: Richard D. Irwin, Inc., 1960), p. 3.
2. Walton Hamilton, "Institution," *The Encyclopedia of the Social Sciences,* vol. 8 (New York: Macmillan, 1932), p. 84.
3. Vincent P. Norris, "Toward the Institutional Study of Advertising," in *Occasional Papers in Advertising,* vol. 1, no. 1 (Urbana, IL: University of Illinois, Department of Advertising, January 1966), pp. 60-61.
4. See in general, Robert L. Heilbroner, "The Economic Revolution," in *The Worldly Philosophers* (New York: Time, Inc., 1961), chap. II.
5. Harry K. Girvetz, *From Wealth to Welfare* (Stanford, CA: Stanford University Press, 1950), chap. 1. Used by permission.
6. Quoted in Otto Friedrich, "The Individual is Sovereign," *Time,* July 21, 1986, p. 80.
7. Winston Churchill, quoted in S. Watson Dunn and Arnold M. Barban, *Advertising: Its Role in Modern Marketing* (Hinsdale, IL: The Dryden Press, 1974), p. 5.
8. "Idealism on Trial," promotional ad, *Time, Inc.,* 1982.
9. Heilbroner, *op. cit.* The authors acknowledge their debt to the ideas expressed throughout Chapters I–III in this excellent work.
10. Thoughts attributed to Sabin Rashid, Professor of Economics at the University of Illinois. See Tom Day, "Author of 'Wealth of Nations' 'borrowed' Many of His Ideas," *IlliniWeek,* April 19, 1984, p. 1.

11.   Quoted in "Revolution of Self-Love," *Time,* April 21, 1980, p. 45.
12.   Heilbroner, *The Economic Problem,* 2d ed. (Englewood Cliffs, NJ: Prentice-Hall, 1970), p. 547.
13.   Quoted in Paul A. Samuelson, "Adam Smith," *Newsweek,* March 15, 1976, p. 86.
14.   Heilbroner, *The Worldly Philosophers,* p. 65.
15.   "The New FTC: Steady as She Goes," *American Advertising,* January 1987, p. 9.
16.   William Leiss, Stephen Kline, and Sut Ghally, *Social Communication in Advertising* (New York: Methuen, 1986), p. 31.
17.   Jerry Kirkpatrick, "A Philosophical Defense of Advertising," *Journal of Advertising,* vol. 15, no. 2, 1986, p. 44.

3

IDEA SYSTEMS ——>INSTITUTIONS ADVERTISING AND NEO-LIBERALISM

Walton Hamilton offers this perceptive observation on the linkage between ideas and institutions:

> In the continuous process of the adaption of usage and arrangement to intellectual environment, an active role is assumed by that body of ideas taken for granted which is called *common sense*. Because it determines the climate within which all others must live, it is the dominant institution in a society.[1]

In the last chapter, we explored the relationship between a particular idea system—classical liberalism—and the types of institutions which would seem to be a "natural" outgrowth (e.g., freedom of the press, representative government, the market system). Of course, the reason for this emphasis was to make clear the extremely supportive role these assumptions about human nature and the relationship between the individual and society played (and play) for the development and maintenance of advertising thought and practice.

But if IDEA SYSTEMS——>INSTITUTIONS, and the ideas (or "common sense") change, how will this affect the expectations that we have for our institutions?

Our purpose in this chapter, then, is to hold up several of the key assumptions of the classical liberal idea system—spawned more than 200 years ago—to the light of some of the prevailing thoughts and practices of America in the last decades of the 20th century. We will attempt to determine what is retained, and what altered, and to draw out conclusions about the effects of our contemporary idea system on institutions, particularly advertising.

We will, of course, be operating on a high level of generalization, attempting not to be exhaustive, but insightful; pointing to events, trends, and prevailing modes of thought that seem modal. First, we'll explore where we may stand today with such critical classical liberal assumptions as egoism, the individual's rationality, the division of power in society, and the role of the market and of government. Then we'll narrow the focus to advertising.

It is, we feel, an important undertaking. For, as we suggested in the first chapter, it would seem that much about advertising in contemporary society can be understood as a clash of different perceptual realities, caused in part by individuals operating from differing sets of assumptions of the world around them.

A REEXAMINATION OF CLASSICAL LIBERAL CONCEPTS

Egoism

Certainly a case can be made that the classical liberal assumption about the driving force of self-interest is alive and well in contemporary America. Author Thomas Wolfe dubbed the 1970s as the "Me Decade," and the 1980s have appeared to be dominated by a kindred spirit. The much-heralded Yuppie life-style has been strong on pursuits of the ego—through narcisstic physical fitness, throw-away romance, self-above-all career moves. The military seem to find appeals of travel, free medical care, and specialized training somewhat more compelling than patriotism; and the world of professional sports may represent the zenith in the naked self-interest business. Deploring the sorry state of affairs in national morals, highlighted by hijinks of government officials, insiders trading schemes on Wall Street, scandals in military procurement and TV evangelism, *ad nauseum,* columnist Cal Thomas suggests:

> The reason the ethical supply is depleted is because our emphasis since the early 1960s has focused on expanding individual "liberties," not on renewing our dwindling ethical resources.[2]

This is certainly a recognition and condemnation of rampant egoism.

Of course, much of the past, present, and pending local, state, and federal legislation dealing with issues such as pollution control, the disposal of toxic wastes, product and worker safety and the like, suggests that these matters will *not* be dealt with convincingly unless a check on self-interest is instituted.

Now, keep in mind that classical liberalism assumed that individuals pursuing their self-interests in single-minded ways would *naturally* result in the good of the whole. Academic Theodore Levitt put it in blunt economic terms in his classic 1958 article, "The Dangers of Social Responsibility": "The governing rule in industry should be that *something is good only if it pays.* Otherwise it is alien and impermissible."[3] But clearly today, there are other currents at work as well.

Although the 1980s have seemed conservative times (particularly in relation to the economy), and business representatives have undoubtedly felt more comfortable making statements such as, "The first responsibility a firm has is to produce a profit for its stockholders" than in the 1960s era of The Great Society, most are also likely to point to other company activities that seem to have no direct "bottom line" payout—at least in the short run. For example, it is certainly not uncommon for companies to underwrite programs designed to retrain minorities, support various community organizations and undertakings, or underwrite advertising dealing with equal opportunity for women, race/civil rights, public education, and other causes. (The Leo Burnett advertising agency reports that in 1987 its employees devoted 6,639 hours to *pro bono* project for 46 organizations.)[4]

Some of this is, of course, clearly enlightened self-interest—e.g., "If we don't help make the downtown area a more attractive place, we'll have difficulty getting employees"—and a recent study indicated that many of the "social responsibility" advertisements from 1967-1985 dealing with such topics as health and safety, consumerism, ecology, and the physical environment were clearly "intended to fulfill marketing strategies."[5] As a former Federal Trade Commission activist observed:

> Americans are under no illusion about business practices. . . . One does not have to be a cynic to conclude that those areas where business is perceived as socially progressive have a striking tendency to coincide with its economic self-interest, while those areas where business is given low marks for moral and civic virtue happen to be those areas where there is little or no (apparent) advantage to be gained.[6]

We can imagine, then, a continuum, polarized by acts of pure self-interest in its narrowest sense and acts of pure altruism at their most selfless. Realistically, although there is still a clustering at the egoism end, that stark position is no longer as easily defensible, in public life at least. Today as we move into what some have termed a "post-yuppie" era, we *may* be more inclined to expect a certain "pulling of the punch" on the part of individuals, groups, and organizations. *To the extent we do, we are assuming that the automatic adjusting mechanisms of the classical liberal world view (e.g., the "invisible hand") cannot consistently be relied upon to produce societal good from self-interested acts.* Thus, as our ideas change, so do our expectations from our institutions.

The implications for advertising are significant.

Intellectualism

With Galileo and Copernicus, humankind ceased to be at the center of the universe attended by the sun and planets. With Darwin, we ceased to be the creature unique in its immunity from the forces of natural selection. With Freud, we learned that we could no longer claim to have our actions determined solely by the reflective deliberations of the conscious mind. And now we must confront "artificial intelligence." All in all, it hasn't been easy sledding for our classical liberal friend, the deliberate and calculating individual.

But we are a nation that has, in important ways, "staked it all" on the individual. Thus, many of our institutions reflect that belief, even while others manifest grave reservations:

Item: The American jury system rests on the premise that ordinary men and women, not the elect or elite, can make reasonable judgments on matters of justice ranging from the trivial to those of life or death. But these same individuals may be required to wear helmets when operating motorcycles, thus casting doubt on their abilities to make sound decisions concerning their *own* well-beings.

Item: Enough faith is placed in the rationality of individuals that we are encouraged to vote for a person (presumed rational as well) who may ultimately have to make a decision that could destroy life as we know it on this planet. Yet, there is grave doubt as to whether or not these same individuals should be allowed to operate their private cars unless first securely strapped to their seats.

Item: High school graduates throughout the land hear speakers congratulate them on their citizenship in a land of freedom and opportunity where all doors are open to inquiring minds. Yet these same students may not have been able to find certain "unfit" books in their school libraries, the removal of which was the result of the agitation of groups offering *their* standards as the norm to which others should attend.

Item: *Consumer Reports* recently informed its well-educated readers that its tests revealed that tested food store brands were equal to or superior to the more costly national brands in 7 out of 10 common categories. Yet a survey of their readers revealed that "80 percent or more preferred a national brand."[7]

As this minuscule sample may suggest, we are apparently uncertain as to exactly what to make of our current version of "human nature." Clearly we have based countless of our institutional systems (e.g., governmental, judicial, communication, religious, etc.) firmly on our classical liberal beliefs. Yet "common sense" has caused us to question.

James Carey, referring to Ernst Cassirer's distinction between *animal rationale* and *animal symbolicum,* observes, "Economic man, buying and selling, and equating cost and utility at the margin, has been replaced by psychological or symbolic man who makes economic decisions on the basis of economic and also noneconomic but equally potent psychological need-want stimuli."[8] This is not to suggest that the modern perception is inferior, only that it is different. Thus, individuals can be seen as less predictable, more complex, and, to some, more vulnerable.

Now, recall that in the absence of any conscious "social responsibility," the two principal forces that would channel the individual's inherent self-interest (egoism) into socially beneficial channels were assumed to be intellectualism and atomism. If today we are apparently uncertain about the individual's inherent rationality, or at least when it is brought to bear, then we can feel less comfortable with the likelihood that the "invisible hand" will turn self-interested acts into socially beneficial consequences.

The implications for advertising, as you can envision, are intriguing.

Atomism

The sum and substance of much of sociology and social psychology is that the individual is, to a considerable degree, molded by society. In contrast to the classical liberal conception of a society composed solely of sovereign individuals who control by their self-interested actions, today we accept a certain level of powerlessness as society and its institutions impose form upon us through their sets of norms or expected behaviors. This sense of being controlled by societal forces is simply not a psychological state that classical liberals could feel comfortable with. For, with the assumption of atomism, individuals (not institutions) were the masters.

If societal power is *not* diffused among all participants then, where *does* it reside? Still with "the people," some would contend. But others assert: big government; big labor; big business; the networks; etc. Clearly seeds of conflict are abundant.

The Justice Department's Antitrust Division was originally established to keep economic competition at least reasonably "atomistic" by preventing mergers ("trusts," etc.) that could presumably nullify competition and pave the way for exploitation. Yet, the head of this division for the Reagan administration was highly critical of the "populist bigness-is-badness notion." William Baxter was apparently willing to assume that companies "got big because they were successful at pleasing customers, not successful at ripping off customers."[9]

By contrast, consumer advocate Ralph Nader believes:

> The contemporary challenge to giant business . . . is almost primitive in its simplicity. It is a call for corporations to stop stealing, stop deceiving, stop corrupting politicians with money, stop monopolizing, stop poisoning the earth, air and water, stop selling dangerous products, stop exposing workers to cruel hazards, stop tyrannizing people of conscience within the company and start respecting long-range survival needs and rights of present and future generations.[10]

In an attempt to counter what he considers to be a condition of "producer sovereignty" rather than the classical liberal ideal of consumer sovereignty, "Nader conjures up a future in which consumers have their own attorneys sitting across the table from the insurance companies negotiating policies; in which leases are written more in favor of the tenant; in which big buying groups will have more leverage and power to set their own terms in the market-place."[11]

Notice the undercurrent of oppressor and oppressed in Nader's arguments. Presumably individuals cannot make their way without joining together—to counter concentrated power with concentrated power, as labor unions confront businesses—atomism elevated from the individual to the group level. This is certainly a far cry from individuals acting in their own self- interests solely as individual entities, not as members of groups.

An interesting parallel is found with the subject of media diversity in our mass communications system. Some contend that diversity in media context can be best achieved by letting the *market* decide. "Underlying this approach is the premise of a fluid, competitive marketplace and a fairly broad distribution of economic power that will permit all sectors to enter the marketplace and provide needed information-communication services."[12] But another position calls for *government* to assume an active role to assure a truly "democratic social structure"—a greater degree of atomism. For, the argument goes, "in this era of giant national and transnational corporate dominance it is absurd to presuppose that there is sufficient equitable distribution of economic power to allow market forces alone to ensure equitable distribution of services. . . . Information should not be considered simply a marketable commodity distributed only to those with the capacity to pay" (p. 7).

There is no question that economic power is becoming more concentrated than diffused, and often, as Leo Bogart informs us, with intriguing international dimensions.

> Most Americans couldn't care less that the two biggest advertising agency organizations are now owned by British companies. It doesn't matter to them that magazines like *Scientific American* and *Parents* are owned by a German firm or that the largest U.S. newspaper chain—in number of daily newspapers—is Thomson, a Canadian company. There was no great furor when UPI was sold to a Mexican publisher. And, except in Akron, it doesn't bother anyone that Firestone, our third biggest tire manufacturer, is being bought by the Japanese. New Yorkers are oblivious to the fact that Saks Fifth Avenue is owned by the British. [13]

But a critical question concerns the *effects* of that concentration. Does big overcome small to the benefit of the few? Or do we exist in a land of enormous countervailing power blocks, where big business is countered by big labor, held in check by big government and big press, so that a hybrid competition is maintained that ultimately benefits all? Or is there collusion among the titans, and, if so, between whom?

Does advertising, then, flow with these currents or, in fact, help channel them? The answers result in strikingly different perceptions of advertising in contemporary society.

The Economy

Depending, then, on the assumptions one makes about the states of egoism, intellectualism, and atomism, an individual can arrive at very different conclusions about how our economy works and what role (if any) government should play in its maintenance and/or direction.

The market, as seen by the classical liberals, was a self-contained, self correcting system in harmony with the "natural laws" of human nature and the relationship of the individual to society.

At the time of this writing, the American economy is subject to decidedly mixed reviews. The Reagan administration took credit for sustained growth, new job creation, and relatively low inflation and unemployment. Yet critics argued that much of this benefited the few rather than the many, that the new jobs created were predominately in the relatively low-paying service sector, and that the national debt represents an "economic time bomb" as the United States assumes the mantle of the world's premiere debtor nation. In addition, at least one economist argued that the "*environmental* deficit" is of even greater concern:

> A pervasive thought underlying the current policy is the notion that the environment is somehow less important than marketable goods and services, that producing things that individual people buy—such as Cadillacs and cosmetics—is more valuable than protecting things that are consumed collectively, such as air and water.[14]

Notice the distinction here between the individual and the collective, and the implicit assumption that individuals pursuing their own self-interests will *not* necessarily result in the good of the whole.

And thus we are an economy of contradictions, attempting a balancing act of relatively uncontrolled economic activity by individuals and momentous actions by mammoth corporations, labor unions, and government bodies. The Reagan government, the most conservative administration of modern times, was unwilling (and/or unable) to make any significant changes in the "Welfare State" programs and mentality that have characterized much of our economic activity since the New Deal. And while actions on the federal level have loosened some regulation strings and placed more fiscal responsibility on the states, the states, hungry for revenue, have stepped up *their* regulatory and revenue-enhancing activities, often at the price of the economic freedom so cherished, at least in word, in Washington.

As we enter the post-Reagan era, there is still some currency given to at least the notion of what is sometimes called an "industrial policy"—generally considered "a program of government planning, protective trade measures and tax concessions or even subsidies to restore some industrial losers to health."[15] The idea has particular appeal to hard-hit industries such as autos, rubber, steel, and textiles. Failure to compete in world markets, the argument goes, is to a great extent due to foreign firms receiving generous subsidies from their governments. Yet, economist Lester Thurow notes the apparent contradictions of American firms claiming that their business failures are frequently due to "too much government" while foreign governments are given credit for making *their* firms highly efficient. The core reason for failure, Thurow contends, may not be the role of government, but "bad management, poor foresight and sloppy organization." [16]

"The market," Robert Heilbroner observed, "has no goal orientation other than to existing demand." [17] The ongoing problem of our economy, then, may be seen as when—if at all—to *force* the direction, to put governmental hands on the economic rudder. There are profound philosophical differences here, ranging from those who see an unfettered economy unleashing the self-seeking energies of individuals and firms for the eventual good of all (George Bush's acceptance speech at the 1988 Republican convention was laced with these ideas), to those who see short-run gains turning to long-run tragedies as resources are misallocated to the advantage of the haves and the disenfranchisement of the have-nots (as in Michael Dukakis's acceptance speech at the 1988 Democratic convention).

This "mixed" market, then, interacts with our mixed visions of human nature to provide fertile grounds for controversy. Advertising, predictably, can be seen as friend or enemy of this mixed system, as mirror or shaper of fundamental economic and social tides.

Government

Lassiez-faire was a term introduced in France in the 18th century and used in the writings of Adam Smith "to argue against the theory of mercantilism and governmental restrictions and regulations of economic activity characteristic of his day." [18] Clearly, the idea that government should not interfere with economic activity is no longer endorsed in unadulterated form by even the most conservative among us. Yet there is ample room for divergence on the matter of how much "assistance or control" should be offered, where, and for what ends.

A reasonable approximation of a middle-range position on the role of government in social and economic matters has been provided by economist Irving Kristol. [19] A "neo-conservative," Kristol contends, would generally hold views such as these:

◆   In general there is approval for those social reforms that, "while providing needed security and comfort to the individual in our dynamic, urbanized society [e.g., social security, unemployment insurance, some kind of national health insurance and family assistance plan] do so with a minimum of bureaucratic intrusion in the individual's affairs."

◆   There is great respect for the market "to respond efficiently to economic realities while preserving the maximum degree of individual freedom."

There is a willingness to interfere with the market for "overriding social purposes," but this, ideally, should be done by "rigging" the market to take advantage of its own dynamics—e.g., housing vouchers for the poor rather than government-built low-income housing.

◆ There is belief in the traditional American value of equality, but not egalitarianism, "as a proper goal for government to pursue." A favoring of equality of *opportunity* (e.g., affirmative action) rather than equality of *outcome* (e.g., "quota" programs). (An interesting current example of the latter is the requirement that the University of Illinois must make at least 10% of its purchases from minority and female owned businesses.)

Now, keep in mind that Kristol's points represent a relatively conservative position. Yet, they still recognize and, indeed, encourage, a significant role for government. It is, then, useful to explore further by considering government's role as *regulator* and *planner*.

The regulating dimension essentially involves government tinkering with what is already present. Often government works in this role to attempt to achieve classical liberal ends—e.g., more competition—even while using decidedly non-classical liberal means—e.g., government antitrust activity. Clearly the popularity of calls to "take government off our backs" and "free the American market system from strangling regulation," suggests widespread doubts about the efficacy of regulation. But we remain ambivalent concerning the proper limits. Writing in the 1980s, economist Robert Samuelson noted:

> Twenty years ago, the vague concepts of "social responsibility" and "consumerism" barely existed; now diluted to be sure, they are the conventional wisdom, even in business. . . . And Reagan notwithstanding, [Ralph] Nader's social regulation—of everything from auto safety to pollution—has triumphed. The boundries of the market have been redrawn.[20]

But government also has played the role of planner—to attempt to chart the course of the economy and the society. For example, income tax programs rest on assumptions of future as well as present states—that is, how income should be redistributed in society, what activities are to be encouraged and which discouraged, etc. But there are those who feel that government needs to play a far more active role in order to avert what they consider to be likely ecological or social disorder on a planetary scale. If the world is going to be a reasonably habitable place for our children and their children, the arguments go, government—perhaps world government—must direct resources toward a sane and just future. From this position, the market, and its narrowly self-interested premises, can no longer suffice in a world that may be poisoning itself ecologically and socially.

In the mid-1980s, a national church organization asserted that if the entire world were a global village of 100 people:

- ◆   47 would be literate.
- ◆   1 would have a college education.
- ◆   67 would be poor.
- ◆   35 would suffer from hunger and malnutrition.
- ◆   50 would be homeless or living in substandard housing.
- ◆   Of the 100 people, six would be Americans, with 33% of the village's entire income. [21]

But the answer to this dilemma, another perspective offers, is not governmental planning with all its ineptitude and strangling bureaucracy, but a vigorous world market, where the benefits will accrue to all through the creation of new economic opportunities.

There is, then, no shortage of positions for government as regulator or planner, locally, regionally, nationally, or even on a planetary scale. What is evident is an acceptance of government's role in significant dimensions of the lives of every citizen of this country. This ongoing governmental presence, of course, assumes that the economy and society cannot be entirely self-regulating without what would seem to be unacceptable social and economic costs—potential exploitation, a widening of the gap between the haves and the have-nots, and so forth.

The role of government is certainly the most obvious deviation from the classical liberal world view. But that, as we have seen, can only be seen properly against the backdrop of changing perceptions of self-interest, the individual's rationality, and the presumed buffering force of competition.

◆   ◆   ◆   ◆   ◆

We can, then, call this series of compromises and uncertainties "neo-liberalism."   They represent, we believe, grafts on the existing classical liberal trunk rather than a new variety. We have, after all, trusted much to the individual, with all that implies, and we are reluctant to abandon our ideological roots, no matter how ambiguous the resulting idea system.

THE IMPLICATIONS OF "NEO-LIBERALISM" FOR ADVERTISING

In the last chapter we investigated the implications of the relationship

CLASSICAL LIBERALISM——>ADVERTISING.

We could, then, begin here with

NEO-LIBERALISM——>ADVERTISING.

Based on the reexamination of several of the key elements of the classical liberal world view (i.e., egoism, intellectualism, atomism, the economy, and the role of government), we could expect an institution regarded with some suspicion. For if advertisers are presumed to be self-interested, and the expected counterforces of the individual's rationality and the purifying effect of atomistic competition are qualified, then the potential for exploitation—economically and socially—exists. Thus, presumably, the need for regulation internally (i.e., within the advertising business) based on "social responsibility," and externally, from government bodies—exists.

But there are obviously disagreements about this perception of advertising in contemporary society. Those associated with the advertising business, for example, feel quite differently about the practice and effects of their craft. They are troubled that advertising is viewed as shaper rather than mirror, sovereign rather than servant of the individual, and they are concerned about their generally low standing in public-opinion polls concerning their business (advertising), its products (advertisements), and themselves as responsible professionals.

One way, we believe, of seeing these different visions of advertising in contemporary society with greater clarity is offered in Figure 3-1.

Note that the range of individual positions encompassing what we call neo-liberalism is represented on a continuum, with those positions toward the top being far closer to the set of classical liberal assumptions we explored in the preceding chapter than those further down the continuum. Basically, then, we suggest:

> That in order to understand advertising in contemporary society, it is useful to examine an individual's assumptions about intellectualism, atomism, and egoism as we have come to understand them. These will likely lead to a compatible view of the economy and the role of regulation. Depending, then, upon where one falls in these dimensions, he or she will "see" advertising very differently.

Now, in order to deepen our understanding, let's examine each of these dimensions separately, offering some notion of the possible implications for advertising.

Depending Upon One's Assumption About "Intellectualism". . . .

In their focus on modern advertising as "privileged discourse through and about objects," William Leiss, Stephen Kline, and Sut Ghally comment on "a wonderfully orchestrated play of social behavior oriented around consumption practices today—our masked ball." They conclude:

> We may think of marketing as the host, and advertising as the master of ceremonies and conductor. Their staging for the spectacle of consumption often is brilliant, so much so that it can distract us from our duty to ensure that we do not sacrifice or neglect other

FIGURE 3-1

Positions in "Neo-Liberalism"

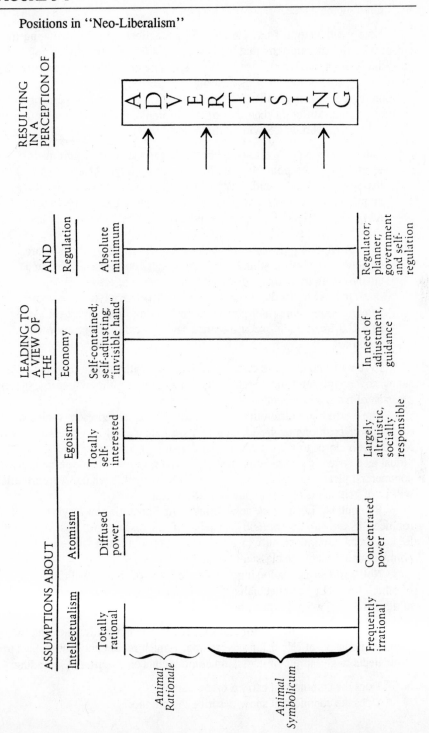

important values and goals just because we have become enraptured by the dance.[22]

Note the deviation from the ideal of the deliberate and calculating individual with the assumptions that we can be "distracted" by advertising from our "duty" such that we can potentially "sacrifice or neglect" other important values and goals, presumably against our own self-interests. This is clearly a position on the "intellectualism" continuum destined to lead to perceptions of advertising quite different than that of, for example, advertising executive Joseph E. De Deo, who, in a Soviet seminar on advertising and marketing, stated:

> The problem is to determine what represents the basic requirements of life at a given point in time, for a given society. As a U.S. professor of marketing said, "When and how does an extension telephone, or a second car, or a VCR, or even an underarm deodorant make that official list of life's necessities, and who determines that?" In an advertised marketplace, the consumer does.
>
> Advertising doesn't manipulate people. It makes them aware of new possibilities, stimulates latent needs, dormant desires, and enables them to enjoy a greater and wider range of tastes.
>
> But these needs, desires, tastes—all originate with the consumer. As an important part of the marketing mix, advertising is, as a U.S. marketing executive once said, "a catalyst but not a determinant."[23]

Here we seem closer to classical liberal turf, with the assumptions of consumer sovereignty and the capable consumer directing the system by the expression of his or her self-interest.

These strikingly different visions of the individual represent something of the range of positions in the idea system we have called neo-liberalism, with Mr. De Deo closer to the classical liberal vision of *animal rationale,* the individual as a sovereign calculating decision maker, quite at home in an arena of commercial pleading, and able to extract from the babble whatever information will be of help in his or her pursuit of self-interest.

By contrast, Leiss *et al.* see the individual operating in a symbolic environment, as *animale symbolicum,* capable of responding to a host of psychological/social/cultural stimuli in addition to the more narrowly defined economic dimensions of the classical liberal.

Not surprisingly, endorsing one or the other of these positions, or a host of others along our "intellectualism" continuum, results in different perception of advertising. Two important considerations:

What Is Meant by "Information"?   In a major study assessing the information content of television advertising, Danish researcher Preben Sepstrup evaluated a large sample of television commercials on 24 criteria, including:

◆   Does the commercial carry a brand name?
◆   Does the commercial show/describe the product?

◆   Does the commercial mention the name of the company behind the
    brand?
◆   Does the commercial quote the price?
◆   Does the commercial mention varieties of the product?

Sepstup concluded, ''From a general consumer point of view, TV advertising
has limited value, since information relevant for purchasing decisions is not
communicated to a degree that would seem to have any practical significance
to consumers.''[24]

It should not surprise us that, based on these and 19 other demanding criteria, television advertisements were found wanting, in the same manner that
most consumer goods advertisements in *all* media seem inadequate sources of
''information'' when compared to the exhaustive evaluations of, say, *Consumer Reports.*

Yet, television advertising thrives because advertisers find it in their self-
interests to use it because, presumably, individuals frequently find it in *their*
self-interests to respond to it.

What we seem to have, then, are two general working definitions of ''information.'' The *first* revolves around criteria that ''information'' should be
product-centered, functional in a mechanistic sense, and relatively objective.
Thus an advertisement could be assumed to have adequate information if it
contained facts about, say, price, durability, performance in a relatively narrowly defined sense, etc.

The *second* definition moves more to the symbolic dimension, suggesting
that a host of psychological/sociological cues serve as ''information'' as well.
As Leiss *et al.* observe, advertising also communicates about such matters as:

> . . . interpersonal and family relations, the sense of happiness and
> contentment, sex role and stereotyping, the uses of affluence, the
> fading away of older cultural tradition, influence of younger gen-
> erations, the role of business in society, persuasion and personal au-
> tonomy, and many others. (Leiss, *et al.,* p. 3)

This, they would contend, certainly represents ''information'' as well, for products and services are frequently not perceived as narrowly functional by consumers. Hence, it is argued, they respond to market information, including
advertising, that matches their own expanded criteria.

Clearly, differing positions on this essential element in the assessment of
the individual's ''deliberate and calculating'' nature will lead to dramatically
different visions of advertising at work in contemporary society. But there is
also the dimension of . . .

How Much ''Information'' Is Enough?   Reviewing several contemporary books on advertising, including works by practitioners David Ogilvy,
John O'Toole, and Jane Maas, the *New York Times'* Roger Draper observes:

> Advertising cannot consistently tell the truth, the whole truth, and
> nothing but the truth. If we are to settle for something less than the

whole truth, so far as it can be known to us, what shall we settle for? "Some of the truth" would be the answer [from] Ogilvy, O'Toole, and Maas. . . . By this they mean not the amount of truth that can reasonably be compressed into a reasonable amount of space, but the product of efforts to suppress an important fact: *the similarity among competing brands.* If "some of the truth" in this sense is an acceptable alternative to all of it, the value of truth itself becomes puzzling. It is easier, and perhaps necessary, for the advertising industry to dethrone truth as a value, much as it is often necessary to distort the truth in advertising.[25]

Yet, there are those who would contend that the "clash of ideas" in the marketplace will inevitably lead to the recognition of truth, since the individual is assumed deliberate and calculating. But what, others argue, if that information *doesn't* emerge? Will not the individual's rationality be thwarted?

These are muddy waters indeed. Consider, for example, that a recent study by the advertising agency BBDO Worldwide revealed that *two-thirds* of consumers surveyed in 28 countries considered brands in 13 major product categories to be *at parity*—i.e., virtually identical.[26] Yet, in many countries, including the United States, more expensive, generally highly advertised brands tend to dominate sales. For example, a *Consumer Reports* assessment of mouthwashes concluded that virtually all are "essentially similar," yet prices per fluid ounce ranged from 3 cents for No Frills Amber, to Listerine (10 cents), and Chloraseptic (29 cents).[27] This could be interpreted to suggest that individuals *are* generally aware of "the similarity among competing brands" but still choose to pay a premium for the often more symbolic rewards offered in manufacturers' brand advertising.

Thus, advertising can be savaged, or praised, from virtually any point on the intellectualism continuum. What seems clear, however, is that, generally, the more the assumption is made that the individual represents *animal symbolicum* rather than *animal rationale,* the more likely it is that the individual will be seen as vulnerable—to advertiser and critic alike. And when advertising practitioners defend their practice, they are more likely to evoke the model of the steely eyed, deliberate and calculating, maddeningly fickle consumer, close to the classical liberal roots.

Depending Upon One's Assumptions About "Atomism". . . .

Remember that the second major buffer to egoism-run-rampant was assumed to be diffused power, so that no single entity, or group of entities, could avoid being brought into line with the wishes of the sovereign consumer because of the relentless forces of competition offering the rational individual cheaper, better alternatives, etc. And that, *because* of this diffused power, individuals controlled institutions, not the other way around.

Referring back to our previous discussion on the neo-liberal dimensions of intellectualism, you can imagine the volatile combination of assumptions of a vulnerable individual subjected to concentrated power. You begin to catch the flavor of this mind-set when encountering articles such as *TV Guide's* recent, "Why You Watch Commercials—Whether You Mean to or Not."[28]

Basically, it can be argued that as an individual's position falls toward the "concentrated power" end of the continuum, he or she is more likely to assume that institutions, rather than individuals, are sovereign, and, hence, capable of influence. Those toward the "diffused power" dimension are, predictably, likely to place more faith in the individual being in charge of his or her destiny. Let's examine some current controversies linked to the question of where power resides.

◆   Assessing the dimensions of the advertising agency field in the U.S. in the late 1980s, Leo Bogart observed:

> The three billion-dollar U.S. advertisers, RJR-Nabisco, P&G, and Phillip Morris, represent 11% of all network TV advertising and 10% of all national advertising in consumer media. . . .
>
> This concentration of power has tremendous social and cultural consequences. A recent trade press item reports that the Saatchi and Saatchi agencies among them account for one out of every five dollars spent on network television. I would be very much surprised if at this time the brothers Saatchi *have* sought to impose any guiding hand of corporate philosophy upon the time-buying practices of all their individual agencies. But could any television network, in its programming decisions, be unresponsive to the prevailing philosophy of Saatchi and Saatchi, of J. Walter Thompson, of Omnicom—of all the other giants of the agency world? (Bogart, pp. 18-19)

◆   Planned Parenthood counted more than 20,000 sexual scenes on prime-time network television in a single year. Using a full-page advertisement, they urged readers to send prepared coupons to the major media power brokers, the presidents of NBC-TV, CBS-TV, and ABC-TV. The coupon read:

> Hyping sex on television while censoring references to birth control is giving a dangerous double message to American teens. The U.S. suffers the highest rate of teen pregnancy in the industrialized world, causing school dropouts, family breakups, and massive welfare. TV industry censorship of birth control is making a bad problem worse. Please reverse your policy. Permit programs *and* advertising to discuss birth control.[29]

◆   The National Coalition on Television Violence states that sales of war
toys increased 700% between 1983 and 1987, due in no small part to
"the toy industry's use of children's programming as 30-minute commercials [e.g., with *He-Man, GI Joe, et al.*] to sell a variety of war toys."[30]
They claim that the linkage of entertainment and selling directed to children has accelerated since 1978 with the popularity of the movie *Star
Wars* and its related merchandise tie-ins.

A spokesperson from the Toy Manufacturers of America responds:

> It's getting into dangerous territory when somebody decides
> what is good for all 44.3 million American children. Ameri-
> can parents, making intelligent parental decisions, have
> purchased *Star Wars* toys in the millions of units.[31]

Where does power reside? If we believe the individual is in charge, there
can be little concern of exploitation. But if those in concentrated power set the
agenda, concerns are raised. Even the deliberate and calculating individual, it
may be argued, can be overmatched if he or she is not in position to set some
priorities of choice. And when it is assumed that the individual is often adrift
in a symbolic universe, alarms become shrill indeed.

Now, One's Assumption About "Egoism" Is Likely to Be Influenced by His or Her Position on Intellectualism and Atomism.

For, predictably, if the individual is considered rational and sovereign,
self-interest will be seen as "natural" and beneficial rather than potentially ex-
ploitive. But if the individual is perceived as potentially vulnerable and at the
mercy of concentrations of power, then calls for restraint on self-interest will
be heard.

Thus, advertisers can be seen in pursuit of their self-interests, which must
"naturally" take into account the self-interests of the potential customers; *or*
advertisers can be called upon to exercise social responsibility to avoid the potential exploitation that could occur if it is assumed (a) the individual is not
always "rational," (b) power is concentrated and thus not channeled in positive ways by the atomistic forces of competition, or (c) both of the above.

To use a topical example, there is currently much concern about alcohol
abuse, particularly among young people. Senator Strom Thurmond recently
waved a Spuds MacKenzie doll on the Senate floor, declaring, "Is this the kind
of responsibility which we can expect from the alcoholic beverage industry in
the future? If so, I think we in Congress should get to work on some major
policy changes."[32] If Senator Thurmond were making assumptions about self-
interest similar to those of the classical liberals, he would probably not have
raised the issue at all. For it would be assumed only natural that firms would
seek their self-interests in whatever manner most benefited their profit interests. Any "responsibility" would be handled by the give-and-take of market

forces. If Anhesuser-Busch offended, they would be punished where it *really* hurt—at the cash register.

There is a *New Yorker* cartoon depicting an executive from the fictional Frizzly Corporation reviewing potential advertising approaches with slogans such as, "It's People We're All About" and "Our Concern is People." "I'm sick of this whole approach," he finally tells the nonplussed advertising man, "Just tell the public we're cold and aloof and we make a damn good carburetor." For better or for worse, most advertisers today are called upon to do more than just make good products or services; because of doubts about intellectualism and atomism, there may also be concerns about how they act as responsible city, state, national, and international citizens—and advertisers.

It's not difficult to see, then, that an individual's assumptions about such a basic matter as the outcome of self-interest can lead to starkly different views about advertising as an institution—servant or exploiter. But there is, we know, other contested ground as well.

Based on the Assumptions About Intellectualism, Atomism, and Egoism, the Individual Is Likely to Have a Compatible View of Advertising's Role in . . .

The economy.   Advertising executive Joseph E. De Deo applauded this definition of advertising in the new *Soviet Encyclopedia:*

> Advertising involves the popularization of goods with the aim of selling them, the creation of demand for these goods, the acquaintance of consumers with the quality, particular features, location of their sales, and the explanation of the method of their use. (De Deo, np.)

"The American Association of Advertising Agencies," he added, "couldn't have said it better." Well, certainly the Soviet definition might imply a somewhat more conservative form of persuasive communication than we've become accustomed to, but it still suggests a relationship between advertising and the economy that many American practitioners could embrace. Note De Deo's later elaboration:

> . . . advertising helps allow a more efficient use of national resources. It is the key link in the marketing process, the aim of which is to produce what the market needs and can absorb. As the means of communication with consumers, it helps guard against the wasteful production of unwanted goods.
>
> Next, without question, advertising is one of the major stimulants to vigorous economic growth and stability. As the Organization for Economic Cooperation and Development recently stated, after a detailed review of all the major industrial economies of the

West, "The secret of economic stability and growth lies in the steady maintenance of demand." (De Deo, np.)

Notice the familiar assumptions of classical liberal thinking—an efficient, self-adjusting economy, ultimately serving the self-interests of all sensible participants. But note also the somewhat jarring references to the "creation" and "maintenance" of demand in the two statements. Surely, this suggests that demand does not simply emerge "naturally" but must routinely be invented and/or constantly reinforced—through advertising as well as other marketing stratagems.

Herein, then, lies the essence of two strikingly different visions of advertising and the economy—advertising as (a) friend or (b) foe of the market system. The arabesques will be explored in much greater detail in Chapter 5, but let's at least acknowledge the positions here.

As a friend of the market, advertising, as De Deo proclaims, is seen to serve as a lubricant for the efficient exchange of goods and services between eager seller and cautious buyer, with power presumably residing in consumer demand. Competition is stimulated by self-interest, with advertising serving as a readily available communication device to reach, and hopefully persuade, the multitudes regarding what educator Charles Sandage refers to as the "want satisfying qualities of products and services."[33] Self-interest is well represented on all sides, thus stimulating the energy so typical of the best market economies.

But to the extent advertising "creates" demand, the power balance begins to shift from the consumer to the producer/supplier, with presumably ever larger advertising budgets carrying ever greater clout. If the market has no direction other than to existing demand, and that demand is in some way contrived by advertising, the scenario suggests large firms having their way, relatively immune to the disciplines of rigorous competition as they joust on the level of brand name rather than price. Clearly, symbolic man is afoot here, easily impressed by the promises of the advertiser and responding accordingly. Consequently, the market is distorted, with a perceived need for government to enter to restore balance and/or fashion direction.

Simply, if one's assumptions involve the self-interested, rational individual, directing the economy through his or her "dollar votes," advertising will generally be perceived as helpful or, at least, not likely to do great harm. But if it is believed that the individual can be unduly influenced, that the power to pursue that influence is not checked by social responsibility, the forces of individual rationality, or diffused power, then advertising can be seen as a worrisome tool of the power brokers.

All of this, in turn, sets the stage for . . .

Regulation.   As we have noted, an acceptance of a major role for government in virtually every facet of our society represents the greatest departure from "pure" classical liberal thought. Predictably, then, those whose positions are likely to fall near the top of the regulation continuum are likely to urge the smallest possible role for government as a regulator in the economy and society at large, with whatever constraints deemed necessary supplied by self-regulation. Indeed, with the companion assumptions of rational individuals exercising their sovereignty in a self-adjusting economy, it would be surprising if it were otherwise. But move down the continuums through *animal symbolicum,* concentrated power, and the subsequent perceived need for a tinkered economy; then, the role of government as regulator/planner to "set things right" becomes equally paramount, as does the vigorous exercise of social responsibility on the part of the advertising community in the form of self- regulation at the advertiser, agency, media, and association level.

The consequences for advertising are enormous, as will be explored in greater depth in Chapter 8. Herewith, a sampling of the implications and consequences.

◆   Consumers Union on a potential ban on all cigarette advertising:

> Given the hazards of tobacco, the addictive nature of nicotine, which makes tobacco use less than voluntary, the sophisticated manipulation of cigarette advertising, the violations of the spirit (if not the letter) of the tobacco industry's own code of advertising conduct, the indication of an inverse relationship between cigarette advertising and media discussions of smoking hazards, the reinforcement of smoking by advertising that portrays cigarettes as not only socially acceptable but desirable—given all these, Congressional action to ban cigarette advertising and promotion is fully justified, in CU's judgment.[34]

John O'Toole, of the American Association of Advertising Agencies:

> The fear underlying the compulsion to censor is groundless. Consumers are protected against untruthful advertising by media and advertising industry self-regulation and, ultimately, by the Federal Trade Commission. Truthful advertising for legal products and services can hurt no one. Indeed, it is inconsistent, if not erratic, to believe that those citizens who can distill the truth from the welter of diverse opinion heaved up each day by a free press cannot be trusted to decide, on the basis of commercial messages, which brand of soap or beer or even cigarettes to purchase—or whether to make such a purchase at all.[35]

The reader is invited to dissect these dramatically different positions in terms of the implicit assumptions of intellectualism, atomism, and egoism.

◆   As should have been clear through simple observation (and will be under-
scored in Chapter 8), the Reagan administration generally pursued a
strong *de*regulation program at virtually every level—including those
areas that impact advertising. Not surprisingly, the resulting federal
regulatory vacuum became filled by the states. Of course, even here
there were different interpretations about the "proper" course:

> When deception occurs that hurts the citizens of our states,
> the state attorneys general cannot turn a blind eye, as the fed-
> eral agencies have done. As the chief law enforcement offi-
> cers of our states, it is our duty to stop deception and we will
> do so.[36]
>
> *James Mattox*
> *Texas Attorney General*

> National advertising guidelines administered by the states re-
> pudiate the wisdom of the founders and bestow upon state of-
> ficials the mantles of both the legislative and executive
> branches of the federal government.[37]
>
> *Hal Stratton*
> *New Mexico Attorney General*

In spite of Mr. Stratton's reservations, the National Association of Attorneys General has voted overwhelmingly to adopt strict guidelines for air-
line advertising, and it is currently considering whether to apply stiff
standards for rental car advertising as well. This, of course, is in addition
to whatever activity may take place within individual states—e.g., New
York and Texas putting aspirin manufacturers on notice that they face
state court action if they promote aspirin as a preventative for heart
attacks.[38]

◆   ◆   ◆   ◆   ◆

In the first chapter, we offered this premise:

Because of its cultural boundness, its complexity of forms and
functions, and the difficulty in ascertaining its outcome, advertising
is highly prone to disparate interpretations.

Given the range of positions we contend are possible under "neo-liberalism," we hope the reader is now in a better position to understand that perceptions of advertising in contemporary society are based in no small part on varying interpretations of such essential concepts as human nature, the seat of
power, and the proper relationship between the individual and the state.
Simply, advertising is "seen" differently, depending on the degree of neo-
liberalism embraced.

SUMMARY

If IDEAS——>INSTITUTIONS, then it is appropriate to inquire into what passes for our contemporary idea system by examining how it may differ from its classical liberal predecessor discussed in Chapter 2. *Intellectualism* has been called into some doubt because of ambiguity about the dimensions of *animal symbolicum;* and *atomism,* the other major counterforce to narrow self-interest, is confronted with an economic and social landscape dominated by enormous power blocs in addition to somewhat atomistic participants. Hence, the notion of *egoism* is now qualified to some extent by the philosophy of "social responsibility," with its inherent assumption that the workings of the "invisible hand" are no longer certain.

Thus the *economy* is now commonly regarded as in need of regulation and, perhaps, direction, often through the role of *government* as regulator and/or planner.

Given this range of ideas under what we have called "neo-liberalism," advertising in contemporary society can be regarded quite differently. As master . . . or servant. As friend of the market . . . or foe. As information dispenser . . . or symbol manipulator.

Much can be better understood through such a perspective.

ENDNOTES

1.   Walton Hamilton, "Institution," *The Encyclopedia of the Social Sciences,* vol. 8 (New York: Macmillan, 1932), p. 85.
2.   Cal Thomas, "Lack of Moral Values Trickling Up," The Champaign-Urbana *News-Gazette,* June 23, 1988, p. A-4.
3.   Theodore Levitt, "The Dangers of Social Responsibility," *Harvard Business Review,* September-October, 1958, p. 48. (Emphasis in original.)
4.   "Burnett's *Pro Bono* Work Through the Years," *The Burnettwork,* May/June, 1988, p. 6.
5.   David Lill, Charles Gross, and Robin Peterson, "The Inclusion of Social-Responsibility Themes by Magazine Advertisers: A Longitudinal Study," *Journal of Advertising,* vol. 15, no. 2, 1986, p. 39.
6.   Michael Perschuk, "The Press and Business: As Biased as a Scream From the Dentist's Chair!" remarks before the Society of Professional Journalists, San Francisco, November 10, 1983.
7.   "How to Save $2500 a Year in the Supermarket," *Consumer Reports,* March 1988, p. 163.
8.   James W. Carey, "Advertising: An Institutional Approach," in *The Role of Advertising,* C. H. Sandage and V. Fryburger, eds. (Homewood, IL: Richard D. Irwin, Inc., 1960), p. 16.

9. "Rewriting Antitrust Rules," *Newsweek,* August 29, 1983, p. 50.

10. Ralph Nader, "Corporate Power in America," *The Nation,* March 29, 1980, p. 367.

11. Jonathan Rowe, "Ralph Nader Reconsidered," *The Washington Monthly,* March 1985, p. 12.

12. "What Kind of Media Diversity?" *Communication Research Trends,* vol. 4, no. 1 (1983), p. 7.

13. Leo Bogart, "Advertising: Art, Science, or Business?" James Webb Young Fund Address, Department of Advertising, University of Illinois, April 7, 1988, pp. 8-9.

14. "Nation's 'Third Deficit' Widening—Dovring," *IlliniWeek,* University of Illinois, Urbana, December 10, 1987, p. 5.

15. "Talking Up an Industrial Policy," *Newsweek,* April 4, 1983, p. 66. Also, see "Issues at a Glance," *Best of Business,* vol. 6, no. 1 (Spring 1984), p. 55.

16. Lester C. Thurow, "Down Without a Fight," *Newsweek,* April 4, 1983, p. 67.

17. Robert L. Heilbroner, *The Worldly Philosophers* (New York: Time, Inc., 1961), pp. 336 ff.

18. George A. and Achilles G. Theodorson, *Modern Dictionary of Sociology* (New York: Thomas Y. Crowell Co., 1969), p. 224.

19. Irving Kristol, "What Is a 'Neo-Conservative?'" *Newsweek,* January 19, 1976, p. 17.

20. Robert G. Samuelson, "The Aging of Ralph Nader," *Newsweek,* December 16, 1985, p. 57.

21. "That All May Have Life," flyer for One Great Hour of Sharing from United Church of Christ, 1985.

22. William Leiss, Stephen Kline, and Sut Ghally, *Social Communication in Advertising—Persons, Products, & Images of Well Being* (Toronto: Methuen, 1986), p. 296.

23. Joseph E. De Deo, *Why Over $109,800,000,000 Was Spent on Advertising in America Last Year* (New York: Young & Rubicam, Inc.), nd.

24. Preben Sepstrup, "Information Content in TV Advertising. Consumer Policy Implications of the Growing Supply of TV Advertising in Europe," *Journal of Consumer Policy,* 8 (1985), p. 250.

25. Roger Draper, "The Faithless Shepherd," *New York Review,* June 26, 1986, p. 18.

26. Nancy Giges, "World's Product Parity Perception High," *Advertising Age,* June 20, 1988, p. 66.

27. "Listings—Mouthwashes," *Consumer Reports,* March 1984, p. 146.

28. *TV Guide,* February 20, 1988, pp. 5-7.

29. "They Did It 20,000 Times on Television Last Year. How Come Nobody Got Pregnant?" Champaign-Urbana *News-Gazette,* December 7, 1986, p. A-15.

30. "War Toys, Cartoons More Violent," *Advertising Age,* September 21, 1987, p. 18.
31. "Action Tales for Kids are Traditional," *Advertising Age,* September 21, 1987, p. 18.
32. "Spuds MacKenzie Meets Strom Thurmond," American Association of Advertising Agencies, Washington Newsletter.
33. Charles H. Sandage, "Some Institutional Aspects of Advertising," *Journal of Advertising,* vol. 1, no. 1 (1973) pp. 6-9 for "essence" of his position.
34. "Ban Cigarette Advertising?" *Consumer Reports,* September 1987, pp. 568-569.
35. John O'Toole, "Advertising and Democracy: Is Advertising Second-Class Speech?" *Gannett Center Journal,* Spring 1987, p. 107.
36. "Should States Regulate Ads?" *Advertising Age,* August 8, 1988, p. 18.
37. *Ibid.*
38. Jennifer Lawrence, "New Attacks on Aspirin Ads, States Threaten Court Action," *Advertising Age,* February 15, 1988, p. 1.

4
PERSPECTIVES ON ADVERTISING AS AN INSTITUTION

In the two preceding chapters we have probed the left side of the IDEAS
——>INSTITUTIONS concept. Here, we turn our attention to the right, as
seen through the lens of several individuals who have asked the following fundamental questions: What functions does advertising perform as an institution
in our society? With what consequences and trade-offs? Their ruminations
deepen our understanding of advertising in contemporary society.

It has been said that, ''We don't know who discovered water, but we're
pretty sure it wasn't a fish.'' That's a useful idea to bring to the study of an
institution. For it's very difficult to appreciate the larger dimensions of something of which we ourselves are a part. Thus, the true impact of the idea ''Island Earth'' did not hit us until the astronauts photographed it from
afar—colorful, but very, very much alone.

And so it is with institutional analysis. We often find it extraordinarily
difficult to understand the full configurations of an institution *of which we are
a part.* Indeed, as Hamilton observes, until the academic community began to
grudgingly accept the idea that the behavior of individuals could not be adequately explained solely as resulting from their own free wills or as the behavior of cells in a well-integrated and predictable organism, institutional analysis
was simply not considered at all.[1]

As we have noted in the preceding chapters, an institution may be seen as
representing a convention, an arrangement, or an answer to a problem considered important by the society. It was also held that the different ''answers''
that various societies choose to deal with the same fundamental problems (e.g.,
what to produce) can, in part, be attributed to their differing idea systems.
Thus, the institution of the market (with its emphasis on resource allocation
through the action of many self-seeking individuals) was seen to be most compatible with the idea system of classical liberalism (with its emphasis on the
sovereignty and rationality of each individual).

WHY INSTITUTIONAL ANALYSIS?

Why bother considering a phenomenon in our society from an institutional perspective? At a minimum, it can give us some view of the forest even as the trees compel our attention. For example, a marriage certificate, a high-school athletic jacket, a jail cell, make little sense in and of themselves unless we see them as parts of the larger institutional whole of marriage, organized amateur athletics, and a system that attempts to define crime and punishment.

Similarly, advertisements for motor oil, perfume, a breakfast cereal, a bowling alley, or an abortion clinic are not readily understood in any significant dimension unless we first understand why it is we consider an impersonal information and persuasion process an acceptable means to attempt to alter the thinking and behavior of individuals; what the generally accepted "rules of the road" between advertiser and receiver are, etc. Charles Sandage has put it this way: institutional analysis lets us be architects as well as bricklayers, with our vision filled with the total structure as well as the roles assigned to its component parts.[2]

Institutional analysis may also aid us in understanding the "conventional wisdom" of advertising as an institution. Hamilton notes:

> As it crystallizes into reputable usages, an institution creates in its
> defense vested interest, vested habit, and vested ideas and claims
> allegiance in its own right. (Hamilton, p. 87)

And thus does every institution create its own apology. The origins of an institution may be very utilitarian—e.g., to tend the sick—but as it flourishes and draws to it individuals whose vested interests lie in its perpetuation and ennoblement, an ideology and apparatus emerge to support it—e.g., the American Medical Association. By way of further example, as the institution of marriage comes under attack, it is frequently defended by references to the Scriptures; while, organized athletics is often charged with no less a noble endeavor than "character building," and so on.

It would thus seem reasonable that this institutional perspective may be useful in helping us to better understand not only the defenses of, but also the attacks on, advertising. For example, some critics proclaim that advertising directed to children is likely to do serious harm to their psyches, or that advertising contributes to a massive waste of human and natural resources, or that advertising is offensive and demeaning to the role of women, the elderly, Hispanics, and others. In a similar mode, it is not uncommon to attend advertising conventions where advertising is described as the consumer's best friend, an indispensable source of relevant market information and, depending on the severity of the critical salvo, the bulwark of the free enterprise system. As we hope we have made clear this far, *all* advertising is—objectively—none of these things, although critic and defender believe the contrary. This tendency to generalize about the activities and purposes of an institution is, apparently, quite natural. We should, then, be on our guard, realizing that the perception of an institution that emerges from its more dedicated critics, *and* ardent defenders, is far more likely to resemble an impressionistic painting than a realistic photograph. Institutional analysis, then, holds the promise to lead us to higher analytical ground while reminding us not to overlook the variations in the terrain below. To see the whole while appreciating the parts is, then, not an unpromising quest.

The following perspectives offer us the opportunity to see advertising as an institution through perceptive eyes. They encompass four decades and are rich in analytical tools and insights. Learn and enjoy.

CAREY—ADVERTISING AS MARKET INFORMATION

James W. Carey, a communications scholar, offers this intriguing interpretation—"the information provided in purely competitive markets and in primitive markets is *advertising*. We here define market information as advertising."[3] But there is much more that needs to be said.

Carey devotes his penetrating 1960 essay to the search for "the ideas and institutions which favor the development of an economic system in which advertising becomes a part of the very logic by which commerce is carried on." (p. 3) He finds the "ideas" in the liberalism of the eighteenth and nineteenth centuries and, particularly, in the influence of Newton (indirectly) and Locke and Smith (directly):

> For our purposes the ideas that were of fundamental importance in justifying the new economic order [the market] were the notions that all was mechanistic, that natural law governed the physical and social world, that the world was characterized by fundamental harmony, that man possessed reason and conscience, that men were equal and endowed with certain fundamental rights—life, liberty, and property. (p. 10)

Sound familiar? The explanatory institutions are thus seen as the market system and, of particular importance, the idea of property rights.

As seen from these classical liberal premises then, an individual expresses the rights to "property"—anything with which he or she has mixed labor—in the free marketplace, where he or she encounters other individuals in the same pursuit. Harmony rather than discord results due to the essentially rational and moral nature of the individual, and—crucially—the great safeguard of competition. And it is *within this system,* Carey argues, that the institutional importance of advertising becomes evident:

> One of the fundamental assumptions underlying theoretical analysis of competitive markets, and the whole concept of economic man, is that all entrants into the economic market shall have perfect knowl-

edge; that is, each should be aware of all prices resulting from supply and demand relationships and should have perfect knowledge of
alternative forms of satisfying demand. *Caveat emptor*—let the
buyer beware—simply means that every individual, being rational,
is assumed to possess the ability to exercise correct judgment by
basing his decisions on available market information. (p. 13)

Under *purely competitive* markets, the task of supplying relevant information is carried out by the "market" itself (contemporary approximations can
be found in the stock market, the grain market, and so on) based on myriad
interpersonal transactions. Thus, this market-supplied information concerning
supply and demand represented the interactions of many buyers and sellers
concerning their property rights and, presumably, led to the "natural" value of
the goods offered. It is here, in the supplying of relevant information, Carey
states, that advertising's institutional birth can be found. It is not, of course,
advertising as we generally know it today (it differs in *content* and *source*) but
it does, he feels, correctly place advertising's origins as a supplier of relevant
information in a market economy in proper institutional perspective.

Advertising in its *modern* form, Carey holds, developed as markets began to lose their interpersonal nature. As production became more centralized,
as branded merchandise developed, the function of supplying market information shifted from the market itself to the firms in the market, with "the old
interpersonal relationships in the marketplace . . . displaced by relationships
mediated by mass communication facilities" (p. 15). Of course, the self-seeking firms were interested in "market information" for persuasive (rather than
simply informational) purposes.

Now, *under the assumption that the individual is rational,* it is quite appropriate to attempt to persuade. For, it is assumed that the rational person will
be able to detect truth in the clashing views of self-interested individuals in the
economic marketplace in the same manner that his or her discerning nature
would enable truth to arise in the political arena. Thus, advertising's basic institutional function of supplying information "to facilitate judgment and free
choice on the part of the consumer" (p. 15) remains intact, but the fact that the
"information" is now supplied by interested parties (firms) has certain consequences:

There is no longer any guarantee that the self-righting process operates to yield the "true value" of goods when individual firms possess a measure of control over the market. Because competition no
longer provides the check on self-interest that it did under atomistic
market organization, control in the market is increasingly being
sought in human and corporate conscience—a conscience expressed through the notion of social responsibility. (p. 15)

Modern-day advertising is seen by Carey as still performing the traditional function of disseminating market information "as a logical corollary of a

market system,'' (p. 16) but also acting ''as an agency of social control providing norms of behavior appropriate to current economic conditions'' (p. 16). Thus, as marketing is conventionally concerned with the development of demand in an abundant society, advertising is called upon not merely to ''sell,'' but also to ''create and develop'' demand for a host of products and services that are well beyond any traditional definition of ''necessity.'' He concludes:

> Consequently, the nub of the ''advertising problem'' really rests on a controversy over who shall supply the necessary market information, what type of information it shall be, and to what ends it should be directed. The reader may then reflect upon the following two propositions: (1) That the source of advertising or market information is determined by the demands of technology and the location of economic power; and (2) that the specific form and nature of advertising messages is dependent on the particular economic problem which the society recognizes as most pressing and, more importantly, on the view that society takes toward the nature of man and to what it is that motivates ''appropriate'' market behavior. (p. 17)

For Carey, then, the key is the source and type of the information necessary for the functioning of a market system and, implicitly, the assumptions about ''human nature'' that lie behind these functions. Advertising's basic institutional function is thus linked to the provision of ''market information,'' however that be interpreted by the society.

◆   ◆   ◆   ◆   ◆

Now, it would seem that considerable understanding is offered by the concept of market information. If the information necessary for the functioning of a market system is provided by the sellers through mass communication, then the content and frequency of that information will be different than that provided by the ''market'' itself, either through interpersonal exchanges (e.g., a flea market) or a formalized system (e.g., the grain market). The comparison can perhaps be made clear in Table 4-1 on the next page.

This is the nub of a great deal of ongoing controversy about the proper role of advertising. The content of modern advertising is directed primarily by the best interests of the seller. Thus, it may or may not include *all* the market information that might be necessary for the model of the rational consumer to make a proper decision. To risk oversimplification, ''consumerists'' generally argue that the informational content of much advertising is not adequate to achieve that purpose, while many advertisers contend that it is. And here the arguments become quite complex indeed.

The consumerist may, for example, argue either (a) that the informational content of the *existing* market information (e.g., advertisements) needs to be

TABLE 4-1

INFORMATION SUPPLIED BY:	CONTENT	MEDIUM/FREQUENCY	EXAMPLE
Market			
(a) formal	Prices, quantities, qualities.	Mass or controlled media. As needed by participants.	Winter wheat information.
(b) interpersonal	Relevant information.	Person-to-person. As controlled by participants.	Flea market.
Sellers	Biased— whatever is in the best interest of the seller.	As desired by seller.	Cosmetics advertising.

enriched (usually through legislation—e.g., the cigarette warning), or (b) that *additional* sources of market information be made more widely available—e.g., the product ratings of government agencies, the judgments of such sources as *Consumer Reports,* "counter" advertising, and so on.

The second contention seems to offer a view of human nature much like that of the classical liberals, with the suggestion that an increase in message sources will better enable the truth-seeking individual to make a wise decision. Certainly, as we have seen, this is the assumption behind much of the ideology and practice of our press, and judicial and political systems. The first assertion, however, can be viewed as suggesting that the individual is *not* a "truth seeker" (or at least is a lazy one) and must be catered to by making present sources of market information (e.g., advertisements) more informative (i.e., less "imperfect") in content.

Advertisers generally argue that the individual is quite capable of making satisfying market decisions on the basis of the existing state of the market information as represented by the advertisements of competing enterprises. The key here is "satisfying." (Remember our discussion of "information" in Chapter 3.) While consumerists often assume that economic/qualitative criteria can be applied that will make some products and services objectively "better buys" over others, advertisers frequently suggest that the *individual* should be the sole judge of what criteria she or he will apply in reaching a purchase decision. Thus, it is reasoned, if an individual *bought* it, he or she must have *wanted* it, for whatever reason. And if the advertisement led in any way to that decision, then it *must* have been satisfying "market information," at least for *that* individual. (Pushed to its limit, this reasoning suggests there is no such thing as an "irrational" decision.)

The matter of the frequency of advertising is, of course, a subject of some contention, particularly in the broadcast media. Carey's perspective enables us to see that the frequency of market information, when supplied by self-interested participants, will be whatever they feel is necessary to achieve their ends. Thus, we find the irritation factor emerging among those who complain of increasingly lengthy interruptions of broadcast programming, repetition of particular advertisements, and so on. Basically, in the classical liberal market, the "deliberate and calculating" individual seeks out "market"-supplied information. With information supplied by self-seeking firms, however, the information frequently *seeks out the individual,* with all the ensuing trade-offs.

Carey's analysis, then, raises a major question for the analysis of advertising: *What should be the proper source, content, and frequency of market information in the United States?* The position an individual takes, as this brief analysis is meant to suggest, is heavily dependent upon such contentions as how rational the consumer is assumed to be.

NORRIS—THE QUEST FOR MARKET POWER

In his 1965 address to the American Academy of Advertising,[4] Vincent P. Norris, another communications scholar, chastised advertising educators for (a) not pursuing institutional analysis in their examination of advertising, and (b) not being aware of the "conventional wisdom" of the institution of advertising that they themselves often embrace (and pass on to their students) in an unquestioning manner—e.g., "The Sunday *New York Times* would cost the reader $5.00 if it weren't for the support of advertisers." (But, Norris points out, without advertising the *Times* would be far less expensive to print, not to mention the savings in the elimination of the advertising department [p. 72].)

"Institutions," Norris reminded his listeners, "are the 'rules' according to which social life is carried on, and consequently our understanding of the life of any society is limited by our understanding of those institutions" (p. 60).

To understand advertising as an institution, Norris holds, one must avoid the temptation to trace it back to Pompeii or medieval Europe. Such a practice, he contends, is "roughly analogous to tracing the history of man back to the paramecium" (p. 63). Advertising, for Norris, was only "on its way" to becoming an institution . . .

> When some sizable segment of the population (namely, the business class) came to look upon advertising not as an emergency measure to be used sporadically, but as the routine manner of solving an omnipresent problem (let us say, the profitable conduct of business). (p. 65)

He argues that it was not until the last thirty years of the nineteenth century in America that advertising emerged as a "full-fledged" institution. It was during this period that advertising volume increased tenfold, but, of far greater importance, the increase was due largely to "an entirely new form of advertising"—the advertising of *producers,* not retailers. Yet, Norris claims, when advertising text writers deal with the subject of the emergence of ''national'' (producer) advertising, they usually handle it somewhat like this:

> As the Industrial Revolution brought technological advances, the output of the factory increased. Soon it was turning out goods in quantities far too great to be consumed in its immediate area; consequently, the manufacturer began shipping his output to more and more distant markets. And of course, *he had to use advertising, because the people in those areas did not know of him or his products.*
> (p. 66, emphasis in original)

This, he asserts, is a gross oversimplification ("to say it as charitably as possible") because: (a) centralized supply had existed for centuries (e.g., the Phoenicians) without advertising; (b) these nineteenth-century producers were essentially operating in a seller's market, so there was no *incentive* to advertise for reputational reasons; and (c) it ignores the role of the wholesaler—''somewhat akin to describing the plot of *Othello* without mentioning Iago'' (p. 66).

To follow Norris's thinking, as producers began to satisfy the demand of their local markets, they faced the question of how to distribute their goods to other cities, towns, and villages. For most suppliers, wholesalers filled the vacuum by serving as the link between a limited number of producers and a much larger number of retailers. As goods were still largely undifferentiated (e.g., the ''cracker barrel'' full of unbranded crackers), the wholesaler was in a position to translate the retailer's wishes (''I need thirty pounds of crackers'') to his own economic advantage by buying from that supplier that would offer the lowest possible price. And, *since the producers needed the wholesaler more than he needed each of them,* the wholesaler was able to play one against the other. This worked out well for the wholesaler. It was, however, quite another story for the producer.

> As a result of this price competition, the revenue of the manufacturers during this period of wholesaler domination was driven down very close to the cost of production. It was to escape from this predicament, to gain bargaining power, that manufacturers toward the end of the 19th century resorted to branding their output and advertising it ''over the heads of the wholesalers to the ultimate buyers, the consuming public.'' To the extent that consumers could be induced to request a particular manufacturer's brand from the retailer, the retailer would order it from the wholesaler, [''I need 30 pounds of Fenstermaker's Crackers''], who in turn would be forced to buy it from that manufacturer and no other. Now the manufacturer, not the wholesaler, was dominant, and he could name his price.[5]

Thus, Norris contends, *the reasons for the growth of national advertising had little to do with problems of selling per se,* for the producer could sell all he or she could produce, as long as there was a willingness to accept the wholesaler's price. "The sole purpose of national advertising, in its early days, was to avoid competing on a price basis" (Norris, p. 68).

Now, this intended function was of great institutional import, because it totally "*changed* the pattern of economic activity" (p. 68). For with national advertising and branding, Norris asserts, competition became much less "perfect." This, in turn, led to certain positive and negative consequences. Briefly:

Negative

◆ Resources were no longer distributed only to the most economically efficient market entrants.
◆ Competition was no longer solely on the basis of price.
◆ There was a tendency for a firm with some market power to withhold production somewhat, thus leading to a "waste of resources."

Positive

◆ Control over product quality, packaging, and innovation shifted from the wholesaler and retailer to the producer. ("A biscuit in an air-tight sanitary package made the cracker barrel obsolete . . . obsolete.") [6]
◆ "Pure" profits provided funds for research and development.
◆ Concentrated industries could be considered more progressive than their more atomistic counterparts.

Basically then, for Norris, advertising became a major institution in the latter part of the nineteenth century. Producer ("national") advertising emerged as an attempt to acquire market power and thus avoid damaging price competition. The market, he contends, was never the same again.

◆   ◆   ◆   ◆   ◆

Norris directs our attention to advertising's institutional functioning in terms of its economic consequences. First, he suggests it is fruitful to consider advertising's institutional functioning in terms of a dominant *type* of advertising—in this case, that of producers. This in itself has interesting implications. At the beginning of this chapter, we suggested that one facet of "institutional behavior" is a tendency to generalize—to see a uniformity among often diverse and conflicting activities. This clearly has pitfalls as well as assets. It may well be that a cogent case can be made—even today—for advertising's role as a provider of relatively factual information if we examine only such forms as retail, business, professional, classified, and so on. Such an argument would, however, seem somewhat dubious when we turn to much consumer advertising from producers—e.g., beer, cosmetics, cigarettes, etc. Thus, Norris suggests there are advantages to understanding in adopting a somewhat narrow analytic field.

Norris leaves little doubt that he feels the market system in this country changed with the emergence of national advertising as the ongoing solution to a problem concerning the acquisition of market power by the firms in the market. The major question raised is whether advertising's effects on the nature of the market system are, on balance, positive or negative.

Interestingly, he has forced us to examine the alteration of one form of a market system, where all entrants are essentially powerless to affect the overall allocation of resources, to a variant where producers can acquire market power through the differentiating of their products with national advertising. Who wins in this "imperfect" market resulting from the emergence of producer advertising?

Supporter

◆   Advertising enables the producer to achieve "pure" profits that can, in turn, be plowed back into product improvement, research and development, etc.

◆   Advertising, as an expression of property rights, is an efficient form of communicating the advantages of the producer's product to a large number of people.

Critic

◆   Advertising enables a producer to manipulate the price of his good to his or her own advantage. The price thus has little relationship to the "real" market value of the product.

◆   Advertising leads to a waste of resources by shifting the reward system away from the standard of pure efficiency and by enabling producers to operate at less than full capacity for their own advantage.

Norris makes his own position clear. "As advertising works better and better," he asserts in a purposefully ungrammatical but telling phrase, "the market works worse and worse." Note that he is working from the assumptions of the "perfect" market and is assuming that the alterations presumably caused by advertising are, overall, dysfunctional. Herein, it can be contended, lies the primary analytical rigor in his analysis.

For Norris is offering a critical economic perspective that explains much about the assumptions behind many of the more persistent economic criticisms of advertising. For example:

◆   "Advertising leads to higher prices"—based on *what standard?*
◆   "Advertising restricts competition—compared to *what?*
◆   "Advertising leads to a waste of resources"—defined *how?*

Basically, it can be contended that these familiar claims are all assuming that "as advertising works better and better, the [perfect] market works worse and worse." At a very minimum, then, Norris's perspective forces us to probe the implicit standard behind critical economic themes concerning advertising and the economy and weight that model with its contender.

Herein, then, is both a more historically precise explanation of the origins of national advertising *and* a critical matrix for examining advertising's performance in differing visions of a market system.

POTTER—SOCIAL CONTROL WITHOUT SOCIAL RESPONSIBILITY

It was really an "outsider"—an historian—who first dealt explicitly with the idea of advertising as an institution in the modern era. David Potter, in his 1954 book, *People of Plenty*,[7] explored the role of abundance in society. Abundance, he contended, must be considered "a major force" in American history. Yet, unlike other major forces such as democracy, religion, and science, abundance had apparently not been considered as having developed its own distinctive institution comparable to representative government, the clergy, and the apparatus of scholarship, for example. However, Potter felt that he had found the appropriate institution of an abundant society:

> If we seek an institution that was brought into being by abundance, without previous existence in any form, and, moreover, an institution which is peculiarly identified with American abundance rather than abundance throughout Western civilization, we will find it, I believe, in modern American advertising. (p. 18)

Advertising, he felt, had been woefully neglected by historians of public opinion, popular culture, and the mass media, even though "advertising created modern American radio and television, transformed the modern newspaper, evoked the modern slick-periodical, and remains the vital essence of them at the present time" (p. 19).

Potter notes the considerable growth of advertising in the last quarter of the nineteenth century, and particularly the rise of the advertising of producers (Norris's emphasis) in an attempt to "create a consumer demand for their brand and thus of exerting pressure upon the distributor to keep their products in stock" (p. 21). Soon, Potter contends, producers were no longer using advertising merely "as a coupling device between existing market demand and their own supply," but rather were trying "to create a demand" (p. 22). This, he feels, altered the nature of the advertising message from one emphasizing information to one focused "upon the desires of the consumer." (He notes the appearance, in 1903, of Walter Dill Scott's article, "The Psychology of Advertising" [p. 22].)

What accounts for advertising's growth? Potter quotes Neil Borden's explanation of the widening gap between producer and consumer, but places particular emphasis on Borden's claim that advertising flourished in part when "the quest for product differentiation became intensified as the industrial system became more mature, and as manufacturers had capacity to produce far beyond existing demand" (p. 22).

Advertising begins to fill its essential function in the society then, Potter holds, when potential supply exceeds existing demand—a condition of abundance. And what, beyond the aims of the individual producers, does advertising accomplish in this capacity?

> ... consumer societies, like all other kinds, seem to fall short of their utopias, and we revert to the question how the citizen, in our mixed production-consumption society, can be educated to perform his role as a consumer, especially as a consumer of goods for which he feels no impulse of need. Clearly he must be educated, and the only institution which we have for instilling new needs, for training people to act as consumers, for altering men's values, and thus for hastening their adjustment to potential abundance is advertising. That is why it seems to me valid to regard advertising as distinctively the institution of abundance. (pp. 24-25)

Thus, Potter contends, advertising's influence is not merely economic. In fact, he asserts it is one of a very few "instruments of social control" that serve to "guide the life of the individual by conceiving of him in a distinctive way and encouraging him to conform as far as possible to the concept." He sees these few "institutions of social control" as follows (p. 25; interpretation based on his statements on that page):

TABLE 4-2

INSTITUTION	CONCEIVES OF THE INDIVIDUAL AS:	APPEALS TO:
The church	An immortal soul.	Salvation, through conscience, spirit.
The schools	A being whose behavior is guided by reason.	Reason, with the hope of a perfected society.
Industry	A productive agent.	Workmanship, personal satisfaction.
Advertising	A consumer.	Desires and wants—cultivated or natural.

The church, schools, and industry, Potter feels, "have tried to improve man and to develop in him qualities of social value...." Advertising, however, attempts none of this.

> It is this lack of institutional responsibility, this lack of inherent social purpose to balance social power which, I would argue, is a basic cause for concern about the role of advertising. (p. 26)

Potter devotes the remainder of his chapter to developing what he considers to be the dimensions of advertising's "power." First, there is the sheer dollar weight—e.g., "Our national outlay for the education of citizens . . . amounted to substantially less than our expenditure for the education of consumers" (p. 26). But of particular concern is advertising's "profound influence on the media" and "through them" on the public (pp. 27-32).

He asserts that as advertising revenues became more and more attractive to publishers—and essential to broadcasters—their products (the magazines, newspapers, television and radio programs) became less and less *ends* in themselves and more *means* to the end of attracting large numbers of potential customers to be exposed to the advertising messages. This necessitated the watering down of the nonadvertising content of the media—the avoidance of controversial themes, the emphasis on the bland "common denominator" that would attract the largest numbers of readers or viewers, and other similar strategies. Thus, he contends, Americans are more frequently titillated by the mass media than educated, and the appeal is to the attention-getting rather than the substantive. The result of all this is thus "to enforce already existing attitudes, to diminish the range and variety of choices and, in terms of abundance, to exalt the materialistic values of consumption" (p. 34). He summarizes:

> Certainly it marks a profound social change that this new institution for shaping human standards should be directed, not as are the school and the church, to the inclination of beliefs or attitudes that are held to be of social value, but rather to the stimulation or even the exploitation of materialistic drives and emulative anxieties and then to the validation, the sanctioning, and the standardization of these drives as accepted criteria of social value. Such a transformation, brought about by the need to stimulate desire for the goods which an abundant economy has to offer and which a scarcity economy would never have produced, offers strong justification for the view that advertising should be recognized as an important social influence and as our newest major institution—an institution peculiarly identified with one of the most persuasive forces in American life, the force of economic abundance.

For Potter then, advertising is an institution of abundance whose important effects are not merely economic but rather "upon the values of our society," (p. 34) as an instrument of social control. Clearly, he does not view the outcome positively.

◆   ◆   ◆   ◆   ◆

Potter links advertising's institutional functioning to the transition from a "producer's culture" to a "consumer's culture." Advertising, he contends, teaches us to be consumers. In this capacity, advertising becomes one of a handful of institutions that exert social control. The problem, as Potter sees it, is that the other major sources of social control—the schools, the church, the business system—have a higher "social responsibility," a noble vision of the individual to go with their social power. Potter contends that advertising does not, and this lack of higher purpose is a cause of considerable concern to him.

Remember that under the classical liberal world view there was *no* explicit expectation of responsibility beyond individual self-interest. Indeed, the "laws" of the market would operate in their self-correcting manner only if each participant pursued his or her self-interest in a single-minded manner. The forces of competition (and the individual's inherent moral sense) would—at least in the long run—assure that all would work out well for the whole due to the "universal harmony of interests" or, if you prefer, the "invisible hand."

To the extent that Potter is chiding advertising for its lack of social responsibility, he is operating from a set of assumptions about "human nature" in the neo-liberalism idea system that are considerably removed from its more classical liberal interpretations. Thus, Potter, by implication, seems to be arguing that the individual will not be able to resist the seductive appeals of advertising to his or her "wants and desires" *in spite of the competition offered by the other major institutions* that he offers for comparison (i.e. the church, the schools, business) as well as those not explicitly discussed but clearly influential (e.g., the family). Under these assumptions, it is not surprising that he calls for less self-interest and more "social" interest on the part of advertisers.

It can further be assumed that from this perspective many of the "natural laws" of the classical liberals are no longer considered operative. Primary among the apparent defections are the decline of man's rationality under the onslaught of high advertising expenditures and the assumption that a "clash of ideas" will emerge from the normal functioning of the media system. (In fact, Potter asserts that because the media depend on advertising, they serve the status quo in a dollar-sensitive quest to offend no one and, thus, maximize the audience size they sell to advertisers.)

More explicitly, Potter's view raises intriguing questions in the very broadest realms of "social control." Are massive doses of advertising necessary to sustain a "consumer culture"? And, if they are, what are their costs—in terms of the cliche-like "leading us to buy things we don't need or want," in the watered-down, status-quo-oriented values that the advertising-dependent media must perpetuate in order to survive? (It is important to note that in today's era of increasing media fragmentation, Potter's assertions of media homogeneity and editorial timidity do not appear as persuasive as they might have in the early 1950s. Yet, as common sense observation will suggest, and Chapter 7 will explicate, the advertising/media relations today are no less troubling. In any event, this should not detract the serious student from careful consideration of Potter's primary contribution to understanding and examination—the idea of advertising's presumed institutional directive to "teach us to be consumers" with all that it implies.)

Now, if Carey offers us analytical perspectives on advertising's communication dimensions, and Norris provides insights into critical economic themes, Potter helps us to understand the assumptions behind the criticisms of advertising as a *social* force.

Consider issues such as:

♦   Does advertising adversely influence children?
♦   Does advertising cause social strains through stereotyping?
♦   Does advertising "cause us to buy things we don't want or need"?

The answers, for the critics, would be *yes*. Why? Because, all critics basically assume, as did Potter, that advertisers' self-interests are *not* channeled toward socially desirable ends by individual rationality or the forces of competition. Thus, in the absence of "social responsibility," exploitation reigns.

In essence, Potter offers us insights into the common occurrence of a perspective on the neo-liberal continuum interacting with an institution that is perceived as operating from another dimension of the same continuum (e.g., an individual doubting the individual's rationality "seeing" advertising exploiting that weakness). Small wonder, then, that Potter's exploration of advertising as an institution has endured, for it illuminates areas of bedrock ideological conflict.

SANDAGE—TO INFORM AND PERSUADE

Advertising educator Charles Sandage addressed his 1973 essay[8] to the climate of criticism that surrounded advertising in the 1960s-70s phase of "consumerism." He makes it clear from the outset that an institutional perspective can enable the practitioner to *respond to criticism* by "understanding the true nature of advertising and concentrating on its positive values" (p. 6).

Thus, he asserts, it is first necessary to distinguish between the institution (advertising) and the instruments (advertisements). Much criticism, and much heated defense, has been spent on individual parts of the larger whole. But what is the nature of the whole?

Advertising, Sandage holds, has been assigned the function of "helping society to achieve abundance" by *informing* and *persuading* members of society in respect to products, services and ideals (p. 6). In addition, another responsibility "that is becoming more and more significant is that of education in consumerism—the development of judgment on the part of consumers in their purchase practices" (pp. 6-7). Once we understand these larger functions, he contends, we will also realize that a great deal of the criticism of advertising is in fact criticism of such basic concepts as abundance, persuasion, and freedom of choice. The classical liberal tone of his argument is perhaps best revealed in the matter of freedom of choice:

In a free society the nature of consumption is determined primarily by consumers themselves. They decide, through their actions in the marketplace, how many people will be employed to supply them with tobacco, clothing, homes, automobiles, boats, golf balls, cosmetics, air conditioners, books and paintings to hang on their walls. They decide, too, how much of their purchasing power will be spent to support preachers, private schools, research foundations, art galleries and symphony orchestras. In a little different fashion but still basic, they determine through their votes at the polls how much they will buy in the form of defense hardware, public school buildings, teachers' services, public parks, highways, help for the less fortunate, and pollution control. (p. 7)

To the extent that individuals do *not* seem to be making choices that, objectively, appear to be in their best interests, the solution rests, he contends, not in "substituting a commissar for the free consumer," but rather in "raising the level of education in consumerism" (p. 7). Thus, Sandage argues, advertising should serve to "implement freedom of choice" by "supplying consumers with adequate and accurate information about all of the alternatives available to them" (p. 7).

He suggests that this necessary flow of information will be accomplished through two processes:

1. Through the ongoing conflict of ideas in the marketplace—e.g., the overweight person is exposed not only to the tempting messages of the confectioners, but also to the persuasive arguments of the products and services of weight reduction.
2. Through "full and honest disclosure, with competition available to provide knowledge of alternatives." This suggests that each message "will provide full disclosure of product characteristics that are important in evaluating its ability to meet a need or want" (p. 8).

By performing these two functions then, Sandage asserts, those who attempt to "inform and persuade" in respect to "things, services, and ideas" are indeed involved in socially beneficial activities. For, "it is a proper and justifiable social goal to help consumers maximize their satisfactions" (p. 8).

Stepping back to an institutional perspective, Sandage contends, offers the practitioner of advertising the opportunity to assess the function that society expects advertising to perform. That function, he asserts, is to help society achieve abundance by informing and persuading its sovereign citizens in relation to products, services, and ideas. Thus, he reasons, "Advertising practitioners who accept this concept are indeed consumer advocates" (p. 8).

◆   ◆   ◆   ◆   ◆

The sovereign consumer is clearly in charge in Sandage's view of the system. It is the individual's decisions that determine what will be produced, in what quantities, of what quality, and so on. In direct contention with Potter's "social control" interpretation, he asserts:

> Advertising is criticized on the ground that it can manipulate consumers to follow the will of the advertiser. The weight of evidence denies this ability. Instead, evidence supports the position that advertising, to be successful, must understand or anticipate basic human needs and wants and interpret available goods and services in terms of their want-satisfying abilities. (p. 7)

The institution is not master here, but servant. This is, in general, quite consistent with the strongly classical liberal perspective of the Sandage analysis.

It should be noted, however, that he also suggests that the quality of the information supplied by advertisers *is not always sufficient to enable the sovereign individual to function rationally.* Thus, he calls for "full and honest disclosure" in advertising. Carried to its full interpretation, this could at times require the disclosure of information by advertisers that is not in their best interests—e.g., the advertisers of smaller cars providing the information that loss of life in event of accident is far more likely in their products than in full-sized models. This would, of course, represent a not insignificant qualification of the classical liberal directive of the pursuit of self-interest. It does not, however, seriously dilute the strength of the contrast between the different philosophical assumptions held by Sandage and the other major theorist of advertising and abundance—David Potter. Sandage, it is clear, inevitably comes down on the side of the *sovereign individual*—the true litmus test for a person with a strong classical liberal orientation.

If Carey offers insights in advertising's dimensions as market information, Norris in economic criticisms, and Potter in social critiques, clearly the Sandage perspective illuminates advertising's defensive posture:

◆   Advertising *cannot* "cause us to buy things we don't want or need."
◆   Advertising *does not* lead to adverse consequences for the consumer, etc.

Why? Because the *individual is capable*—capable of seeking, capable of evaluating, capable of finding satisfaction from the market. Advertising, then, can do no more than the individual finds meaningful.

These sentiments, as we have seen, are easily found in the advertising business. Their basically classical liberal orientation is, again, apparent.

SCHUDSON—ADVERTISING AS CAPITALIST REALISM

Perhaps the central conceptual contribution from sociology/communications scholar Michael Schudson's 1984 book, *Advertising, the Uneasy Persuasion,*[9] is the contention that advertising in America (at least the national consumer goods variety) can be seen as "capitalist realism."

Unlike efforts of personal selling, Schudson argues, advertising "is part of the establishment and reflection of a common symbolic culture" which "connects the buyer to an assemblage of buyers through words and pictures available to all of them and tailored to no one of them" (p. 210). He then explores the dimensions and consequences of that culture.

In advertising, he contends, experience is "flattened" in the sense that advertisements depict life that is relatively timeless and placeless. Even models/actors in advertisements are meant to be regarded not as distinct individuals, but rather as representations of a "social type or a demographic category" (e.g., the "career woman" and the "senior citizen") with which the reader or viewer can identify. These neither real nor totally fictional messages are then seen as linked "to the political economy whose values they celebrate and promote" (p. 214). Hence, "capitalist realism."

Advertising as a form of symbolic value expression can be seen with greater clarity, Schudson states, by comparing it to socialist realism, and the guidelines for socialist realist art:

1. Art should picture reality in simplified and typified ways so that it communicates effectively to the masses.
2. Art should picture life, but not as it is so much as life as it should become, life worth emulating.
3. Art should picture reality not in its individuality but only as it reveals larger social significance.
4. Art should picture reality as progress toward the future and so represent social struggles positively. It should carry an air of optimism.
5. Art should focus on contemporary life, creating pleasing images of new social phenomena, revealing and endorsing new features of society and thus aiding the masses in assimilating them. (p. 215)

The parallels, Schudson continues, are striking:

American advertising, like socialist realist art, simplifies and typifies. It does not claim to picture reality as it is but reality as it should be—life and lives worth emulating. It is always photography or dramas or discourse with a message—rarely picturing individuals, it shows people only as incarnations of larger social categories. It always assumes that there is progress. It is thoroughly optimistic, providing for any troubles that it identifies a solution in a particular product or style of life. It focuses, of course, on the new, and if it shows some signs of respect for tradition, this is only to help in the assimilation of some new commercial creation. (p. 215)

Of course, unlike socialist realism, advertising is not state art, except in the sense that it is accepted as a significant phenomenon in society. Yet, its functions are similarly linked to the supporting culture, as, "without a master-plan of purposes [advertising] glorifies the pleasures and freedoms of consumer choice in defense of the virtues of private life and material ambitions'' (p. 218). Thus, the satisfactions portrayed in this idealization of the consumer are ''invariably private'' as individuals are ''encouraged to think of themselves and their private worlds'' rather than any form of collective values (i.e., what's good for society) (p. 221).

Advertising as an art form, Schudson contends while citing Krugman and others, need not necessarily command belief to be effective. Indeed, ''it may shape our sense of values even under conditions where it does not greatly corrupt our buying habits'' (p. 210). Advertising is frequently not taken seriously by individuals, hence our ''perceptual defenses'' are relatively open (p. 227).

This openness becomes even more plausible because advertising is essentially confronting us with values with which we already basically agree. Thus advertising's institutional function can be seen as *materializing a way of experiencing a consumer way of life*. ''Making the implicit explicit is necessary to engage and renew a whole train of commitments, responsibilities, and possibilities (p. 231). In the same way that married couples continue to make the ''implicit explicit'' by stating, ''I love you,'' advertising, Schudson contends, ''is capitalism's way of saying 'I love you' to itself'' (p. 232).

And what are the consequences of this reaffirmation of widely shared values?

> Advertising does not make people believe in capitalist institutions or even in consumer values, but so long as alternative articulations of values are relatively hard to locate in the culture, capitalist realist art will have some power. (p. 232)

Advertising, of course, has no monopoly in the symbolic marketplace, Schudson adds, but ''advertising has a special cultural power'' since:

- No other cultural form is as accessible to children.
- No other form confronts visitors and immigrants to our society so forcefully.
- Only professional sports surpass advertising as a source of visual and verbal cliches, aphorisms, and proverbs. (p. 233)

Advertising, Schudson concludes, is not a *shaper* of our values. Yet the values presented so relentlessly

> are not the only ones people have or aspire to, and the pervasiveness of advertising makes us forget this. Advertising picks up some of the things people hold dear and re-presents them to people as *all* of what they value, assuring them that the sponsor is the patron of common ideals. (p. 233)

◆   ◆   ◆   ◆   ◆

There are some clear parallels between Schudson's perspective and that of at least two other theorists discussed here. First, like Norris, he limits his analysis to one form of advertising—that selling national consumer goods —while recognizing the different functions of other types—e.g., retail. Second, with his concentration on advertising's relationship to values, he is akin to Potter. What, then, does his perspective assume, and what analytical tools does it offer?

Interestingly, there seem to be mixed signals in relation to atomism or the seat of societal power. Schudson makes it clear that the values advertising embodies are widely diffused through the society, thus suggesting the expected classical liberal interpretation of institutions being shaped by the individuals—i.e., the "individual in the society" rather than the "society in the individual." Yet, he is also troubled that "alternative articulations of values are relatively hard to locate" (p. 232), implying that other sets of values do not receive comparable institutional representation—a clear contradiction to atomism.

It can be argued that at the base of the argument is a vision of the individual that suggests a passiveness in responding to values other than those articulated so relentlessly through advertising's ubiquity. Thus advertising re-presents "some of the things that people hold dear as *all* of what they value" (p. 233). If individuals are willing to accept the reinforcement of some values to the diminishment of alternatives which they also "have or aspire to," then advertising is powerful indeed, and the power shifts to the institution.

Schudson's perspective, then, suggests several analytical modes. Among the more interesting:

1. Advertising's economic impact is not nearly as important as its potential interaction with the societal value structure.
2. Although it could be considered relatively benign in the sense that its values are generally our values, advertising's long-run effect is troublesome due to its pervasiveness and the singularity of its value themes.
3. Its influence is particularly magnified in certain population segments —e.g., children, immigrants—and becomes even more powerful because of its assimilation as part of popular culture through comedy routines, movies, books, commonplace daily exchanges, etc.
4. Advertising's effect may be all the more influential because it is so easily accepted as part of our institutional environment and *not* taken seriously, largely because its forms are often subject to derision, and, perhaps of greatest importance, *because we are so comfortable with its values.*

So we are offered the perspective of advertising as capitalist realism. The individual messages are clearly the stuff of the self-interests of individual advertisers. Yet the advertising aggregate makes an important—and certainly controversial—contribution to our symbolic marketplace.

POLLAY AND HOLBROOK—THE MIRROR CONTROVERSY

Students of advertising in contemporary society are well served by two substantial and insightful articles appearing in the *Journal of Marketing* in

1986 and 1987. In "The Distorted Mirror: Reflections on the Unintended Consequences of Advertising," Professor Richard Pollay offers a sweeping review of scholarly thought from "all North American authors known to have written on the cultural character of advertising."[10] Their ideas, he contends, "constitute a major indictment of advertising" (p. 31). Somewhat over a year later, Professor Morris Holbrook responded with, "Mirror, Mirror, on the Wall, What's Unfair in the Reflection of Advertising?"[11] As with our other works in this chapter, the serious student is encouraged to read the originals. Herewith, however, is an attempted summary and commentary.

Pollay

By "unintended effects" Pollay means those consequences of advertising that transcend "the pedestrian one of effecting [sic] sales, and despite the fact that many of the forms of advertising are transparent in intent to even quite unsophisticated subjects."[12] The array of scholars whose assessments are reviewed include psychologists, sociologists, anthropologists, educators, communication specialists, linguists, semanticists, philosophers, theologians, political scientists, economists, and historians (p. 19). A summary statement of the general range of criticisms is afforded by this segment from the 1980 MacBride UNESCO report:

> Regarded as a form of communication, it [advertising] has been criticized for playing on emotions, simplifying real human situations into stereotypes, exploiting anxieties, and employing techniques of intensive persuasion that amount to manipulation. Many social critics have stated that advertising is essentially concerned with exalting the materialistic virtues of consumption by exploiting achievement drives and emulative anxieties, employing tactics of hidden manipulation, playing on emotions, maximizing appeal and minimizing information, trivializing, eliminating objective considerations, contriving illogical situations, and generally reducing men, women, and children to the role of irrational consumer. Criticism expressed in such a way may be overstated but it cannot be entirely brushed aside. (p. 21)

Certainly an entire course could be devoted to the dissection of this litany, but it does provide an inventory of some of the concerns Pollay's scholars have expressed. Clearly, of course, some of these matters are not "unintentional" at all—e.g., playing on emotions, maximizing appeal, minimizing information, and so forth are conscious sales tactics—but certainly many others would seem to be beyond the usual narrow intent of most sales-seeking advertising messages. Why the concern? In part, Pollay contends, because advertising is (1) *pervasive,* appearing in many modes and media; (2) *repetitive,* reinforcing the same or similar ideas relentlessly; (3) *professionally developed,* with all the attendant research sophistications to improve the probabilities of attention, comprehension, retention, and/or behavioral impact; and

(4) *delivered to an audience that is increasingly detached* from traditional sources of cultural influence like families, churches, or schools (p. 21).

Focusing on the common defense of advertising that it must, of necessity, "be in harmony with its culture"—hence acting as a cultural mirror—Pollay qualifies that (1) any culture is a mosaic of multiple values; (2) a culture is characterized in substantial measure by the relative importance of these values; and (3) not all cultural values are employed and echoed in advertising (p.32).

"To most observers," he asserts, "the image presented in the cultural mirror of advertising is not unambiguously worth imitating." Among other concerns, it's heavy on the seven deadly sins, and light on the seven cardinal virtues (p. 26).

Recognition of the historical forces other than advertising (e.g., urbanization, industrial expansion) that can lead to the same outcome (e.g., the ascendancy of materialistic values) "does not alleviate our concern about advertising's continuing cultural role" (p. 31).

Not surprisingly, then, Pollay calls for research to compliment the deductive conclusions of the surveyed scholars, which "constitute the conventional wisdom of nonbusiness academics and are better thought of as hypotheses than conclusions" (p. 31). If advertising, he argues, "reflects" some values at the expense of others, "it becomes a serious research question which values are subjected to this selective reinforcement and which suffer from neglect, however benign" (p. 33).

Holbrook

Calling Pollay's lengthy exploration "a unique and valuable contribution to the marketing literature," Morris Holbrook counters that "if we search through Pollay's discussion to find the slender logical threads that underlie the attack on advertising, we might discover that they fail to support its heavy weight."[13] Figure 4-1 on page 76 depicts the conceptualization Holbrook uses to address the issues.

Monolithic vs. Pluralistic

Holbrook contends that an "emergent assumption" from Pollay's analysis is that

> advertising works like a collective, univocal, and global force in which media, ad agencies, and marketing strategists somehow manage (whether intentionally or unintentionally) to create television commercials, print ads, and other promotional communications that join in concert to foster certain communication ends and objectives. (p. 98)

Yet, Holbrook contends, the institutions involved in advertising are "bastions of pluralism" with explicit agendas to "(1) be different; (2) seek a unique

FIGURE 4-1

Holbrook's perspective on Pollay's "The Distorted Mirror."

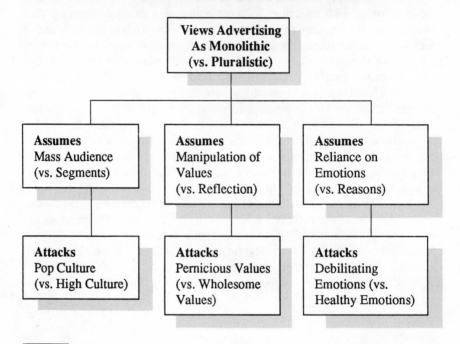

Source: Morris B. Holbrook, "Mirror, Mirror, on the Wall, What's Unfair in the Reflections on Advertising?" *Journal of Marketing* July 1987, p. 97.

niche; (3) avoid head-to-head competition; and (4) protect proprietary secrets." He adds, "A communication system based on self-interest rather than central planning could not be otherwise" (p. 98). Thus, he contends, the thrust of the Pollay argument is perhaps fatally weakened with such a challenge to what he sees as its central underlying assumption.

Mass Audience vs. Segments

Modern advertising practice, Holbrook contends, emphasizes a "general repudiation of mass marketing" (p. 98) upon which, he contends, the Pollay argument depends. As audiences are considered as segments rather than a homogeneous mass, differences, rather than similarities, are emphasized, and the prospects for monolithic control are weakened.

Pop Culture vs. High Culture

"We cannot safely conclude," Holbrook asserts, "that advertising appeals only to the lowest common denominator of pop culture by dealing excessively in social stereotypes.'' Thus, the "difference" argument reasserts itself, when, depending on the segment addressed, it is in the advertiser's best interest to shatter rather than support stereotypes (e.g., the tough-minded little old lady asking, "Where's the beef?"). Likewise, "some advertising escapes the pop-culture level of entertainment to approach the high-culture status of Art." This should not, he adds, be surprising, "in light of the tremendous creative talent and energy" involved (p. 99).

Manipulation vs. Reflection of Values

Citing the work of Boyd, Ray, and Strong,[14] Holbrook contends that generally advertisers find it an easier communication task to "augment or reposition" existing beliefs rather than attempt to substitute one belief for another. (For example, these days it's easier to convince individuals that economy is important in choosing a car than to persuade them that conspicuous consumption is desirable and that low fuel-wasting should be preferred.)[15] Thus, he contends, "most advertising appears to mirror or reflect rather than to mold or shape the values of its target audience" (p. 100).

Pernicious Values vs. Wholesome Values

"For Pollay's version . . . reading print ads or watching TV commercials is the moral equivalent of sticking one's head in a toilet" (p. 100). In sharp contrast, Holbrook responds that most ads seem to reflect "fairly wholesome values," including sociability, affection, generosity, health, patriotism, ecumenism, personal enrichment, security, and temperance (p. 101).

Reliance on Emotions vs. Reason

Holbrook cites research and the viewpoints of practitioners that "emotional appeals work best for some situations, products, or people, whereas rational appeals work best for others" (p. 101). Certainly, he argues, there is ample evidence that "reason why" approaches are still prevalent in American advertising practice.

Debilitating vs. Healthy Emotions

Even if emotional appeals are not the sole staple of advertising appeals, Holbrook agrees with Pollay that the *consequences* of those emotional appeals that are utilized should be of concern. Although he concurs that some emotional responses to television commercials do encourage sentiments of sadness, fear, and disgust, he also finds commercials eliciting feelings of anticipation, acceptance, joyfulness, happiness, gratification, pride, love, and appreciation. "Ask yourself," he concludes, "which would leave you feeling more cheerful, watching two hours of randomly selected television commercials or viewing 10 minutes of the evening news?''

Thus, Holbrook contends, the views represented in Pollay's article ''form a weak logical thread that snaps in several places from the burden of trying to tie together its multifarious attacks on advertising'' (p. 102).

◆   ◆   ◆   ◆   ◆

Pollay and Holbrook share common ground with several of our other theorists. Like Potter, they concentrate not on advertising's narrow economic effects, but rather on advertising and values. Like Potter, Pollay's scholars apparently share the view that advertising *shapes* values (advertising ''trains us to act as consumers'' as Potter put it) as well as sharing the concern of Schudson that advertising *reinforces* some values to the exclusion of others.

By contrast, Holbrook could seem to be aligned to some extent with Sandage, who contended that advertising's institutional function is to ''inform and persuade.'' And in the process of implementing this highly self-interested directive, Holbrook could contend that advertisers emphasize differences rather than similarities, reasons as well as emotions, uplifting as well as worrisome appeals, etc.; therefore, undermining the presumed ''monolithic'' assumption central to Pollay's position.

Both also share a fundamental interest with Leiss and colleagues in advertising's ''nonintended'' consequences, such as advertising's implicit communications concerning

> interpersonal and family relations, the sense of happiness and contentment, sex roles and stereotyping, the uses of affluence, the fading away of older cultural traditions, influences of younger generations, the role of business in society, persuasion and personal autonomy, and many others.[16]

Again, Pollay would contend that advertising works to both shape these dimensions, as well as reinforce those aspects of these facets of everyday life that are in concert with the overarching agenda of business—establishing and reinforcing materialistic values. Holbrook, by contrast, could contend the advertisers' agendas are varied, with techniques ranging along a range of emotional and ''rational'' appeals, many quite laudatory.

Holbrook states that Pollay, ''rather than revealing his own views,'' simply portrays the ''conventional wisdom'' of those he analyzed.[17] Yet Pollay's own ideological assumptions seem reasonably apparent: ''Polemic stands on all sides of this issue are potentially tempered by research findings, which should illuminate our understanding of both the institution of advertising and the character of its target, the consumer.''[18]

And in calling for future research, Pollay states:

> Critical inquiry does not require researchers to believe that adver-
> tising will be absolved of all charges as much as it requires having
> faith that all institutions of advertising have some potential for self-
> correction and a capacity for moral action in the light of new
> knowledge. (pp. 33-34)

Thus, in one case, the consumer is considered advertising's "target," with all
the one-sided force that suggests; and in another, advertising is clearly posi-
tioned as guilty-until-proven-innocent, with the only possibility for redemption
through self-corrective "moral action."

Holbrook's continuing theme of the diverse intents of advertisers undermining the "monolithic" assumption of Pollay's position can, on the other
hand, be seen to raise as many questions as it addresses. For example, if marketing directives do suggest "difference" as a desirable strategy and the transmission of "fairly wholesome values" to aid the process, could these not also
be considered merely the *means to the end of selling the product,* therefore reinforcing the agenda of goods = happiness implicit in so many of the objections
of Pollay's scholars? And when Holbrook writes of advertising's intent to
"augment or reposition people's beliefs" while concluding that "most advertising attempts to mirror or reflect rather than to mold," the question can be
raised of *what* is repositioned and *what* reinforced—e.g., a broad representation
of the American value system or, as Pollay contends, *some* commercially compatible values to the exclusion of many others?

Both researchers conclude with a call for value-free research that can rise
above "microphenomena" and replace it with macro concerns where, as Pollay puts it, "we should study the consumer in the marketing environment as the
biologist studies the fish" (p. 34). Neither, however, seem particularly optimistic, with Pollay expressing repeated concern that academics are "servants
to marketing practice," and Holbrook noting the "contrasting ideological origins" that lead these two researchers to their jousting.[19]

The "mirror" issue is, as we have seen, one which is in many ways an
ideological litmus test, with those to the classical liberal end of the neo-liberal
spectrum seeing advertising as a reflection of the will of the sovereign consumer, while those seeing advertising as shaper/selective reinforcer, envision-
ing a vulnerable populace.

Pollay's scholars, and Pollay himself, seem to contend that because advertising is value laden in what they assume is an undesirable dimension, that
individuals are influenced accordingly; on the other hand, Holbrook seems to
be assuming that self-interested business practice, presumably directed by correctly reading potentially powerful "markets," will result in a reasonably representative value mix by the "natural" adjustment processes of the market.
Pollay's focus is, to a great extent, on the product of the process (the *ads*), and
Holbrook's focus is on the business *motives* behind them.

Given the ideologically sensitive nature of advertising thought and the
arabesques of its practice that we have encountered in preceding pages, there

seems little doubt that there is unlikely to be any convergence on truth, as the Phoenix from the flames, in the near future.

In the meantime, we are, we believe, well served by the paths to understanding illuminated by the theorists of this chapter.

◆

SUMMARY

In an attempt to deepen our understanding of the nature of institutional analysis in relation to advertising, we've examined the views of a number of insightful theorists.

James Carey sees advertising performing the historically necessary function of providing market information, with the nature of that information, and its potential effects, clearly affected by its source and by attendant assumptions about human nature.

Vincent Norris sees advertising emerging as an institution in the late 19th century with the rise of national (producer) advertising in an attempt to avoid price competition and seize market power from the dominant wholesalers.

David Potter finds advertising the distinctive institution of abundance, training people to act as consumers in an abundant economy, but without social responsibility to counter social control.

Charles Sandage envisions advertising informing and persuading individuals in order that they may make satisfying decisions in a largely responsive market.

Michael Schudson suggests advertising as an expression of capitalist ideals—capitalist realism as compared to socialist realism—with significant influence due to its possibility of overwhelming other competing values with its sheer ubiquity and the comfort of its themes.

Finally, Richard Pollay and Morris Holbrook address the vexing question as to what extent advertising mirrors or shapes our society. Pollay enlists the "conventional wisdom" of major scholars to characterize advertising as a "distorted mirror" with troubling images. Holbrook finds advertising practice leading to diversity, with relatively benign consequences and an image of reasonable fidelity.

Each perspective, along with the visions offered in the preceding three chapters, provides us with analytic tools for arriving at greater understanding of the various dimensions of advertising in contemporary society. And it is to a tighter focus on several of these dimensions that we now turn.

ENDNOTES

1. Walton Hamilton, "Institution," *The Encyclopedia of the Social Sciences,* vol. VIII (New York: Macmillan, 1932), p. 89.
2. Charles H. Sandage, "Some Institutional Aspects of Advertising," *Journal of Advertising,* vol. 1, no. 1 (1973), p. 9.
3. James W. Carey, "Advertising: An Institutional Approach," in C. H. Sandage and V. Fryburger, eds., *The Role of Advertising* (Homewood, IL: Richard D. Irwin, Inc., 1960), p. 14. (Emphasis in original.)
4. Vincent P. Norris, "Toward the Institutional Study of Advertising," *Occasional Papers in Advertising* (Urbana, IL: University of Illinois Department of Advertising, 1966), pp. 59-73.
5. *Ibid.,* p. 67, Quote beginning "over the heads . . ." from Nicholas Kaldor, The Economics of Advertising," *The Review of Economic Studies,* vol. XVIII (1), no. 45 (1949-1950), pp. 1-27.
6. The reader may recall these lyrics from the opening number of *Music Man.*
7. David M. Potter, "The Institution of Abundance: Advertising," printed in Sandage and Fryburger, *op. cit.,* pp. 18-34. Originally chap. viii in Potter's *People of Plenty* (Chicago: University of Chicago Press, 1954). All subsequent citations from the Sandage and Fryburger chapter.
8. Charles H. Sandage, "Some Institutional Aspects of Advertising." *Journal of Advertising,* vol. 1, no. 1 (1973), pp. 6-9. Reprinted with permission by Board of Directors, *Journal of Advertising.*
9. Michael Schudson, *Advertising, The Uneasy Persuasion* (New York: Basic Books, Inc., 1984).
10. Richard W. Pollay, "The Distorted Mirror: Reflections on the Unintended Consequences of Advertising," *Journal of Marketing,* April 1986, pp. 18-36.
11. Morris B. Holbrook, "Mirror, Mirror, on the Wall, What's Unfair in the Reflections on Advertising?" *Journal of Marketing,* July 1987, pp. 95-103.
12. Pollay, p. 21.
13. Holbrook, p. 96.
14. Boyd, Harper W., Jr., Michael L. Ray, and Edward C. Strong, "An Attitudinal Framework for Advertising Strategy," *Journal of Marketing,* April 1972, pp. 27-33.
15. Holbrook, pp. 99-100.
16. William Leiss, Stephen Kline, Sut Ghally, *Social Communication in Advertising—Persons, Products, & Images of Well Being* (Toronto: Methun, 1986), p. 3.
17. Holbrook, p. 95.
18. Pollay, p. 31.
19. Pollay, p. 34; Holbrook, p. 102.

PART 2

◆

ISSUES OF CONSEQUENCE

5
ADVERTISING AND THE ECONOMIC DIMENSION

Why have so many studied the economic effects of advertising for such a long period of time? The reasons are probably quite simple:

1. Advertising is a major industry in the United States, with over $90 billion spent annually.
2. Advertising is a highly visible institution, its messages touching most businesses and consumers everyday.
3. There is a common belief among many business people that advertising "sells" the product or service. If sales are down, the blame is laid on advertising; if sales are increasing, advertising gets the credit.

BASIC LIMITATIONS OF MANY ECONOMIC STUDIES

Before beginning a discussion of some of the issues concerning the economic effects of advertising, it is necessary to look at some basic underpinnings of many economic studies related to advertising. In many of the studies, there is an implicit assumption that advertising works in isolation rather than in concert with other elements of the marketing mix (product, place, price, and promotion) and the promotion mix (advertising, personal selling, sales promotion, and public relations). However, if one examines expenditure patterns within the promotion mix it becomes clear that examining just advertising expenditures can lead to erroneous results. Compared with the over $90 billion spent annually on advertising, business firms spend approximately $172 billion on personal selling[1] and approximately $85 billion on sales promotion efforts.[2] It is difficult to imagine that anything but a synergistic effect on sales could be expected from the combination of the marketing and promotion mixes.

Other studies fail to take into account the many external factors that influence the effectiveness of a firm's advertising. For example, the advertising and promotion activities of competitors can dramatically affect a firm's advertising effectiveness.

Another critical factor often ignored in studies attempting to determine the economic effects of advertising is the cooperative advertising allowance made to retailers. Rachman has reported that for many household items, over one half of all retail advertising is sponsored by some type of cooperative funding, the expenditure total being $4.8 billion.[3]

An additional handicap to research into the economic effects of advertising was pointed out by Morgenstern, who found that necessary data are often unavailable and, when available, are often inaccurate or untrustworthy.[4] For example, the industry classifications used in government data may group together firms producing unrelated products, or firms may switch classifications without any change in the kinds of goods they produce.[5]

It is also unlikely that individual firms over time or firms within a particular industry are equally effective in the development and transmission of their advertising.[6] Not all copy platforms, basic research programs, or media strategies are equally productive.

Lastly, few scholars in the economics area are conversant with basic material on consumer behavior such as that presented in Chapter 6 of this book, "Advertising and Its Audience." Definitions of what is information or how it is processed by the consumer are often ignored. In other instances, consumer behavior concepts are defined in a manner to suit a more "economic" view of the research process.

TWO SCHOOLS OF THOUGHT ABOUT THE ECONOMIC EFFECTS OF ADVERTISING

Albion indicates there are two principal models that economists use to describe the effects of advertising: the advertising = market power school and the advertising = market competition school. The first model views advertising as a persuasive communications tool that marketers use to make consumers less sensitive to price. This decreased price sensitivity will subsequently increase the firm's market power. The second model regards advertising as informative in nature and contends that it increases consumers' price sensitivity and stimulates competition among firms.[7]

The market power school believes advertising is capable of changing consumer tastes and building brand loyalty. A brand-loyal customer is not very price sensitive, as he/she does not perceive that there are acceptable alternatives in the marketplace. Once the firm has been able to differentiate its product/service through advertising expenditures, the firm should be able to increase its prices to consumers, subsequently increasing its profits and reducing competition in the marketplace.

The market competition model holds that advertising provides basic information to the marketplace, information that will increase price sensitivity, lower prices, and reduce any potential monopoly power. Ornstein described the market competition model as follows:

> The essence of this new view is that advertising provides information on brands, prices, and quality, thus increasing buyer knowledge, reducing consumers' search costs, and reducing the total costs to society of transacting business. By increasing information, advertising increases the number of substitutes known to buyers, thereby increasing price elasticity of demand and reducing price-cost margins. Far from being a barrier to entry, advertising facilitates entry by allowing previously unknown products to gain rapid market acceptance. . . . Advertising serves consumers by increasing product variety and by permitting firms to exploit economies of scale in production and distribution—which in turn yield lower consumer prices.[8]

Table 5-1 summarizes the two approaches.

These two approaches have some major flaws. As discussed by Albion,[9] the market power model assumes that advertising is probably the sole cause of brand loyalty and price insensitivity. But there are other elements in the marketing mix or promotion mix such as packaging, better product quality, personal selling, and sales promotion that could contribute to the development of brand loyalty. The market competition school assumes that consumers engage in a thorough and extensive search of produce/service alternatives which is facilitated by advertising. The school also assumes that consumers are excellent judges of the merits of competing brands. Given our discussion in Chapter 6, this assumption does not necessarily hold true.

SOME NEWER APPROACHES

Porter and Steiner have each developed new approaches to studying the economic effects of advertising. The main contribution of these two models has been the recognition of the retailer's role in both the sale of and the dissemination of information about the manufacturer's product to the ultimate consumer.

Porter divides retail goods into two sectors, convenience and nonconvenience. Convenience goods retailers (gasoline stations, convenience food stores, traditional supermarkets) provide display space for the manufacturer's product, but that is about the only service they offer. The manufacturer has already differentiated the product with the advertising to create demand and eventually develop brand loyalty among consumers. The manufacturer subsequently increases prices to the retailer, thereby reducing trade margins. Retailers will be willing to accept price increases because of higher product turnover. Consumers engage in limited information search because of the lower cost of these items.[10]

TABLE 5-1

Two Schools of Thought on the Role of Advertising in the Economy

ADVERTISING = MARKET POWER		ADVERTISING = MARKET COMPETITION
Advertising affects consumer preferences and tastes, changes product attributes, and differentiates the product from competitive offerings.	Advertising	Advertising informs consumers about product attributes and does not change the way they value these attributes.
Consumers become brand loyal and less price sensitive, and perceive fewer substitutes for advertised brands.	Consumer Buying Behavior	Consumers become more price sensitive and buy best "value." Only the relationship between price and quality affects elasticity for a given product.
Potential entrants must overcome established brand loyalty and spend relatively more on advertising.	Barriers to Entry	Advertising makes entry possible for new brands because it can communicate product attributes to consumers.
Firms are insulated from market competition and potential rivals; concentration increases, leaving firms with more discretionary power.	Industry Structure and Market Power	Consumers can compare competitive offerings easily and competitive rivalry is increased. Efficient firms remain, and as the inefficient leave, new entrants appear; the effect on concentration is ambiguous.
Firms can charge higher prices and are not as likely to compete on quality or price dimensions. Innovation may be reduced.	Market Conduct	More informed consumers put pressure on firms to lower prices and improve quality. Innovation is facilitated via new entrants.
High prices and excessive profits accrue to advertisers and give them even more incentive to advertise their products. Output is restricted compared to conditions of perfect competition.	Market Performance	Industry prices are decreased. The effect on profits due to increased competition and an increase in efficiency is ambiguous.

Reprinted with permission of the publisher from Mark S. Albion, *Advertising's Hidden Effects: Manufacturers' Advertising and Retail Pricing* (Boston, Mass.: Auburn House, 1983), p. 18.

Nonconvenience goods retailers (auto dealers, appliance stores, furniture stores) play a more significant marketing role. The retailer is often asked to provide information about the product, to demonstrate it, and relate it to the store's image. More manufacturer advertising dollars are spent promoting the product to the trade (push strategy) in order to gain additional outlets. Consumers spend more time looking for the "best buy." The brand name, developed through manufacturer advertising, may not be all-important; store advertising and cooperative advertising may be just as important. As a result, manufacturer prices may be lower to maintain distribution in critical stores.[11]

The contributions of this model are clear. It stipulates that studying the economic effects of advertising is at best situational (convenience vs. nonconvenience goods) and that advertising as economists generally study it may be more important for the convenience goods sector. It also involves the retailer as an important element in the system.

Steiner's dual-stage model also indicates that the retailer must be viewed as an integral part of the economics of advertising.[12] A scenario for Steiner's model would be as follows:

In the early stages of a product, it is generally unadvertised, and consumers exhibit no particular preference among a wide variety of close substitutes. Then as Steiner describes the process:

> If a dealer in an unadvertised product category carries, say, 5 to 6 items, he is likely to be offered 100 by the manufacturers and finds he can select and substitute between them quite freely without a noticeable impact on his sales volume. As the retailer puts it, he can live without virtually any manufacturer product. Consequently, he plays one maker off against the next and ends up carrying the factory brands that afford him the greatest margin between retail list and factory invoice price. This causes factory demand curves to be extremely elastic and price to be depressed close to average unit cost.[13]

Consumer prices may well remain high because of the lack of competition at the retail level.

> If Manufacturer X now begins successfully to advertise his brand, the terms of trade shift decisively in his favor. Dealers find that the public expects them to handle the item. Hence, the trade's ability to stock a competing article in place of Brand X or to beat down the latter's price as a condition for carrying it is substantially diminished. As advertising expands the popularity of Brand X, its maker therefore finds he can increase its retail distribution with progressively fewer price concessions.[14]

Consumer prices may fall because of the increased competition at the retail level. Intense price competition could follow, driving retail margins to the new zero level, as retailers begin offering heavy discounts on the items or offer them as loss leaders to generate store traffic. Retailers will use these heavily advertised products in this way because consumers tend to use them as benchmarks in price comparisons. Factory prices at this stage might remain relatively constant or even increase.

At this point, Steiner indicates that one of three situations will probably occur:[15]

1. Manufacturer's brand domination
2. Mixed regimen
3. Private label domination

In the case of manufacturer's brand domination, it is possible that, from the point of view of the market power school, the heavily advertised brands will dominate the market and thus create major barriers to entry by new firms. Those controlling the market may see opportunities to offer a variety of new brands and advertise them heavily. Product differences would be relatively minor. Consumer prices would rise given the successful new differentiation effort. The aspirin and detergent markets might be good examples of this situation.

In the mixed regimen situation, private labels may develop as the retailer attempts to challenge the manufacturers to restore some of their gross margins. Retailers can often negotiate low manufacturer prices for their own labels because manufacturers want to put excess plant capacity to use. The resulting competition between private and national brands keeps factory and consumer prices of national brands at reasonable levels. The retail prices of the advertised brands are lower than prices would be without advertising because of the low gross margins continually earned by retailers. The replacement tire market is an example of this situation, with 50 percent of the market being held by private labels. Many of the traditional canned goods in supermarkets probably also follow this scenario.

Few examples of the private label domination situation can be cited. If this situation did exist, it would mean high margins for retailers and consumer prices slightly below prices found when there is manufacturer's brand domination but above those in the mixed regimen.

In Steiner's model, advertising can be seen as increasing distribution and thus potential users while diminishing the gross margin earned by retailers. At the same time, it allows factory prices to increase more than consumer prices.[16]

THE BASIC ECONOMIC ISSUES

As the basic economic issues are reviewed, it will become evident that the phrase "It depends" will play an important role. Often, only mixed conclusions will be reached for many of the issue areas. These mixed conclusions probably arise from the limitations discussed earlier in this chapter—viewing advertising as an isolated function, using inaccurate data, etc.—or from failing to recognize the thrust of the Porter and Steiner models.

Advertising and Price

Does advertising lead to lower prices or does it make items the consumer purchases more expensive? Before the price question can be answered, as Norris indicates, one must inquire about what kind of advertising is being discussed, retail or national.[17] His distinction between national and retail advertising is the same one that Porter and Steiner have made.

A number of studies have indicated that high levels of retail advertising increase price competition and may subsequently lower relative consumer brand prices.[18] Product groups including gasoline, drugs, eyeglasses, and eye care are often cited as examples. As for national advertising, Norris concluded in his review of the economics literature that national advertising probably raises the price of goods and services.[19] Studies by Comanor and Wilson [20] and Lambin[21] concluded that advertising decreases factory price sensitivity. The factory price vs. consumer price (retail price) conclusions of these studies seem to be in agreement with the assumptions of both the Porter and the Steiner models.

Economies of Scale

In advertising, an examination of the economics of scale (for example, a doubling of inputs may yield an output that is more than doubled) reveals a mixed set of results. Many economists and marketers have assumed that there are increasing returns to advertising expenditures. A campaign must reach a certain level of expenditure to generate the most efficient level of response.[22] It is assumed that large firms can more easily reach this level of response than can firms with more limited resources. But it does not necessarily mean that large firms can support their market share with relatively lower advertising costs than can smaller firms.[23]

Economies of scale in advertising can occur because there is a threshold of awareness that advertising must cross. Though it is assumed that a certain amount of message repetition is necessary before consumers become aware of a product or service, unfortunately no one knows exactly what that threshold is. The exact amount of message repetition needed to communicate effectively to consumers is often a function of such factors as risk, novelty, perceived differences in product alternatives, degree of confidence about a purchase, and the type of decision-making rules consumers employ (see Chapter 6). If a high rate of repetition is required, many smaller firms could be excluded because they lack a substantial promotion budget.

Can larger firms produce ''better'' advertising? Through the use of marketing research and copy-testing procedures combined with the excellent creative departments at major advertising agencies, it may be possible for the large advertiser to produce more "effective" advertisements. No studies that the authors are familiar with have been conducted in this area.

Evidence that larger advertisers receive dramatically different media discounts than smaller advertisers is also lacking.[24] Although such differentials did apparently occur as late as the 1970s, the differentials now seem rather small.

Advertising's Effects on Profits

Jeffres correctly pointed out: "Many economists believe that the true measure of market power is the price elasticity of demand. However, since it is so difficult to measure this factor, economists concentrate on the profit rates of manufacturers."[25]

Unfortunately, conclusions regarding the effect of advertising on profits are also clouded by measurement problems, cause-and-effect issues, and definitions of basic terms. Some authors have concluded that advertising has little effect on profit rates,[26] while others have found that advertising leads to higher profit rates.[27] Albion and Farris conclude that there is no overwhelming evidence to substantiate either the market power or market competition model, though a majority of the empirical studies find a positive relationship between advertising and profitability.[28] Because of these confusing results, researchers have often turned to another measure of the market power of advertising: concentration.

Advertising and Concentration

The concentration ratio which has been used in most of the studies in this area of research is based upon a ranking of the firms in an industry by order of size (usually sales or employees), beginning with the largest. The percentage of each firm's sales to the total industry sales is first derived. Then the top X firms' percentages are added to obtain a concentration ratio. Published statistics usually give concentration ratios for the largest four, largest eight, and sometimes the largest 20 firms in the industry.[29]

It is assumed, especially by the market power school, that advertising expenditures are related to these measures of market concentration. Advertising would cause these high concentration levels because:

1. Economies of scale in advertising would enable large-scale advertisers to push smaller advertisers out of the market.
2. Increased capital requirements and brand loyalty would discourage potential entrants.[30]

Norris indicates that the trend of increased concentration in this country has been much more severe in some industries than in others. Between 1947 and 1963, the number of firms increased in 64 percent of producer goods industries and decreased in 33 percent. In consumer goods industries, the number of firms increased in only 33 percent but decreased in 67 percent. Within this consumer goods sector, Norris also states that the number of firms decreased in 57 percent of the industries in which brands are only slightly differentiated but decreased 88 percent in the highly differentiated industries.[31]

Scherer,[32] Mann,[33] Blair,[34] Lancaster et al.,[35] and Mueller[36] found that advertising inequalities explain the largest share of the variance in market concentration. Many of these studies found the electronic media, especially television, to be a prime factor in leading to increased levels of concentration. However, Comanor and Wilson,[37] Albion,[38] Ornstein and Lustgarten,[39] and Vernon[40] found no significant relationships between advertising and concentration. An interesting finding by Caves et al. was that advertising was highest in medium concentrated industries and lower in high and low concentrated industries.[41]

Norris would conclude that advertising does lead to higher levels of concentration in consumer goods industries.[42] There is, however, enough mixed evidence to indicate that the relationship may not be so simple.[43] Again, there are probably specific industries and situations when advertising can lead to higher levels of concentration, but a sweeping statement that advertising always develops concentration may not be possible at this time.

Advertising and Aggregate Consumption

Several studies have investigated the effect of advertising on aggregate consumption. Schmalensee found high correlations between advertising and aggregate consumption, correlations that were improved when advertising was moved from cause (preceding consumption) to effect (lagging behind consumption).[44] He points out, however, that in spite of an increase in the ratio of advertising to GNP, the ratio of household spending to household disposable income has remained stable over the long term.[45] He concludes that national advertising does not affect total spending for goods and services.[46]

Other researchers, however, disagree with Schmalensee. Indications that advertising does affect aggregate consumption have been reported by Taylor and Weiserbs[47] and Cowling et al.[48] Quarles and Jeffres examined data for more than 50 nations to test the Galbraithian notion that advertising raises consumption to fit the needs for the industrial system against the competing argument that advertising is caused by consumption (see Figure 5-1).[49] Income and industrial development were seen as factors affecting advertising and consumption. They conclude:

> We find little evidence for Galbraith's view of advertising as a high priest of materialism with the persuasive force to alter the spending and savings habits of people and nations. Instead, our analysis yields a picture of spending severely constrained by disposable income—a world where advertising has little room to maneuver in any efforts to draw spending from savings.[50]

Most of the evidence would seem to indicate that advertising is the result rather than the cause of consumption. The conclusion that advertising does not increase aggregate consumption may be based on the way that advertising budgets are traditionally established at the manufacturers' level. Many firms continue to use a percentage-of-sales method, which will always view sales as the cause of advertising rather than as the result. Also, the studies on aggregate consumption have made an implicit assumption that advertising affects consumer attitudes and values concerning their saving and spending patterns. The two confounding factors introduced above can only lead to the conclusion that it simply is not clear whether advertising affects aggregate consumption patterns.

FIGURE 5-1

Competing View on the Relationship between Advertising & Consumption

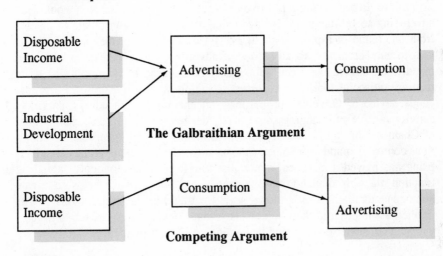

Source: Leo W. Jeffres, *Mass Media: Processes and Effects* (Prospect Heights, IL: Waveland Press, 1986), p. 317.

Advertising's Effect on Primary Demand

Primary demand is the demand for all the brands, advertised or unadvertised, within a given product category. Borden's 1942 study concluded:

> [So far as primary demand is concerned] from the many cases analyzed and from the industry studies, one clear and important generalization can be made, namely, that basic trends of demand for products, which are determined by underlying social and environmental conditions, are more significant in determining the

expansion or contraction of primary demand than is the use or lack of use of advertising.[51]

Grabowski concluded that "the main impact of advertising is on a consumer's choice of brands or products within a particular class rather than across product classes."[52] Lambin probably best critiqued knowledge in this area:

In only four product markets out of ten have statistically significant (barely, at low levels) industry advertising effects been observed on primary demand. . . . Those four product classes are all in the early stages of the life cycle, where product-related social, economic, and technological forces are favorable to the spontaneous expansion of demand.[53]

The finding that advertising can speed growth rates (not cause dramatic shifting between product categories) under favorable conditions within a given product category gives the critics of advertising another reason to condemn the institution. In fact, either a positive or negative finding in this area would lead advertising to be damned. If advertising simply leads consumers to change from one brand of aspirin to another or from one brand of dishwashing detergent to another, it is a social waste. If advertising does increase primary demand, then advertising "can quite easily be accused of being nothing more than an antisocial tool, the properties of which range from those of a propaganda device of Orwellian proportions, an uncontrolled, insidious, pervasive activity capable of changing consumers' 'desires' to the more academic ideas of Chamberlain and Galbraith that it is a means by which capitalist corporations control demand."[54] Some Marxists and radical scholars argue that advertising has played a historical materialist role in making monopoly capitalism function through demand management[55]—e.g., advertising helps to create homogeneous markets on a global scale for transnational corporations.[56] The implicit assumption in their arguments is that "advertising is effective in reorganizing consumer demand and in creating artificial wants."[57]

SUMMARY

Is advertising a social waste or does it benefit society and the individual consumers who comprise that society? There is no firm answer to the question. As Norris states, "The most obvious and perhaps the only certain conclusion to be drawn from this plethora of studies is that there is manifold disagreement among the students of the economic effects of advertising."[58]

Chiplin and Sturgess underscore the point at the end of *Economics of Advertising:*

> Our discussions have indicated that there is no consensus in economics concerning the net benefit or cost of advertising to society. Much here depends on the value judgments of the particular individual. There are, therefore, no clear-cut policy recommendations. In the remainder of this chapter, we shall discuss the forms of policy towards advertising that have been suggested, while leaving the reader to decide whether any or all of the policies are necessary and if so, the precise way in which they should be implemented.[59]

There is hope of finding more definitive results through the recent contributions made by Porter, Steiner, and Albion and Farris. They have broadened the economic horizon by adding the retailer component, recognizing that there are different types of consumer goods, and explicitly recognizing the difference between demand at the retail and factory levels with regard to price. Advertising is here to stay; it is to be hoped that future research will provide better ways to refine this social institution.

ENDNOTES

1. Philip Kotler, *Marketing Management: Analysis, Planning, and Control* (Englewood Cliffs, NJ: Prentice-Hall, 1988), p. 663.
2. Kevin T. Higgins, "Sales Promotion Spending Closing in on Advertising," *Marketing News,* July 4, 1986, p. 8.
3. David J. Rachman, *Retail Strategy and Structure* (Englewood Cliffs, NJ: Prentice-Hall, 1975) and "Partnership Perks Up Profits," *Advertising Age,* August 17, 1981, p. S-1.
4. Oskar Morgenstern, *On the Accuracy of Economic Observations* (Princeton: Princeton University Press, 1963).
5. Richard Schmalensee, *The Economics of Advertising* (Amsterdam: North Holland Publishing Co., 1972), p. 146.
6. David Ogilvy and J. Raphaelson, "Research on Advertising Techniques That Work and Don't Work," *Harvard Business Review,* 60 (July/August 1982), pp. 14-18.
7. Mark S. Albion, *Advertising's Hidden Effects: Manufacturers' Advertising and Retail Pricing* (Boston, MA: Auburn House, 1983), pp. 16-17.
8. S. I. Ornstein, *Industrial Concentration and Advertising Intensity* (Washington, DC: American Enterprise Institute, 1977), pp. 2-3.
9. Albion, pp. 17-21.
10. Mark S. Albion and Paul W. Farris, *The Advertising Controversy: Evidence on the Economic Effects of Advertising* (Boston, MA: Auburn House, 1981), p. 139.

11. *Ibid.*

12. *Ibid.,* pp. 144-145.

13. Robert Steiner, "A Dual Stage Approach to the Effects of Brand Advertising on Competition and Price," in *Marketing and the Public Interest,* John Cady, ed. (Cambridge, MA: Marketing Science Institute, 1978), p. 131.

14. *Ibid.,* p. 134.

15. Albion and Farris, p. 148.

16. *Ibid.,* p. 149.

17. Vincent P. Norris, "The Economic Effects of Advertising: A Review of the Literature," in *Current Issues of Research in Advertising,* James H. Leigh and Claude Martin, Jr., eds. (Ann Arbor: Division of Research, Graduate School of Business Administration, University of Michigan, 1984), p. 93.

18. See Norris, pp. 93-94; and Albion and Farris, *op. cit.,* pp. 153-170.

19. Norris, p. 105.

20. William S. Comanor and Thomas A. Wilson, *Advertising and Market Power* (Cambridge, MA: Harvard University Press, 1974).

21. J. J. Lambin, *Competition and Market Conduct in Oligopoly over Time* (Amsterdam: North Holland Publishing Co., 1976).

22. Albion and Farris, p. 103.

23. Kenneth D. Boyer and Kent M. Lancaster, "Are There Scale Economies in Advertising?" *Journal of Business,* 59 (July 1986), pp. 509-526.

24. John L. Peterman, "Differences Between the Levels of Spot and Network Advertising Rates," *Journal of Business,* 52 (October 1979), pp. 549-562.

25. Leo W. Jeffres, *Mass Media: Processes and Effects* (Prospect Heights, IL: Waveland Press, 1986), p. 319.

26. See R. Ayanian, "Advertising and Rate of Return," *Journal of Law and Economics,* 18 (October 1975), pp. 479-501; and H. Block, "Advertising and Profitability: A Reappraisal," *Journal of Political Economy,* 82 (March/April 1974), pp. 267-286.

27. See Comanor and Wilson, *op. cit.,* and John M. Vernon and Robert E. M. Nourse, "Profit Rates and Market Structure of Advertising Intensive Firms," *Journal of Industrial Economics,* 22 (September 1973), pp. 1-20.

28. Jeffres, p. 319.

29. Richard Caves, *American Industry: Structure, Conduct, Performance* (Englewood Cliffs, NJ: Prentice-Hall, 1964), p. 8.

30. Albion and Farris, p. 60.

31. Norris, p. 88.

32. F. Scherer, *Industrial Market Structure and Economic Performance* (Chicago: Rand McNally, 1980), chap. 14.

33. H. Mann, "Advertising, Concentration, and Profitability: The State of Knowledge and Directions for Public Policy," in *Economic Concentra-*

tion, *The New Learning,* Harvey Goldschmid, H. Mann, and J. Weston, eds. (Boston: Little, Brown, 1974).

34. John Blair, *Economic Concentration: Structure, Behavior and Public Policy* (New York: Harcourt Brace Jovanovich, 1972), pp. 311, 321-331.

35. K. Lancaster, R. Batra, and G. Miracle, "How the Level, Intensity, and Distribution of Advertising Affect Market Concentration," in *Proceedings of the 1982 Conference of the American Academy of Advertising,* Alan Fletcher, ed. (Lincoln, NE: American Academy of Advertising, 1982).

36. W. Mueller, "Changes in Market Concentration of Manufacturing Industries 1946-1977," *Review of Industrial Concentration,* 1 (Spring 1984), pp. 1-14.

37. Comanor and Wilson.

38. Mark S. Albion, "The Determinants of the Level of Advertising and Media Mix Expenditures in Consumer Goods Industries," unpublished manuscript, Harvard University, January 1976.

39. Stanley I. Ornstein and Steven Lustgarten, "Advertising Intensity and Industrial Concentration—An Empirical Inquiry, 1947-1967," in *Issues in Advertising: The Economics of Persuasion,* David G. Tueruck, ed. (Washington, DC: American Enterprise Institute for Public Policy Research, 1978), pp. 217-253.

40. John M. Vernon, "Concentration, Promoting, and Market Share Stability in the Pharmaceutical Industry," *Journal of Industrial Economics,* 19 (July 1971), pp. 146-266.

41. Richard E. Caves, Michael E. Porter, and A. Michael Spence, with John T. Scott, *Competition in the Open Economy* (Cambridge, MA: Harvard University Press, 1980).

42. Norris, pp. 88-92.

43. E. Woodrow Eckard Jr., "Advertising, Competition, and Market Share Instability," *Journal of Business,* 60 (October 1987), pp. 539-552.

44. Richard Schmalensee, "Advertising and Economic Welfare," in *Advertising and the Public Interest,* S. F. Divita, ed. (Chicago: American Marketing Association, 1974), p. 266.

45. *Ibid.,* p. 264.

46. *Ibid.,* pp. 58, 85-86.

47. L. Taylor and D. Weiserbs, "Advertising and the Aggregate Consumption Function," *American Economic Review,* 62 (September-December 1971), pp. 642-655.

48. Keith Cowling *et al., Advertising and Economy Behavior* (London: Macmillan, 1975).

49. Jeffres, p. 316. For a discussion of Galbraith's view on advertising, see Michael Schudson, "Criticizing the Critics of Advertising: Towards a Sociological View of Marketing," *Media, Culture and Society,* 3 (January 1981), pp. 3-12.

50. Rebecca C. Quarles and Leo W. Jeffres, "Advertising and National Consumption: A Path Analytic Re-examination of the Galbraithian Argument," *Journal of Advertising,* 1983 12(2), p. 13.

51. N. H. Borden, *The Economic Effects of Advertising* (Chicago: Irwin, 1942), p. 433.

52. H. Grabowski, "The Effects of Advertising on Intraindustry Shifts in Demand," *Explorations in Economic Research: Occasional Papers of the National Bureau for Economic Research,* 4 (Winter 1977-Spring 1978), pp. 675-701.

53. Lambin, p. 136.

54. P. Kyle, "The Impact of Advertising on Markets," *International Journal of Advertising,* 1 (October-December 1982), pp. 345-359.

55. Dallas W. Smythe, "Communications: Blindspot of Western Marxism," *Canadian Journal of Political and Social Theory,* 1 (Fall 1977), pp. 1-27.

56. Noreene Z. Janus, "Advertising and the Mass Media: Transnational Link between Production and Consumption," *Media, Culture and Society,* 3 (January 1981), pp. 13-23.

57. See Editorial, *Media, Culture and Society,* 3 (January 1981).

58. Norris, p. 116.

59. B. Chiplin and B. Sturgess, *Economics of Advertising* (London: Holt, Rinehart and Winston with the Advertising Association, 1981), p. 134.

6
ADVERTISING
AND ITS
AUDIENCE

This chapter will depart from many others written on the same topic. We will not discuss basic demographic characteristics of audiences, identify the types of consumers who tend to watch more television, or include any of the wealth of information that syndicated services provide on media and product usage patterns.

Instead of focusing on the advertising audience in general terms, we will center our discussion on the concept of information. The views of Carey and Sandage, reviewed in Chapter 4, suggest that advertising is an institution that attempts to transmit different types of market information, information that presumably matches buyers and sellers in the marketplace. This information can be functional in nature, such as the amount of hot water that various kinds of dishwashers use. It can also be aesthetic or symbolic, such as whether a cologne or after-shave lotion suits the self-image of a consumer.

We will focus on the impact of advertising information on the individual consumer. By individual consumer, we mean the average consumer who must enter the marketplace to buy anything from salt to a new automobile. This definition excludes those who buy professionally for others—e.g., purchasing agents. These institutional buyers have been excluded because we wish to focus our discussion on typical consumer advertising, for it is here that advertising's role is most praised and damned.

Since this chapter will view advertising as an informational medium, we will see how individual consumers acquire information and subsequently evaluate it in order to make final purchase decisions. Advertising's role in the process will be examined as well. It is felt that this perspective offers potential for considerable understanding of the interaction between advertising and the individual.

THE BASIC INFORMATIONAL FUNCTIONS OF ADVERTISING

Sheth believes that advertising fulfills four basic functions—precipitation, persuasion, reinforcement, and reminder.[1] *Precipitation* induces consumers to move from a state of indecision to one where purchase of a particular brand is a definite possibility. It attempts to intensify existing needs and wants. Its main function is to create general awareness and brand knowledge among large groups of potential customers.

When new products are introduced to the marketplace, there is usually an initial burst of advertising. The advertising usually indicates that a new product is available, tells something about its unique features, and indicates where it may be purchased. This is typical of the precipitation function.

Persuasion is seen as the mechanism by which advertising actually induces purchase. By using appeals to basic human emotions, such as love, hate, fear, and self-esteem, or by using appeals to reason by discussing product attributes as benefits, the advertisement attempts to induce purchase.

For example, advertisers of home-security systems hope their messages reach those who have recently been victimized by crime or know of someone who has. By utilizing a strong appeal to fear combined with product attributes and benefits, there is an attempt to get these potential consumers to move to an immediate purchase of the security system, based on their past disturbing experience with crime.

The *reinforcement* mechanism provides information that will legitimize *previous* choices. Information is given that indicates the wisdom of the existing choice or validates a previous decision to reject a particular product.

Automobile companies often do an excellent job of reinforcement advertising. Usually, after a new car has been purchased, the buyer is made a member of a special club formed by the company. Each month he/she receives a magazine that offers glowing information about the car just purchased.

Finally, the *reminder* mechanism is said to act as a triggering cue for habitual brand behavior (brand loyalty) learned from prior experiences and exposure to information. With products that are purchased frequently, customers need to be reminded about a particular brand because of the many conflicting messages they will hear about competing brands. The large volume of advertising done for the popular soft drinks and fast-food establishments is an example of reminder advertising.

Figure 6-1 demonstrates the sequential nature of the four advertising mechanisms. It is hypothesized that consumers move through these four mechanisms in making initial purchases. Not all consumers, however, will cycle completely through to the reminder stage. Some will remain at reinforcement. This usually occurs for infrequently purchased products such as autos and color television sets. Some consumers will become satiated or bored with an existing product. When satiation or boredom occurs, it is suggested that they will enter the first stage of the cycle again and begin to search for new

FIGURE 6-1

Basic Advertising Mechanisms

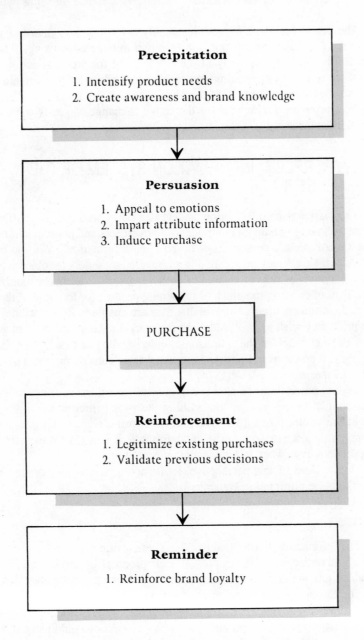

product alternatives. For example, a person may become "tired" of a sofa and seek to buy a new one, feeling it will "liven up" the living room. Others will perceive there to be a "better offer" in the marketplace and thus will also recycle.

The key to the Sheth model presumably is information. It seems apparent that the four functions are performed in part through advertising. The consumer can be seen as constantly in the marketplace for products and services. Thus, there is a constant sending and receiving of advertising information fulfilling various functions for both the consumer and the advertiser. This process, then, provides the impetus for the active exchange of goods and services in the marketplace.

THE "IMPERFECT" INFORMATION SYSTEM OF THE MARKETPLACE

The marketplace information system can be viewed in a simplified perspective as having two major components—advertisers and consumers. Matching of advertisers and consumers is based upon information. Yet, the market does not exhibit a "perfect" matching of buyers and sellers by objective standards. Hundreds of new products fail each year, retail outlets constantly have the problem of carrying too much of the wrong product (or too little of the right one), and consumers often complain that they are unable to find what they want at the price they wish to pay. Although the market clearly "works" in a satisfactory manner much of the time, some understanding can be gained by suggesting it still performs at less than an optimal level considering the quality and quantity of messages available. Why?

Several possibilities exist: (1) Advertisers are not transmitting *enough* information; (2) Advertisers are transmitting the *wrong* information to the audiences at the wrong times; (3) Advertisers transmit too much information; (4) Consumers do not *seek* out sufficient information; and (5) Consumers make poor decisions even when *given* adequate information.

On the basis of this perspective, let us now examine the components of the marketplace information system.

Advertisers

The information transmitted by advertisers is often of a persuasive nature. Since all advertisers attempt to present their products or services in the most favorable light, the information transmitted will not be perfectly objective.

For example, auto manufacturers do not emphasize in their advertising that driving is dangerous. Nor do food product advertisers discuss the presence of certain additives in their products, as such a discussion could make the product less appealing.

Critics have often taken issue with the persuasive nature of advertising, claiming that it subverts the consumer's "rational" decision processes. But, as

Borden has argued, "Whether one likes persuasion or not, it appears inevitable in a free society."[2] As Carey suggested, the persuasive nature of advertising communications is an institutionally understandable part of our market economy. The market economy basically presumes that firms will operate in their own self-interest to produce sales and profits; persuasive advertisements are thus a vehicle to achieve that end.

Closely related to the persuasion issue is the issue of frequency. Frequency—the intrusive repetition of many commercial messages—is something that all consumers are aware of and many are annoyed by. Recognizing that their messages are among hundreds attempting to attract the attention of consumers, advertisers use the technique of repetition to attract their share of attention. They are trying to be "heard above the crowd."

Although advertisers view repetition as an important technique in selling products, they are often unsure about how much repetition to use. Sometimes an ad is repeated too many times and sometimes not repeated often enough. It is usually quite difficult to determine the optimal expenditure of media dollars.

Related to repetition is the issue of occasion—the time of day that an advertisement is presented. Many consumers complain about the promotion of certain kinds of products at the dinner hour—laxatives or hemorrhoid preparations, for example. Again, however, the advertiser is presumably acting on self-interest. Large numbers of people are viewing television during the dinner hour, and many of these people are users or potential users of these products. Since advertisers want to reach as many potential customers as possible, they see the dinner hour as an ideal time for them to transmit their messages.

In addition to "puffing" their products, repeating their ads too often, or placing them at "inappropriate" times, advertisers may direct their message to the wrong audience. The advertiser may have perceived the market to be the twenty- to thirty-year-old group when, in fact, the major market for the product is consumers forty to fifty years of age. This misdirected information may not effectively reach the "prime market" and consequently will be of little value to either advertiser or consumer.

At other times advertisers send messages that consumers do not understand or interpret incorrectly. For example, consumers may have seen an ad for a paint sale at a local hardware store. The ad may have failed to state clearly enough that only certain colors were on sale, leaving some consumers with the impression that the sale prices applied to all colors of paint. The subsequent visit to the hardware store will prove unsatisfactory for both the advertiser and the consumer.

In sum, advertisers do not always transmit "perfect" information for either their own or the consumer's interests. Because of practices such as attempting to induce purchase through partial information, making mistakes in frequency rates and timing, developing poor messages, and transmitting information to the wrong audience, less than optimal information may be offered by advertisers to consumers.

Consumers

Consumers, as well, are "imperfect" in the way they go about gathering and processing information. They are not the rational people that classical economists had hoped they were. Although there is evidence that consumers approach some buying decisions in a deliberate manner, there is also good reason to believe that a good deal of purchasing behavior involves little conscious decision making.

Much decision making does not follow the systematic approaches presented in formal consumer behavior models. Rarely does a consumer proceed smoothly from need recognition, to information acquisition, to purchase. The decision process may take place over a long period of time with incomplete and often ambiguous data, and the final decision may be made with something less than total confidence.[3]

A consumer's ability to process bits of information is also imperfect. At any given time, individuals can probably actively process only a limited amount of information.[4] When the buying environment is very complex, it is easy to become confused. Take, for example, the process of deciding which house to buy. After looking at many different houses and collecting a myriad of data, how many consumers base their final decision on an essentially minor feature, such as whether a fence is part of the property? For some home buyers, the mass of information about unique support features, insulation, wiring, landscaping, fireplaces, size of lot, and heating and cooling systems can be too much to deal with.

Consumer behavior is aptly described in March and Simon's concept of "bounded rationality": Faced with a very complex environment and limited resources (time, money, cognitive capabilities), consumers attempt to resolve buying problems in ways that are satisfactory rather than optimal.[5] In Bauer's view of consumer behavior, "Consumers characteristically develop decision strategies and ways of reducing risk that enable them to act with relative confidence and ease in situations where their information is inadequate and the consequences of their actions are in some meaningful sense incalculable."[6]

Thus, it appears that neither consumers nor advertisers always operate in an optimal manner in the marketplace. Yet, given this less than ideal performance on the part of both major components of the market information system, it is interesting to note that the system continues to function and has given apparently adequate service to many consumers and advertisers. The *perfect* marketplace has never existed—and never will. That does not mean, of course, that it is fruitless to search for ways to improve the existing mechanism.

One approach may be to look more closely at exactly *how* consumers use the information available to make buying decisions. Given some kind of descriptive model, it may be possible to better understand the "human" workings of the market, and thus be more adequately equipped to offer suggestions for improvement.

HOW CONSUMERS GATHER AND PROCESS INFORMATION

Of course consumers do not rely solely upon advertising to gather product brand information. There are five primary sources of information, both internal and external, available to consumers:[7]

1. *Memory* of past searches, personal experiences, and low-involvement learning (internal information).
2. *Market-dominated sources* such as advertising, personal selling, etc.
3. *Consumer-dominated sources* such as family and friends.
4. *Neutral sources* such as *Consumer Reports* and various state and local government publications.
5. *Experiential sources* such as inspection or product trial.

These sources are shown in Figure 6-2.

FIGURE 6-2

Information Sources for a Purchase Decision

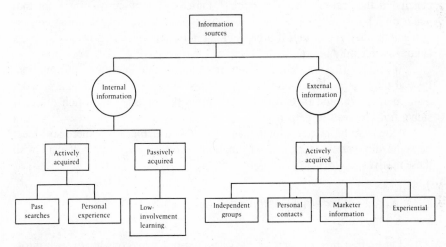

Source: Adapted from H. Beales, M. B. Mazis, S. C. Salop, and R. Staelin, "Consumer Search and Public Policy," *Journal of Consumer Research*, June, 1981, p. 12.

When Are These Information Sources Used?

The internal information sources are the primary ones used by consumers, especially in cases where the consumer is involved in a very limited problem-solving situation or is brand loyal.[8] Mass media or market-dominated sources have been found to be important in the early stages of the decision process, when the buyer is informing himself/herself about possible alternatives

(Sheth's precipitation function);[9] but these sources are frequently found to be of limited direct value in consumer decisions (Sheth's persuasion function).[10] Although little research has been done concerning Sheth's reinforcement and reminder functions, it is reasonable to predict that consumers use some combination of internal and market-dominated sources.

There has been some research on the effect of product characteristics on information sources used. Research on the diffusion of information indicates that there is a tendency for buyers of new and high-involvement products to prefer consumer-dominated sources.[11] Settle found that for complex and socially visible products the preferred sources of information were conversations with experts and close friends. For durable and multipurpose products, the preferred information source was personal experience.[12]

The neutral channels are vastly underutilized. One study found 6 percent or less of female consumers utilize neutral sources in the purchase of small appliances, clothing, and food items;[13] while other researchers found that neutral sources were valued sixth (out of six choices) in importance in the purchase of men's shirts and television sets.[14] Beatty and Smith found that a search of neutral sources was influenced by time, availability, and ego involvement. They concluded that people perceive neutral sources as time-consuming, and that under time pressure, people may avoid this type of search. Examining ego involvement, they found that if a product is really important to a person's ego, a neutral source may be sought out.[15]

It is clear that consumers rarely rely on a single source of information. Instead they use multiple information sources which are complementary rather than competitive, and their use depends upon the situation in which the consumer finds himself or herself.

However, no matter which channel(s) the consumer uses, there still must be some motivation to gather information. The next section will deal with these motivating forces.

Determinants of External Search Effort by Consumers

Let us first turn to some of the basic reasons why consumers seek information before making a purchase. The area of external search activity has a long history of study. Beatty and Smith have developed a rather complete analysis of many of these works. Their conclusions for over seventy reviewed articles were:

1. Consumers tend to engage in more search when purchasing higher priced, more visible, and more complex products—i.e., products that intrinsically create greater perceived risk.
2. Search is also influenced by individual factors, such as the perceived benefits of search (e.g., enjoyment, self-confidence, role), demographic aspects, and product knowledge possessed.

3.   Search effort tends to be further influenced by factors in the marketplace such as time pressure impinging on the shopper.[16]

Although it would not be appropriate for this text to review all the possible determinants of external search activity in depth, some of the more interesting findings which supplement and extend Beatty and Smith will now be reviewed.

Risk.   In every buying decision, consumers have identified (however vaguely) a need and a product or service that will satisfy that need. Many buying decisions involve some perceived risk: as Bauer puts it, "Consumer behavior involves risk in the sense that any action of a consumer will produce consequences which he cannot anticipate with any approximate certainty."[17] How many times have we thought about buying something and yet been very unsure which purchase would be most satisfactory for the money involved?

Perceived risk is apparently a function of at least two factors—uncertainty and consequences.[18] Consumers may be uncertain about their goals. For example, a consumer who has identified the need for a new car might be unsure whether economy or comfort is a more important goal. Even if the consumer has established economy as the basic goal, there is still uncertainty about exactly what type of car will be best. A Ford Escort? A Honda? Thus, uncertainty deals with basic buying goals (economy vs. comfort) as well as with final specification of an exact product (Escort vs. Honda) that will satisfy the overall goal.

The consequences of a purchase are the second factor which can generate perceived risk. Consequences can be defined as "the amount that would be lost if the consequences of the act were not favorable."[19] If you buy the Escort, will it impress your friends as you hoped? You may also have had certain expectations of how well the Escort would perform. For example, you may be fearful that the actual maintenance experience will not be as good as you might have expected.

The major types of risk that consumers may perceive in making product/ service decisions have been categorized as follows:[20]

1.   FUNCTIONAL RISK. The product/service will not perform as expected. "Will the Honda get excellent highway gas mileage?"
2.   PHYSICAL RISK. Using the product will involve risk to oneself or others. "Will the lawn mower be safe for my teenage son to operate?"
3.   FINANCIAL RISK. The product/service will not be worth its cost in terms of money to acquire it. "Will buying a new home cause financial hardship?"
4.   SOCIAL RISK. The product/service will be an embarrassment to oneself. "Will others like my new entertainment center?"
5.   PSYCHOLOGICAL RISK. The consumer's final choice will bruise the ego. "Will I really be happy in this apartment?"
6.   TIME RISK. The time spent in search may be wasted if performance is not as expected. "Will the consumer have to return the product and engage in a new shopping trip?"

7. OPPORTUNITY LOSS. Risk that by taking one action the consumer will miss out on doing something else he or she would prefer doing. "Instead of purchasing a BMW the consumer could have taken a trip to Europe."[21]

In general, consumers can reduce perceived risk by (a) reducing the amount at stake or (b) decreasing uncertainty through information acquisition. Reducing the consequences (the amount at stake) of a decision is a somewhat more difficult strategy to follow for most consumers than reducing uncertainty. To use our earlier example, it may be very difficult for a person to say that she does not care what her friends think of her new Escort if social esteem is important to her. It would also be difficult for her to minimize a poor maintenance record when it has cost her dearly to make repairs. Therefore, it appears more likely that consumers will tend to seek to reduce uncertainty through information acquisition or to avoid the uncertainty altogether.

Some more specific risk-avoidance strategies include the following:[22]

1. Information seeking from memory, market, consumer, or neutral dominated sources of information.
2. Development of brand loyalty toward a product/service instead of purchasing new or untried products/services.
3. Trusting of well-known brand names when experience has been minor in a product category (brand image).
4. Trusting of stores to provide only good-quality products/services (store image).
5. Choosing of the most expensive item or model.
6. Reliance upon private laboratory tests, money-back guarantees, warranties, and prepurchase trial (reassurance).

One study, however, found that risk-reduction strategies employed by consumers vary by product class. Brand loyalty was the best strategy for shampoos, detergents, and canned mushrooms; while money-back guarantees and store images were the best risk-reduction strategies for electric appliances. Comparison shopping was the reduction strategy for dresses and dishes.[23]

The impression should not be left that all consumers act to reduce or avoid risk. Different individuals have different levels of tolerance for risk, each acting to reduce risk to a personally acceptable level. Certain consumers, in fact, have been found to act in a way that increases risk.[24] The Sheth model, discussed earlier, indicated that consumers who become satiated or bored by a product will accept the risk involved in seeking new product alternatives. Thus, consumers can have two entirely different strategies concerning risk: acting to decrease it or acting to increase it. The novelty factor below will expand the discussion on increasing risk.

Novelty, Variety Seeking.   Novelty is a second factor that motivates consumers to seek information.[25] All dimensions of newness in the market, such as new products or new advertising (appeals, media) can be viewed as stimuli that will motivate consumers to seek information. For many consumers, novelty is a change of pace from the usual way of doing things and thus holds intrinsic appeal. The new safer tire, the newly designed auto, or the unusual advertisement may all attract the initial attention of the consumer. Quite often, the consumer will attempt to find out more with the possibility of eventually buying.

Number of Alternatives. The greater the number of alternatives (products, stores, brands) available to the consumer to resolve a particular problem, the more external search there is likely to be.[26]

Store Distribution. The number, location, and distances between retail outlets can affect the number of store visits a consumer will make to gather information.[27] When stores are clustered together, as often happens with auto dealers, or appliance stores, or in shopping malls, the consumer will generally visit more of them, since there will be a reduction in the time and energy to make such visits.

Greater Differences in Product Alternatives. When the consumer perceives important differences between brands based on differences in features, style, or appearance, more external search for information will occur.[28] Dissimilarities in products/services may lead consumers to perceive substantial benefits from searching for information. Such benefits may not be as evident when products/services are perceived as parity. Highly differentiated products for which consumers engage in an extensive information search included clothing,[29] new furniture,[30] and autos.[31]

Education, Occupation, and Income of Consumers. The external search for information has been found to be related to education, occupation, and income.[32] A direct relationship has been found between levels of education and amount of information search for such items as major appliances,[33] homes,[34] and food products;[35] while a negative relationship was found for sporting equipment, shirts,[36] and homes.[37] The more elevated the occupation, the more external search that was found for the purchase of durable goods;[38] while for income, a negative relationship existed for small appliances.[39]

Age of the Consumer. External search tends to decrease as the age of the consumer increases.[40] This may in part be that the older consumer has become more familiar with a host of products/services that the younger consumer is just encountering.

Attitudes Toward Shopping. "Attitudes toward shopping reflect the individual's beliefs about the value and benefit achieved through shopping activities for the product category being purchased. This variable is not equivalent to simple shopping enjoyment, but it is a strong motivating predisposition to shopping and could be viewed as indicating 'shopping involvement.'"[41] The literature shows a strong positive relationship between attitudes toward shopping and actual search behavior.[42]

Degree of Confidence.   If consumers are confident about a purchase, they are not likely to seek much information. An example would be a consumer who is loyal to a particular brand of coffee. When coffee is on the grocery list, a favorite brand is automatically chosen from the supermarket shelf. Because of previous satisfactory experience with the brand, there is no motivation to seek information about the purchase. Many new car buyers, based on a satisfying experience with a brand of auto, repurchased that brand with very little information.[43] Conversely, a consumer who is not confident about a purchase (e.g., buying a home computer for the first time) will probably seek information about both the product class and the brands available.

Moore and Lehmann found that the greater the number of previous purchases, the less information required.[44] However, Bennett and Mandell found that past experience with a product reduces the need for information only as long as the consumer is satisfied with the product.[45] It may be that confidence and risk are closely related. If the consumer is very confident about an upcoming purchase, it may also be that little or no risk is perceived. Thus, in either instance, little information seeking will occur.

Involuntary Situation.   A final factor that motivates information seeking is the involuntary situation. When the refrigerator or dryer breaks for the last time, consumers are forced into the marketplace to gather information. Generally, consumers perceive more risk than is actually present in the involuntary situation.[46]

Given these ten motivations for information seeking, we shall attempt to review some of the factors that affect how much information consumers will gather.

How Much Information Do Consumers Gather?

We do know that consumers are active in the marketplace in terms of gathering information. Often, however, the amount of information that *could* be gathered and processed is overwhelming. For example, on any drugstore shelf, there are a dozen or more brands of shampoo. Each has a different price, different ingredients, different functions (for dry, normal, or oily hair; for dandruff; for body), and different quality-price associations. Information is readily available on the shampoo package and from prior learning about the products through advertisements and personal experience. Friends may have offered advice on what products are good. Hence, with little effort, the consumer can be exposed to a plethora of valuable product information.

Although the amount of external search that consumers undertake before making a purchase has been measured in a number of ways in the literature (number of stores visited, number of information sources consulted, number of alternatives considered, number of different types of information used, and time duration of the purchase decision), it is clear that for most consumers the amount of external research conducted is very limited. We shall review the first two of these measurement types.

Newman found that one-stop shoppers accounted for approximately 60 percent of the purchases of new autos; 60-80 percent of the purchases of various items of apparel and small appliances; and 85 to 90 percent of the purchase of cookware, towels, sheets, and toys.[47]

Westbrook and Farnell reported on retail store shopping patterns used by purchasers of major appliances and found that 31 percent of all buyers visited only one outlet, while 15 percent visited two stores and 19 percent visited three retail outlets. Thirty-five percent visited four or more stores.[48]

Concerning the number of information sources utilized for the purchase of autos, Newman and Staelin[49] reported the following:

1. Fifteen percent of the buyers consulted no external information source.
2. Thirty percent of the buyers consulted only one external information source.
3. Twenty-six percent consulted two information sources.
4. Eighteen percent used three information sources.
5. Twelve percent utilized four or more information sources before purchase.

Hawkins et al.[50] suggest that buyers can be classified into three groups in terms of the search they engage in before making a major durable purchase:

1. NONSEARCHERS. Fifty percent of the consumers conduct little or no search prior to purchase.
2. LIMITED INFORMATION SEARCHERS. Thirty-eight percent of the consumers are associated with limited information search.
3. EXTENDED INFORMATION SEARCHES. Only about 12 percent are involved in extensive information search prior to purchase. These individuals tend to have higher incomes, are heavy users of a variety of media vehicles, are opinion leaders, and have favorable overall attitudes toward business.

Other equally important factors are the time and money it takes to gather information. How many times have we bought the first item we saw because we simply did not have the time or inclination to "look around"? We may have known about a store that offered the same product at a better price, but it was "just too far away." Thus, in many instances, information is not sought by consumers because the added costs of search (time and money) are too high in light of the expected benefits this information will provide for making a final decision.[51]

One note of caution is appropriate. It would appear from the previous studies that many consumers, because they conduct little or no external search, are engaging in no search at all. What many of these studies fail to note is the amount of internal search (memory) each consumer engages in prior to making a purchase.[52] Visiting few stores and reviewing only a few brands may also indicate that consumers have various decision-making rules that immediately limit their set of store and brand alternatives. We will now discuss these decision-making rules.

Decision-Making Rules That Consumers Use

Consumers use decision-making rules when they attempt to evaluate and select alternatives they have discovered in the search process. Some consumers average out some of the very good features with some of the less attractive features of a product in determining overall brand preference. The brand that rates highest on the sum of the consumer's judgment of the relevant evaluative criteria will be chosen. This is known as the *linear compensatory rule*.[53] This form of decision making appears to be used in more complex high-involvement situations.

The following rules are called *noncompensatory*, since very good performance on one evaluative criterion cannot compensate for poor performance on another evaluative criterion:

1. THE DISJUNCTIVE RULE. This rule establishes a minimum level of desired performance for each relevant attribute. The number of attributes will be small, and the level of desired performance will generally be high. All brands that surpass the performance for any attribute are considered acceptable. The consumer would say, "I'll consider all (or buy the first) brands that perform really well on any attribute I consider to be important."[54]

2. THE CONJUNCTIVE RULE. A consumer will consider a brand only if it meets acceptable standards on all key attributes. If the washing machine meets the consumer's requirements for amount of water utilized and permanent-press features but is above a set limit on cost, it will be eliminated from the alternatives.[55]

3. THE LEXICOGRAPHIC RULE. The consumer rank-orders all the key brand attributes in terms of their perceived importance. After comparing the brands on the most important attributes, the one that is highest is selected. If there is a tie, brands are then evaluated on the second most important attribute.[56]

Certainly, these are not the only decision-making rules that consumers employ. For many purchase situations, prior learning as a result of product trial may be utilized. Assessment of attributes may not be important, and the consumer may choose the brand with the best overall impression. Schiffman and Kanuk call this the *affect referred rule*.[57]

Consumers may use only one rule or combine them in a myriad of ways to reach final purchase decisions. Low-involvement purchases probably involve simple decision-making rules, such as the conjunctive, the disjunctive, or the lexicographic, since consumers may attempt to minimize the mental cost of such decisions.[58] High-involvement decisions may utilize complex rules such as linear compensatory and may involve different rules at different stages of the decision-making process.[59]   Table 6-1 may help to clarify the above discussion.

TABLE 6-1

Use of Decision-Making Rules in Choosing a Brand of Automobile

RULE	VERBAL DESCRIPTION	PERCENTAGE USING RULE
Disjunctive	I chose the car that had a really good rating on at least one characteristic.	0%
Conjunctive	I chose the car that didn't have any bad ratings.	0.6%
Lexicographic	I looked at the characteristic that was most important to me and chose the car that was best in that characteristic. If two or more of the cars were equal on that characteristic, I then looked at my second most important characteristic to break the tie.	60.7%
Compensatory	I chose the car that had a really good rating when you balanced the good ratings with the bad ratings.	32.1%
Disjunctive-conjunctive	I first eliminated any car that didn't have at least one really good score and then chose from the rest the product that didn't have a really bad score on any characteristic.	0%
Conjunctive-disjunctive	I first eliminated the cars with a bad rating on any characteristic and then chose from the rest the one with a high score on any characteristic.	0%
Disjunctive-compensatory	I first eliminated any car that didn't have at least one really good rating and then chose from the rest of the cars that seemed the best when you balanced the good ratings.	1.1%
Conjunctive-compensatory	I first eliminated the cars with a really bad rating on any characteristic and then chose from the rest the one that seemed the best overall when you balanced the good ratings with the bad ratings.	5.4%

Source: Derived from M. Reily and R. Holman, "Does Task Complexity or Cue Intercorrelation Affect Choice of an Information Processing Strategy: An Empirical Investigation," in *Advances in Consumer Research* IV, ed. W. D. Perrault, Jr. (Chicago: Association for Consumer Research, 1977), p. 189.

How Does Information Influence Purchase?

There are many conflicting views of how information can influence a purchase decision. We shall review five theories that have received some support from a host of studies conducted in the area. The approaches to be discussed view the influence process as occurring through the interaction of cognitive, affective, and conative elements. The cognitive component includes attention, awareness, comprehension, learning, interest, and beliefs; the affective component is concerned with interest, attitude, feeling, and evaluation; the conative factor deals with behavior—trial, action, and adoption.

The Learning Hierarchy.   One view of the process, the learning hierarchy, states that information transmitted and subsequently gathered by consumers must first create changes in the cognitive component (awareness, attention, comprehension). In other words, the consumer must first attend to and understand the information. If this is successfully accomplished, then changes in the affective component (attitude) may occur (reorganization of belief structure). Once a favorable attitude toward purchase of the brand occurs, changes in the conative component (intentions to behave, trial, etc.) will occur (see Figure 6-3). Ray refers to this sequence as the "learn-feel-do" hierarchy.[60]

As Ray indicates, the learning hierarchy exists only in special circumstances. It is most likely to occur in situations in which there are audience involvement, product differentiation, emphasis on the mass media in communication, and where the product is in the early stages of the product life cycle.[61] Product examples include portable television sets, autos, washing machines, and pocket calculators.[62]

The Dissonance-Attribution Hierarchy.   Another view of the organization of the cognitive, affective, conative structure is called the dissonance-attribution hierarchy. This is the exact reverse of the learning hierarchy—"do-feel-learn" instead of "learn-feel-do"; in the dissonance-attribution hierarchy behavior occurs first, then attitude change, and finally learning[63] (see Figure 6-4 on page 116).

Although studies in dissonance theory have been applied to this model, Ray indicates that attribution theory may be a more adequate explanation of this hierarchy. The reasoning for this approach would be as follows: The basic idea is that people determine that they have attitudes by perceiving their own behavior. If someone has made a brand choice, this person will say, "I must have a positive attitude toward that brand because I have chosen it." If, after choice and attitude change, individuals are exposed to marketing messages, they will tend to choose the information that will support their attitude. Product examples might be autos and home-entertainment equipment.[64]

The dissonance-attribution hierarchy has been found to occur when the following conditions exist:

1. Low differentiation for complex alternatives
2. Non-mass media, personal sources important

FIGURE 6-3

The Learning Hierarchy

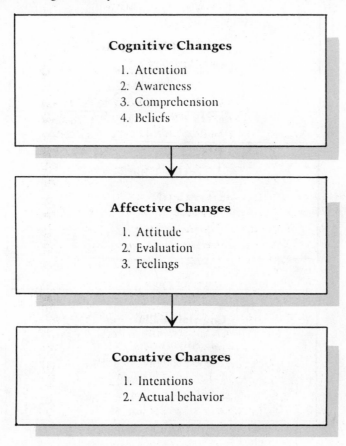

3.   Mature stage in the product life cycle
4.   Involving situation[65]

   The Low-Involvement Hierarchy.   A third approach is called the
low-involvement hierarchy, or ''learn-do-feel''[66] (see Figure 6-5 on page 117).
The low-involvement hierarchy views information as first changing the cognitive component, then bringing about actual behavior changes, and then finally
affecting attitude.   The view holds that television viewers, for example, are not
involved with the advertising.   Thus, there is little perceptual defense against
the commercial messages.   Although television commercials will probably not
change attitudes, they may, after a great deal of repetition, make possible a
shift in cognitive structure.   Consumers will thus be better able to recall the
name of a product or service that has been advertised.   The next time they are
in a store, that name could come to mind and result in a purchase.   After the

FIGURE 6-4

The Dissonance Attribution Hierarchy

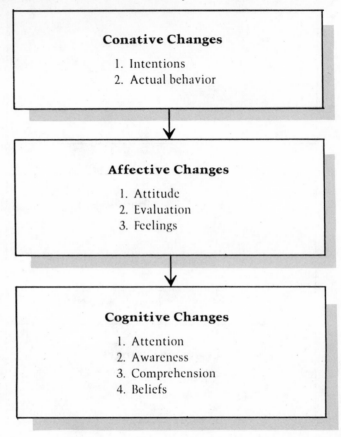

consumer has used the product, it is contended, attitude shift will occur. If product usage is satisfactory, a more favorable attitude toward the product will develop; if usage is unsatisfactory, a negative attitude will develop. Examples of products that often fit this profile are soaps, mouthwashes, and gum—often heavily advertised products.

Low involvement is likely to occur under the following conditions:[67]

1. Low differentiation
2. Mass media important
3. Mature stage in the product life cycle

The Batra-Ray model[68] (shown in Figure 6-6 on page 118) is another more recent view of how information can influence a purchase decision. The first stage in the model, affective responses, indicates that determinants of attitude towards the ad, A_{ad}, are not all cognitively based reactions to the

FIGURE 6-5

The Low-Involvement Hierarchy

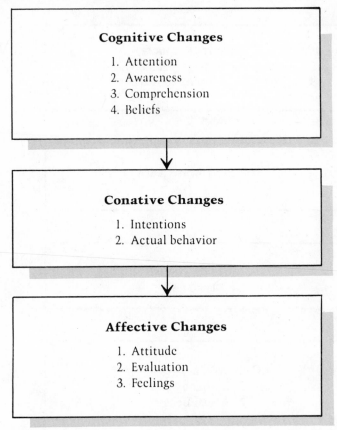

advertising stimulus.[69] Advertisements, in addition to providing product, benefit, or attribute information, can also provide "music, humor, affectionate vi-
gnettes, story elements, role portrayals, and the like."[70] These later elements
can evoke moods within the consumer which are simply the consumer's affective state at the time of exposure.[71]

Given that advertisements can "set the right mood, through some emotional appeal," these affective responses will influence A_{ad}. A_{ad} can best be
defined as liking the advertising execution or production. The model then indicates that A_{ad} could influence attitude toward the brand, A_b, which in turn could
lead to some conative changes, such as more positive behavioral intentions or
actual behavior.

More recent research indicates that the model may work best in situations
where the consumer is unfamiliar with the brand.[72] For familiar brands, it may

FIGURE 6-6

The Batra-Ray Model

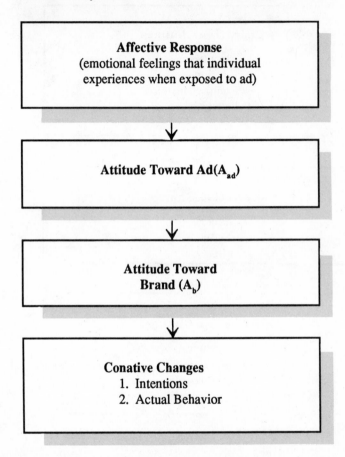

be that the emotional execution acts by changing the level of confidence or degree of accessibility that the consumer has in the A_b.[73]

In sum, this model implies that it is not always what you say but how you say it that is important. This emotional strategy utilized by many advertisers is often viewed as a ''say nothing'' message by critics of advertising, but the Batra-Ray model indicates that these messages can indeed communicate with the audience.

The Experiential-Based Model

Our last model of how information can influence decision is shown in Figure 6-7. This model is based upon an alternative view of the buying process; one that emphasizes the experiential side of consumption rather than the view that consumers actively process information in a rational, thoughtful

FIGURE 6-7

The Experiential-Based Model

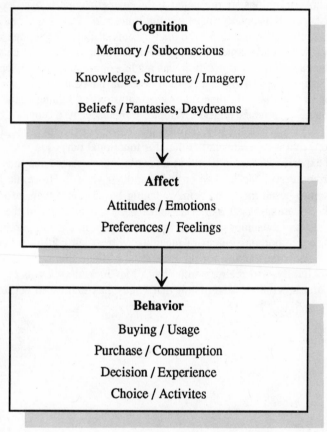

Cognition

Memory / Subconscious

Knowledge, Structure / Imagery

Beliefs / Fantasies, Daydreams

Affect

Attitudes / Emotions

Preferences / Feelings

Behavior

Buying / Usage

Purchase / Consumption

Decision / Experience

Choice / Activites

Note. Terms on left-hand side indicate traditional terms used in information processing, while those on the right-hand side indicate experimental concepts.

Source: Morris B. Holbrook and Elizabeth C. Hirschman, "The Experimental Aspects of Consumption: Consumer Fantasies, Feelings, and Fun," *Journal of Consumer Reseach*, vol. 9, September 1982, p. 133.

manner. The experiential model views consumers as feelers, in addition to thinkers, who consume many types of products for the sensations, feelings, images, and emotions they generate.[74]

Shtola believes that products/services/events should be classified into utilitarian and esthetic groups.[75] Utilitarian products/services/events might include many traditional food products, soaps, garbage bags, and motor oil; while esthetic products/services/events might include movies, art, novels, opera, and casinos.[76] The experiential view, then, focuses on the symbolic, hedonic, and esthetic nature of consumption and regards the consumption experience as a phenomenon directed toward the pursuit of fantasies, feelings, and fun.[77]

Some additional examples might help to clarify the model. When women look to purchase nail polish or eye makeup or men look to purchase cologne, a host of options are presented at the cosmetic counter of a department store. Observing consumers reviewing the hundreds of shades of nail polish and eye makeup or "consuming" the many scents of the cologne, one wonders how a decision is made concerning a particular shade of blue or scent of cologne. When asked how the decision was made, comments often arise such as: "It's me!" or "It is just right!" Is it a decision based entirely upon bits of information or one that is influenced by the fantasies and feelings generated by the individual? Women's lingerie, whether purchased by a female or a male for a significant other in his life, is often purchased for the fantasies, feelings, and emotions that it generates rather than for functional purposes.

This experiential model is still in its evolutionary stages and thus open to many interpretations. McCracken provides another view.[78] He would describe the experiential based model as being meaning-based rather than information-based. The meaning-based model assumes purchase is made in the broader cultural context. Consumer goods, in their anticipation, choice, purchase, and possession, are important sources of meaning with which consumers construct their lives. They are looking for things that help shape the meaning of themselves, their family, and their communities. McCracken's view is compatible with the cultural view of advertising that Carey has expressed earlier in the book.

◆

SUMMARY

We have attempted to look at the information system in the marketplace via advertisers and consumers. Advertisers send messages to consumers with varying degrees of efficiency and professionalism. Consumers in turn receive some of the messages from advertisers, but they also look to their own memories, the advice and opinions of friends, and neutral sources of information.

If we take an "objective" stance, such as that of classical economists, we would have to say that the system of information flow in the marketplace leaves much to be desired. Advertisers, predictably, operate in their own self-interest by sending only the information they wish to send, when they wish to send it, and often with uncertain guidance as to the proper "mix" of message content and frequency.

Consumers, for their part, frequently fail to meet the standards of "economic person." They do not always collect all the information they could when deciding which product to buy. Often they rely on shortcuts; they may look to price as an indicator of quality or they may become brand or store loyal. They not infrequently stop processing information when they become confused and may make "snap" decisions just to "get it over with." They may buy in pursuit of fantasies, feelings, and fun.

But from another vantage point, the market of information flow tends to operate in a generally acceptable manner. If we accept our existing economic system, it is perfectly logical for advertisers to operate in their own self-interest by transmitting persuasive communications which are repeated often. They are attempting to induce sales to ensure the continued existence of the firm.

Although consumers do not always try to find perfect solutions to their purchase decisions, they operate in ways that often lead to subjective satisfaction on their part. Consumers will often informally balance the cost of seeking additional information with the benefits they hope it will bring to the final purchase decision. If it appears that additional information is not needed, they will not collect it. This does not necessarily mean that they are not "rational," but only that they are operating from a set of decision-making rules that they have found acceptable in making purchases. If consumers attempted to behave in the rational manner that classical economists have posited, they probably would spend a great deal of their time gathering information. Consumers are constantly seeking products and services that will allow them more leisure time. It is not different with information seeking. Consumers are always seeking ways to reduce search time, yet still reach acceptable decisions.

This is not to say that consumers do not buy products that are unacceptable for their existing needs. When this happens, it is very difficult to determine whether it is the fault of the "imperfect" market sources or the fault of the "imperfect" consumer. For example, if you make a mistake in a purchase decision, it may be easier to blame the advertising system than to accept the blame yourself.

Advertising can be seen to be involved in a market service. It provides a type of information that helps match buyers and sellers in a general system emphasizing the self-interest of the participants. It is clearly not "perfect," and could certainly be improved. But any steps toward improvement must rest on an understanding of the ways consumers actually utilize information.

More and more information is apparently not the answer. Consumers will continue to use shortcuts in their purchasing behavior. What is apparently needed is not more, but better, information. Unfortunately, neither critics nor supporters of advertising are exactly sure what "better" information is. There is little prospect that we can make the consumer the perfect information procuring and processing system. All we can hope for is to make the consumer a better information system, given the "recalcitrance and perversity" of human nature.

Advertising can be constantly improved in terms of information output, but that is only one side of the issue. The consumer must also be improved through better consumer education, learning not only how to obtain information but how to use it. Most of all, the consumer must *want* to use the information.

ENDNOTES

1. Jagdish N. Sheth, "Measurement of Advertising Effectiveness: Some Theoretical Considerations," *Journal of Advertising,* vol. 3, no. 1 (1974), pp. 8-11.

2. Neil H. Borden, *The Economic Effect of Advertising* (Chicago: Irwin, 1942).

3. Raymond L. Horton, *Buyer Behavior: A Decision-Making Approach* (Columbus, OH: Charles E. Merrill Publishing Co., 1984), p. 12.

4. See Jacob Jacoby, Donald E. Speller, and Carol A. Kohn, "Brand Choice Behavior as a Function of Information Load," *Journal of Marketing Research,* 11 (February 1984), pp. 63-69; William L. Wilkie, "Analysis of Effects of Information Load," *Journal of Marketing Research,* 11 (November 1974), pp. 467-468; and Gerald Zaltman and Melanie Wallendorf, *Consumer Behavior: Basic Findings and Management Implications,* 2d. ed. (New York: John Wiley & Sons, Inc., 1983), pp. 351-353; Thomas E. Muller, "Buyer Response to Variations in Product Information Load," *Journal of Applied Psychology,* 69 (1984), pp. 300-306.

5. James A. March and Herbert A. Simon, *Organizations* (New York: John Wiley & Sons, Inc., 1958), pp. 203-204.

6. Raymond A. Bauer, "Consumer Behavior as Risk Taking," in *Dynamic Marketing for a Changing World,* Robert S. Hancock, ed. (Chicago: American Marketing Association, 1960), pp. 389,398.

7. Del I. Hawkins, Roger J. Best, and Kenneth A. Coney, *Consumer Behavior: Implications for Marketing Strategy* (Plano, TX: Business Publications, Inc., 1986), p. 574.

8. E. C. Hirschman and M. K. Mills, "Sources Shoppers Use to Pick Stores," *Journal of Advertising Research,* February 1980, pp. 47-51.

9. Carol A. Kohn Berning and Jacob Jacoby, "Patterns of Information Acquisition in New Product Purchases," *Journal of Consumer Research,* 1 (September 1974), pp. 8-12; George Kotona and Eva Mueller, "A Study of Purchase Decisions," in *Consumer Behavior: The Dynamics of Consumer Reactions,* L. H. Clark, ed. (New York: New York University Press, 1955), pp. 35-87.

10. D. F. Midgley, "Patterns of Interpersonal Information Seeking for the Purchase of a Symbolic Product," *Journal of Marketing Research,* February 1983, pp. 74-83; T. A. Swartz and N. Stephens, "Information Search for Services," in *Advances in Consumer Research XI,* T. C. Kinnear, ed. (Chicago: Association for Consumer Research, 1984) p. 31.

11. Horton, p. 271.

12. Robert B. Settle, "Attribution Theory and Acceptance of Information," *Journal of Marketing Research,* 9 (February 1972), pp. 85-88.

13. Thomas S. Robertson, "The Effect of the Informal Group Upon Member Innovative Behavior," in *Marketing and the New Science of Planning,*

Robert L. King, ed. (Chicago: American Marketing Association, 1968), pp. 334-340.

14.   Ben M. Enis and Gordon W. Paul, "Store Loyalty as a Basis for Market Segmentation," *Journal of Retailing,* 46 (Fall 1970), p. 46.

15.   Sharon E. Beatty and Scott M. Smith, "External Search Effort: An Investigation Across Several Product Categories," *Journal of Consumer Research* 14 (June 1987), pp. 83-95.

16.   *Ibid.,* p. 84.

17.   Bauer, p. 87.

18.   Leon G. Schiffman and Leslie Lazar Kanuk, *Consumer Behavior* (Englewood Cliffs, NJ: Prentice-Hall, 1987), p. 214.

19.   Donald F. Cox, *Risk Taking and Information Handling in Consumer Behavior,* Donald F. Cox, ed. (Boston: Division of Research, Graduate School of Business Administration, Harvard University, 1967).

20.   List of risks taken from Schiffman and Kanuk, *op. cit.,* pp. 214-215, unless otherwise noted.

21.   John C. Mowen, *Consumer Behavior* (New York: MacMillan, 1987), p. 75.

22.   Schiffman and Kanuk, *op. cit.,* pp. 217-218.

23.   C. Derbaix, "Perceived Risk and Risk Relievers: An Empirical Investigation," *Journal of Economic Psychology,* 3 (1983), pp. 19-38.

24.   Cox, *op. cit.,* p. 9.

25.   M. Venkatesan, "Cognitive Consistency and Novelty Seeking," *Consumer Behavior: Theoretical Sources,"* Scott Ward and Thomas S. Robertson, eds. (Englewood Cliffs, NJ: Prentice-Hall, 1973), pp. 355-384; L. McAlister and E. Pessemier, "Variety Seeking Behavior: An Interdisciplinary Review," *Journal of Consumer Research,* December 1982, pp. 311-22.

26.   D. R. Lehmann and W. L. Moore, "Validity of Information Display Bounds: An Assessment Using Longitudinal Data," *Journal of Marketing,* November 1980, pp. 450-59.

27.   P. Nelson, "Advertising Is Information," *Journal of Political Economy,* July-August 1974, pp. 729-754; G. S. Cost and L. V. Domingurz, "Cross-Shopping and Retail Growth," *Journal of Marketing Research,* May 1977, pp. 187-192.

28.   D. Cox and S. Rich, "Perceived Risk and Consumer Decision Making—A Case of Telephone Shopping," *Journal of Marketing Research,* November 1964, pp. 32-39.

29.   W. Dommermuth and E. Cundiff, "Shopping Goods, Shopping Centers, and Selling Strategies," *Journal of Marketing,* October 1967, pp. 32-36.

30.   B. Le Grand and J. Udell, "Consumer Behavior in the Marketplace—An Empirical Study in the Television and Furniture Fields," *Journal of Retailing,* Fall 1964, p. 32.

31.   J. Newman and R. Staelin, "Prepurchase Information Seeking for New Cars and Major Household Appliances, *Journal of Marketing Research,*

August 1972, pp. 249-257.

32. N. Capon and M. Burke, "Individual, Product Class, and Task-Related Factors in Consumer Information Processing," *Journal of Consumer Research,* December 1980, pp. 314-326.

33. Katona and Mueller, "Study of Purchase," *Cooking Appliance Purchase and Usage Patterns* (New York: Newsweek, 1978), p. 27.

34. D. Hempel, "Search Behavior and Information Utilization in the Home Buying Process," in *Marketing Involvement in Society and the Economy,* P. McDonald, ed. (Chicago: American Marketing Association, 1969), pp. 241-249.

35. J. Pearce, "Are Americans Careful Food Shoppers?" *FDA Consumer,* September 1976.

36. George Katona and E. Mueller, "A Study of Purchasing Decisions," in *Consumer Behavior: The Dynamics of Consumer Reaction,* Lincoln H. Clark, ed. (New York: New York University Press), pp. 30-87.

37. D. Hempel, pp. 241-249.

38. Katona and Mueller, "Study of Purchase."

39. Jon C. Udell, "Prepurchase Behavior of Buyers of Small Electric Appliances," *Journal of Marketing,* 30 January, pp. 50-52.

40. D. Hempel, pp. 241-249; Katona and Mueller, "Study of Purchase"; and Newman and Staelin, pp. 249-257.

41. Howard Schuman and Michael P. Johnson, "Attitudes and Behavior," *Annual Review of Sociology,* vol. 2, 1976, pp. 161-207.

42. Beatty and Smith, pp. 83-95; Calvin P. Duncan and Richard W. Olshausky, "External Search: The Role of Consumer Beliefs," *Journal of Marketing Research,* 19 (February 1982), pp. 32-43; Girish N. Punj and Richard Staelin, "A Model of Consumer Information Search Behavior for New Automobiles," *Journal of Consumer Research,* vol. 9 (March, 1983), pp. 366-380.

43. Peter D. Bennett and Robert M. Mandell, "Prepurchase Information-Seeking Behavior of New Car Purchases—The Learning Hypothesis," *Journal of Marketing Research,* 6 (November 1969), pp. 430-433.

44. William L. Moore and Donald R. Lehmann, "Individual Differences in Search Behavior for a Nondurable Product," *Journal of Consumer Research,* 7 (December 1980), pp. 296-307.

45. Bennett and Mandell, pp. 430-433.

46. B. Fishhoff, P. Slovic, and S. Lichtenstein, "Which Risks Are Acceptable?" *Environment,* 21 (January 1971), pp. 17-38.

47. J. W. Newman, "Consumer External Search: Amount and Determinants," in *Consumer and Industrial Buying Behavior,* A. Woodside, J. Sheth, and P. Bennett, eds. (New York: Elsevier North Holland, 1977), pp. 79-94.

48. R. A. Westbrook and C. Farnell, "Patterns of Information Source Usage Among Durable Goods Buyers," *Journal of Marketing Research,* August 1979, pp. 303-312.

49. Newman and Staelin, pp.249-257.

50. Hawkins *et al., op. cit.,* pp. 577-579.

51. Joseph W. Newman, "Consumer External Search: Amount and Determinant," in *Consumer and Industrial Buying Behavior,* A. G. Woodside, J. N. Sheth, and P. D. Bennett, eds. (New York: North Holland Publishing Co., 1971), pp. 79-94; B. Marby, "An Analysis of Work and Other Constraints on Choice Activities," *Western Economic Journal,* September 1970, pp. 213-225; and T. Lanzetta and U. Kanareff, "Information Cost, Amount of Payoff, and Level of Aspiration as Determinants of Information Seeking in Decision Making," *Behavioral Science,* 1962, pp. 459-473.

52. James R. Bettman, *An Information Processing Theory of Consumer Behavior* (Reading, Mass.: Addison-Wesley, 1979), chap. 5.

53. Hawkins *et al.,* p. 625-626.

54. *Ibid.,* pp. 622-623.

55. *Ibid.,* pp. 620-621.

56. *Ibid.,* pp. 624-625.

57. Schiffman and Kanuk, pp. 644-645.

58. S. M. Shugan, "The Cost of Thinking," *Journal of Consumer Research,* September, 1980, pp. 99-111.

59. N. K. Malhotra, "Multi-Stage Information Processing Behavior," *Journal of the Academy of Marketing Science,* Winter 1982, pp. 54-71.

60. Michael L. Ray, *Advertising and Communication Management* (Englewood Cliffs, NJ: Prentice-Hall, 1982), pp. 184-185.

61. *Ibid.*

62. Michael L. Ray, "Marketing Communications and the Hierarchy-of-Effects," in *New Models for Mass Communications,* Peter Clarke, ed. (Beverly Hill, CA: Sage Publications, Inc., 1973), p. 1152.

63. Ray, *Advertising and Communications Management,* pp. 185-186.

64. *Ibid.,* p. 186.

65. *Ibid.,* p. 187.

66. *Ibid.*

67. *Ibid.*

68. Rajeev Batra and Michael Ray, "Affective Responses Mediating Acceptance of Advertising," *Journal of Consumer Research,* vol. 13, no. 2, September 1986, pp. 234-249.

69. Richard J. Lutz, "Affective and Cognitive Antecedents of Attitude Toward the Ad: A Conceptual Framework," in *Psychological Processes and Advertising Effects,* Linda Alwitt and Andrew Mitchell, eds. (Hillsdale, NJ: Lawrence J. Erlbaum, 1985), p. 47.

70. Batra and Ray, pp. 234-235.

71. Lutz, "Affective and Cognitive Antecedents of Attitude Toward the Ad," p. 54.

72. Karen A. Machleit and R. Dale Wilson, "Emotional Feelings and Attitudes Toward the Advertisement: The Roles of Brand Familiarity and

Repetition," *Journal of Advertising,* vol. 17, no. 3, 1988, pp. 32-33.

73. Russell H. Fazio and Mark P. Zanna, "Direct Experience and Attitude-Behavior Consistency," *Advances in Experimental Social Psychology,* (14), pp. 161-202.

74. M. P. Venkatraman and D. J. MacInnis, "The Epistemic and Senovy Exploratory Behaviors of Hedonic and Cognitive Consumers," in *Advances in Consumer Research XII,* Elizabeth Hirschman and Morris Holbrook, eds. (Ann Arbor, MI: Association for Consumer Research, 1985).

75. Olli T. Shtola, "Hedonic and Utilitarian Aspects of Consumer Behavior: An Attitudinal Perspective," *Advances in Consumer Research XII,* Elizabeth Hirschman and Morris Holbrook, eds. (Ann Arbor, MI: Association for Consumer Research, 1985), pp. 7-10.

76. Morris B. Holbrook and Elizabeth C. Hirschman, "The Experiential Aspects of Consumption: Consumer Fantasies, Feelings, and Fun," *Journal of Consumer Research,* vol. 9, September 1972, pp. 132-140.

77. *Ibid.,* p. 132.

78. Grant McCracken, "Advertising: Meaning or Information?" in *Advances in Consumer Research XIV,* Melanie Wallendorf and Paul Anderson, eds. (Provo, UT: Association for Consumer Research, 1987), pp. 121-124.

7
ADVERTISING AND THE MEDIA

In this chapter, we will discuss the media as social institutions, the functions society expects them to perform, the influence they have in our daily lives, and their relationship to advertising.

Our discussion will pertain primarily to television, radio, newspapers, and magazines. Given this perspective, the reader should not expect this chapter to deal with the more functional media material, such as factors in media selection: reach, frequency, media exposure models, and the differences between the various media vehicles.

Nor will we concentrate on issues such as the alleged bias toward the interest of advertisers in editorial content or the economic implications of the advertising "subsidy." These are covered elsewhere, and the curious reader is encouraged to pursue more specialized sources.[1]

Instead, we will focus on the advertising message as a part of the larger media institutional directive of serving as a forum for learning and debating the character of our culture.[2] It is an area of advertising's evolution in this country that has received particular attention in the last 15 years, and is, we feel, deserving of particular analysis here.

MEDIA-GOVERNMENT RELATIONSHIPS

Two basic theories of media-government relationships are generally recognized, the authoritarian and libertarian theories. The *authoritarian theory*, the older of the two, has its origin associated with the era of authoritarian governments. Under this theory, the media are, in essence, controlled by government and are used to inform people of what the authorities want them to know. Furthermore, the government functions as a gatekeeper to keep out of the media any information that it feels might be detrimental to its authority. The media are thus servants of the state. This theory is still held by most totalitarian governments and is, at times, embraced by democratic regimes when the position of the party in power is endangered.

The *libertarian theory* (i.e., based on classical liberalism) characterizes the manner in which the media presumably function in a democratic society. Although libertarian writings refer mainly to "the press," Siebert's summary of the theory can be readily extended to pertain to all the media:

> The press is not an instrument of government, but rather a device for presenting evidence and arguments on the basis of which the people can check on government and make up their minds as to policy. Therefore, it is imperative that the press be free from government control and influence. In order for truth to emerge, all ideas must get a fair hearing; there must be a "free market place" of ideas and information. Minorities as well as the strong must have access to the press. This is the theory of the press that was written into our Bill of Rights.[3]

Under the libertarian theory, the free press (media) is expected to perform certain functions for the benefit of society. Theodore Peterson has detailed these functions as follows:

> (1) servicing the political system by providing information, discussion, and debate on public affairs; (2) enlightening the public so as to make it capable of self-government; (3) safeguarding the rights of the individual by serving as a watchdog against government; (4) servicing the economic system, primarily by bringing together the buyers and sellers of goods and services through the medium of advertising; (5) providing entertainment; (6) maintaining its own financial self-sufficiency so as to be free from the pressures of special interests.[4]

No specific mention of freedom of speech is included in the functions listed above. This may seem strange in light of the fact that freedom of speech and freedom of the press (media) have been, almost universally, linked together. Scholars have generally held that the reason for constitutional guarantees of freedom of the press was that the press provided the basic machinery for transmitting information and ideas to the people. However, there would be little value in upholding the freedom to speak if the instruments for distributing speech could be curtailed or controlled.

THE MEDIA AS DISTRIBUTORS OF "SPEECH"

Members of the media have generally conceived freedom of speech to be freedom for the media to speak as they wish without fear of government restraints or penalty. Such freedom would then prohibit government from acting as a gatekeeper to open or close the gate at its will in respect to what news, ideas, and concepts should be passed on to the people.

But even then, it is idealistic to expect the media to speak for (or to) all citizens, including the corporate ones. Given this perspective, it can be contended that there must also be freedom for the lay citizen to speak—to place what sentiments he or she pleases before the public. Perhaps society, then, should expect the media not only to be free to speak as they wish but also to serve as distributors of speech by lay citizens who wish to reach large numbers of people. In light of this concept, a seventh function of the media may be suggested as an addition to the six functions given by Peterson—providing facilities for distribution of messages by citizens and making such facilities available without discrimination.

A consideration of various aspects of this seventh function—why it is important and how it might be implemented—is in order. If people are to be kept informed, not only of current news but also of divergent ideas, it is essential that the antiestablishment person, the muckraker, the protester, and the "crackpot," as well as "members of the club," have access to the eyes and ears of the public.

Is this not possible now? Arguably it is not, because of (a) media concentration, (b) the media as gatekeepers, (c) diversity, (d) agenda-setting, (e) spiral of silence, and (f) cultivation theory. *Is* concentration (i.e., inadequate representativeness) a problem? Let us turn to some data dealing with the issue. We will review data for newspapers, magazines, television, and radio.

Media Concentration

Overall, American media ownership has been contracting. The emergence of some new media, such as cable, is inviting more people into the media area; but the general trend is for fewer companies to own more media enterprises and for fewer companies to own more than one aspect of the media business.[5] Some of the relevant facts are:

1. "The top ten newspaper chains own one-third of the nation's dailies; group owners (companies that own more than one newspaper) hold two out of three newspapers published everyday."[6] In 1986, 73 percent of the daily newspapers were chain-owned, while 80 percent of the total daily circulation was chain-owned.[7] Of the 1645 dailies left in the United States, only 489 were still individually owned.[8]
2. "Twenty corporations control more than 50 percent of annual magazine revenue."[9]
3. "Ten corporations control more than 50 percent of radio revenue."[10]
4. "Seventy percent of the nation's TV stations are network affiliates."[11]

Reviewing these quantitative data, it appears that concentration of media ownership is strong. How does this affect the quality of the media?

Eversole found that newspapers that were once competitive but were made monopolies by chains produced "higher prices and lower quality."[12] The Brookings Institution, on the other hand, showed that though chain-owned papers charge 7 percent more for ads than independent papers, chains operating in areas where there are competitive papers have advertising rates 15 percent lower than those for their other chain-owned papers.[13] Keller found that there was 23 percent less new content in chain-owned than in independent papers,[14] while Wackman *et al.,* found that 85 percent of chain papers publish uniform political endorsements.[15] Hess found that chains have about 1/3 the number of correspondents that individual papers have and that chain correspondents have significantly less education than those working for independent newspapers.[16]

Are the media being adversely affected by the increase in media concentration? There would appear to be cause for concern.

The Media as Gatekeepers

In many respects, the media function as gatekeepers. Recent court decisions have interpreted freedom of the press to mean freedom to publish or broadcast, therefore solidifying the idea that publishers and broadcasters make the ultimate decisions concerning what should and should not go into or on their newspapers or magazines, radio or television stations. This certainly includes advertising space and air time. The basic premise that the media use in rejecting news or advertising materials is the "best interest" concept. Presumably, materials that are not in the "best interest" of the particular media vehicle or the public it serves should not be utilized. The problem is whether media management is in a position to (or should) judge what is in the best interest of the public.

What is interesting, however, is that the courts have generally placed many restrictions on the government concerning actions it might take to influence news or editorial content, as well as the advertising placed in the media. Both areas have been granted some First Amendment protection. In its purest form, this principle is expressed in the statement that "above all else, the First Amendment means that the government has no power to restrict expression because of its message, its ideas, its subject matter, or its content."[17]

Although advertising or commercial speech has more limited First Amendment protection than news or editorial material,[18,19] it seems ironic that advertising messages protected from government interference can subsequently not appear because media decide they should not.

Have the media utilized their gatekeeping function? That is, have they interjected their subjective (personal or arbitrary) judgments in the news gathering function, as well as in the selection of which advertisements to run? White,[20] Gieber,[21] and Hetherington[22] seem to believe they have.

The *Baltimore Sun* killed a story describing imminent labor negotiations between hospital workers and the management of Johns Hopkins Hospital in

Baltimore. Apparently, a director of the *Sun* was a director of Johns Hopkins Hospital and also a director of the Mercantile Safe Deposit & Trust Company, which held 61.3 percent of the shares of the newspaper company.[23] In another example, the head of Panax Corp., a chain of eight dailies, fired two editors who refused to run a shoddy story about Jimmy Carter which contained insinuations about sexual activities.[24]

The media can also exercise their gatekeeping function when it comes to traditional advertisements. In the classic case, *Shuck v. The Carroll Daily Herald,* the court held:

> The newspaper business is an ordinary business. It is a business essentially private in its nature—as private as that of the baker, grocer, or milkman, all of whom perform a service on which, to a greater or lesser extent, the communities depend, but which bears no such relation to the public as to warrant its inclusion in the category of business charged with a public use. If a newspaper were required to accept an advertisement, it could be compelled to publish a news item. If some good lady gave a tea, and submitted to the newspaper a proper account of the tea, and the editor of the newspaper, believing that it had no news value, refused to publish it, she, it seems to us would be a person engaged in business to compel a newspaper to publish an advertisement. . . .
>
> Thus, a newspaper is strictly private enterprise, the publishers thereof have a right to publish whatever advertisements they desire and refuse to publish whatever advertisements they do not desire to publish.[25]

The many decisions since have added nothing to this principle. Other cases have established that publishers can classify advertisements as they see fit[26] and change an ad to meet their standards of acceptability.[27] Therefore, barring a pattern of refusal that points to an intent to harm a competitor, any news medium may refuse commercial advertising for any reason or for no reason.[28]

There are occasions when individuals or groups in our society perceive they have a serious grievance and wish to make those grievances known to the larger population. Besides seeking more traditional press coverage of their concerns, they may also wish to purchase space or time in the media for an advertisement to explain their cause. Just as traditional ads may be rejected by privately owned media, so may cause advertisements. Any attempt by the government to tell an owner of a privately held media vehicle that an ad must be accepted could be taking of property without due process of law, violating the Fifth Amendment. Further, an attempt by the state to tell media owners that they must accept an advertisement violates the freedom of the press guaranteed by the First Amendment.[29] Thus, anti-Vietnam war messages, ads by gay rights activists, and information about family planning have regularly been rejected by many media owners over the past decades.

Have the media exercised their gatekeeping function concerning new stories, traditional and cause advertising? There is sufficient evidence to suggest that they have.

The Key Question of Diversity

It may be contended that the central issue in the dissemination of ideas and information in the libertarian or neo-liberal media environment is that of diversity. The essence of diversity is best stated by Jeffres:

> Diversity as a goal is not merely a matter of philosophical or legal niceties. It is grounded in the lessons of experience. First, a free flow of ideas is essential to the political liberty and is essential in developing ideas of potential value to society. The notion of diversity in communication is not new; the challenge is in implementing diversity. Viewed as communication systems rather than industries, the major function of the mass media is to circulate ideas which have consequences for every aspect of society. The circulation of ideas is an evolutionary process. From an enormous variety of possibilities, some ideas are introduced into the system; some are developed or modified as they circulate and some are deleted. Writers introduce ideas but so do producers and directors, networks and advertisers, and local outlets. Public officials may introduce ideas when they give speeches, hold press conferences, or generate interest to attract coverage. Members of the public who normally serve as audiences may also introduce ideas when placed before the microphones and cameras in the studio or on the street.[30]

Of all the ways ideas enter the social discussion, the mass media may be the most important.

Two schools of thought can be found as to how to achieve Jeffres's description of diversity. The first school is skeptical of any regulation, and it assumes that the free and open marketplace is the best possible environment in which diversity can flourish. The premise of this position is that a fluid, competitive marketplace will permit all sectors of the population to enter the system and provide needed information-communication services. The real problem is how to provide profit incentives to attract the risk capital that will be needed to accomplish the goal of additional information-communication services. The key measurement criterion to judge success would be the quantity of channels. This school believes that if there is a sufficient quantity of channels, and the freedom to open new ones, an acceptable level of diversity can be achieved.[31]

The second school argues:

> . . . that in this era of giant national and transnational corporate dominance, it is absurd to presuppose that there is sufficient equitable distribution of economic power to allow market forces alone

to assume equitable distribution of services. The political decision-making process is so manipulated by powerful corporations that it is virtually impossible for citizens' groups, consumers, minorities and the poverty sector of society to participate significantly in the policy-making process. Access to information is such a basic human right and communication so central in the development of national cultures that these should be considered a common good and a public trust. Information should not be considered simply a marketplace commodity distributed only to those with capacity to pay.

For this group the starting point of research on economic concentration should be the problem area of content bias: images of women and minorities, the presence of poverty and other injustices.[32]

The question here, then, is how the economically and socially less powerful can be given access to the media. For this school of thought, what is important is not the *quantity* of channels but their *quality*.

Thus, a case may be made that in order to achieve true diversity in the sense of individuals being confronted with challenging (new, provocative, unfamiliar) points of view, access needs to be gained in a qualitative sense. In short, rather than striving for *more* media vehicles, the aims of diversity might best be served by attempting to enrich the "marketplace of ideas" *within* the existing media structure. And that, of course, requires a fresh look at the media as gatekeepers.

Agenda-Setting

As the issue of diversity was concerned with the free flow of ideas or the knowledge base of the audiences, so does the issue of agenda-setting deal with the distribution of knowledge. The simplest definition of agenda-setting might be this: The media don't tell you what to think, but they do tell you what and whom to think about. The evidence for this statement consists of data showing a correspondence between the order of importance given in the media to issues and the order of significance attached to the same issues by the public.[33] Such a phenomenon has been found for both the press and advertising.[34]

The relevance of agenda-setting for advertising is that a major goal of many advertisers is to focus consumers' attention on what values, products, brands, or attributes to think about rather than try to persuade consumers what to think of these.[35] Sutherland and Galloway proposed a two-step model: Prominence of products or ideas in the media, accomplished through heavy advertising, should increase the salience of the brand; and second, this salience should influence such behavioral outcomes as purchasing. Products that are prominent in the media (heavily advertised) would have a status conferred upon them and would be seen as the more popular products. Just as the ordinary person does not appear on television, neither does the ordinary product.[36]

To test their theory that media advertising can engage in such agenda-setting and produce images that advertised products are superior, the authors surveyed homemakers about a variety of products. No less than 25 percent of the respondents indicated that what they thought was a popular brand was related to advertising frequency. The brand thought to be the most popular was also shown to bear a strong relationship with top-of-mind awareness.[37]

Ghorpade, in his study of the 1984 Helms-Hunt senatorial campaign in North Carolina, found that the respective advertising campaigns of the two candidates did transfer advertising salience to salience in the public mind; and second, from salience in the public mind to behavioral outcome (voting).[38]

Could it be that such large advertisers, such as Procter & Gamble, Ford Motor Company, RJR/Nabisco, McDonald's Corporation, and Anheuser-Bush Co., have achieved such predominant market share in some product categories because they have "set the agenda" for the consumer? When it comes to hamburgers, cigarettes, and beer, we know what to think about!

Spiral of Silence

Noelle-Neumann stated that because journalists in the media tend to concentrate on the same major news stories, the audience receives similar information from many fronts. The media, as a result, tend to present a consensus of opinion to the public. As this opinion gains ascendancy, others will be perceived as losing ground. If members of the audience believe that their opinions are in accordance with the dominant trend, they will feel their opinions can be expressed openly and publicly outside of their family and immediate friends. If these same individuals feel that their opinions have become in the minority, they may well be less confident of their positions; and therefore, will be less likely to express their opinions openly. The more frequently the topic arises, the weaker their positions appear, and in a spiral-like process, opinions become increasingly suppressed as these individuals fear that expressing their opinions could result in negative judgments from others.[39] Glynn and McLeod lend additional support for this theory.[40]

Although no research has been conducted to determine the relationship between the spiral of silence and advertising, speculation on the relationship is possible. As the press, over the past several years, has come to a "consensus" concerning the clear superiority of Japanese products (such as autos and electronic equipment) over American built products, it has become less and less popular to voice any opinion among consumers concerning the quality of American products. Has this suppression of opinion led to less purchase of American products because they are really inferior or because it is not the popular thing to do?

Relationship Between Agenda-Setting and Spiral of Silence.   There may be a relationship between agenda-setting, as previously discussed, and the spiral of silence. A paradigm adopted from Sutherland and Galloway is shown in Figure 7-1 on page 135.

FIGURE 7-1

Relationship Between Agenda-Setting And Spiral of Silence

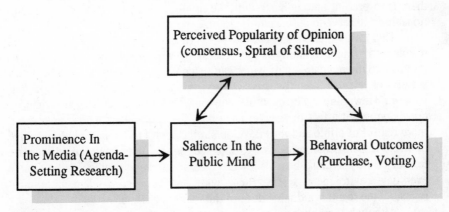

Adapted from Max Sutherland and John Galloway, "Role of Advertising: Persuasion or Agenda-Setting?" *Journal of Advertising Research,* Vol. 25, No. 5 October, 1981, p.29.

This model indicates that the producer could follow a two-fold strategy to bring about purchase: (1) develop sufficient advertising frequency to help set the agenda for the consumer, and (2) cultivate strong relation with the business and popular press to develop a perceived consensus of the superiority of the product. Thus, advertising and public relations are necessary compliments of the communication process.

Sufficient advertising frequency would be quite dependent upon the financial resources of the producer, although the development of highly creative, memorable advertisements could offset limited resources. Cultivation of the press to develop consensus would be more difficult for the popular press than the business press due to the sheer diversity of the popular press. For the business press, however, there are often only a few key publications. Getting positive recommendations in these publications could well trigger the Spiral of Silence. One example might be computer software; a few critical recommendations from lay editors or feature writers might well develop the consensus feeling among potential buyers.

The Cultivation Process

Gerbner's thesis is that television is a centralized system of storytelling. It is part of our daily lives; its drama, advertisements, news, and other programs bring a relatively coherent world of common images and messages into every American home.[41] "Television cultivates from infancy the very predispositions and preferences that used to be acquired from other primary sources. Transcending historic barriers of literacy and mobility, television has become the primary common source of socialization and everyday information (mostly in the form in entertainment) in an otherwise heterogeneous population. The repetitive pattern of television's mass-produced messages and images form the mainstream of a common symbolic environment.''[42] What television does, then, is to present the audience with the myths, ideologies, ''facts,'' and relationships that serve to define and legitimize the social order.[43]

This cultivation process takes place in two ways: mainstreaming and resonance.[44] Mainstreaming is the process by which television brings diverse groups into the mainstream of American values. These groups tend to be heavy viewers of television and by this heavy viewing tend to develop common outlooks or viewpoints. For example, viewing heavy doses of violent crime on television might affect those who have had little experience with it to become more fearful of crime and thus develop similar views to those who already live in crime-ridden neighborhoods. Resonance, on the other hand, could increase fear of crime for those heavy viewers who are already afraid. ''When one's everyday environment is congruent with and reinforces television's messages,''[45] the result is a double dose of the reality of crime.

Although Gerbner and other researchers have mainly focused on television programming, there is no reason to believe that advertising messages do not play the same role. Advertisers are storytellers who convey common messages and images. Although the advertisements may appear diverse, the common messages of ''Buy! Buy!, Buy!'' ''Thin is Beautiful!'' ''Things Can Make You Happy!'' ''You Deserve the Best,'' ''You Deserve a Break,'' and ''You Are What You Consume,'' have cultivated the images of what Americans should be like. The American consumer has, to some extent, been as mainstreamed by American advertisements as it has been by television programming.

SUMMARY

The provision, by the media, of facilities for the distribution of messages by citizens and making such facilities available without discrimination was a key point in this chapter. The issues of concentration and media diversity were discussed as possible impediments to the provision of this function. It was also made clear that the media can act as gatekeepers for many of the issues that concerned citizens would like to transmit. The media and advertising institutions can set the agenda for the consumer about what and who to think about, bring him/her to a consensus on many matters, and help to establish a common set of images and values. It should be noted, however, that these influences are not all pervasive. Many other factors continue to influence the consumer when he/she is in the marketplace, such as friends, family, peers, reference groups and one's own individuality. The key word is "can" influence and not will influence.

ENDNOTES

1. For further information see Vincent P. Norris, "Consumer Magazine Prices and the Mythical Advertising Subsidy," *Journalism Quarterly* 59:2 (Summer 1982); and R. C. Smith, "The Magazines' Smoking Habit," *Columbia Journalism Review,* January/February 1978.

2. The reader is also referred to Charles H. Sandage, Vernon Fryburger, and Kim Rotzoll, *Advertising Theory and Practice* (New York: Longman, 1989) pp. 181-196.

3. Frederick Siebert, in *Four Theories of the Press,* Frederick Siebert, Theodore Peterson, and Wilbur Schramm, eds. (Urbana: University of Illinois Press, 1956), pp. 3-4.

4. *Ibid.,* p. 74.

5. Shirley Biagi, *Media Impact: An Introduction to the Mass Media* (Belmont, CA: Wadsworth Publishing Company, 1988), p. 276.

6. *Ibid.,* p. 276.

7. *Ibid.,* pp. 277, 377.

8. R. E. Hiebert, D. F. Unguvat, and T. W. Bohn, *Mass Media V* (New York: Longman, 1988), p. 64.

9. Biagi, p. 276.

10. Biagi, *Ibid.*

11. Biagi, *Ibid.*

12. Pam Eversole, "Consolidation of Newspapers: What Happens to the Consumer?" *Journalism Quarterly,* Summer 1971, p. 245.

13. *Strass Editor's Report,* December 13, 1968, p. 1.

14. Kristine Keller, "Quantity of News in Group-Owned and Independent Papers: Independent Papers Have More," Master's Thesis, Graduate School of Journalism, University of California, Berkeley, 1978.

15. Daniel B. Wackman, Donald M. Gilmore, and Cecile Graziano, and Everett E. Dennis, "Chain Newspaper Autonomy as Reflected in Presidential Campaign Endorsement," *Journalism Quarterly,* Autumn 1975, pp. 411-420.

16. Stephen Hess, "Chains Tend to Hire," *The Washington Reporters* (Washington, DC: Brookings Institution, 1981), pp. 136-166. Also see D. Weaver and C. G. Wiholt, *The American Journalist* (Bloomington: Universtiy of Indiana Press, 1986).

17. *Police Dept. of Chicago v. Mosley,* 408 U.S. 92, 96 (1971).

18. *Virginia State Board of Pharmacy v. Virginia Citizens Consumer Council,* 425 U.S. 748 (1976).

19. *Central Hudson Gas & Electric Corp. v. Public Service Comm'n,* 433 U.S. 350 (1977).

20. D. M. White, "The Gatekeeper: A Case Study in the Selection of News," *Journalism Quarterly,* 27, pp. 383-90.

21. W. Gieber, "Across the Desk: A Study of 16 Telegraph Editors," *Journalism Quarterly,* 33, pp. 423-33.

22. A. Hetherington, *News, Newspapers, and Television* (London: MacMillan, 1985).

23. Ben H. Bagdikian, *The Media Monopoly* (Boston: Beacon Press, 1983), pp. 3-4.

24. Leo W. Jeffres, *Mass Media: Processes and Effects* (Prospect Heights, IL: Waveland Press, Inc., 1986), pp. 84-85.

25. *Shuck v. The Carroll Daily Herald,* 247 N.W. 813 (1933).

26. *Staff Research Associates v. Tribune Co.,* 346 F. ad 372 (7th Cir. 1965).

27. *Camp-of-the-Pines v. New York Times,* 53 N.Y.S. ad 475 (S. Ct., Albany Co., 1945).

28. Ralph L. Holsiger, *Media Law* (New York: Random House, 1987), p. 428.

29. Holsiger, pp. 428-429. Also see *Chicago Joint Board, Amalgamated Clothing Workers of America, AFL-CIO v. Chicago Tribune Co.,* 307 F. Supp. 422 (N.D. Ill. 1969).

30. Jeffres, p. 76.

31. Robert A. White, "What Kind of Media Diverstiy?" *Communication Research Trends* (London: Centre for the Study of Communication and Culture, 1983), vol. 4, no. 1, p. 7.

32. *Ibid.,* p. 7.

33. Dennis McQuail, *Mass Communication Theory: An Introduction* (Beverly Hills: Sage Publications, 1987), p. 275. Also see G.E. Lang and K. Lang, *The Battle for Public Opinion: The President, the Press, and the Polls During Watergate* (New York: Columbia University Press, 1983) for an expanded version of this concept.

34. Jeffres, p. 296.

35. Max Sutherland and John Galloway, "Role of Advertising: Persuasion or Agenda Setting?" *Journal of Advertising Research,* October 1981, 25(5), p. 26.

36. *Ibid.,* p. 27; Jeffres, p. 296.

37. Ibid., p. 28. See also P.M. Carrick, "Why Continued Advertising Is Necessary," *Journal of Marketing,* vol. 23, 1959, pp. 386-398.

38. Shailendra Ghorpade, "Agenda Setting: A Test of Advertising's Neglected Function," *Journal of Advertising Research,* vol. 26, no. 4 August/September 1986, p. 26.

39. Elizabeth Noelle-Neumann, "The Spiral of Silence: A Theory of Public Opinion," *Journal of Communication* vol. 24, 1974, pp. 43-51; Elizabeth

Noelle-Neumann, "Turbulences in the Climate of Opinion: Methodological Applications of the Spiral of Silence Theory," *Public Opinion Quarterly,* vol. 41, 1977, pp. 143-158; Leo W. Jeffres, p. 281.

40. Carrol J. Glynn and Jack M. McLeod, "Public Opinion du Jour: An Examination of the Spiral of Silence," *Public Opinion Quarterly,* vol. 40, pp. 731-740.

41. George Gerbner, Larry Gross, Michael Morgan, and Nancy Signorielli, "Living With Television: The Dynamics of the Cultivation Process," in *Perspective on Media Effects,* Jennings Bryant and Dolt Zillman, eds. (Hillsdale, NJ: Lawrence Erlbaum Associates, 1986), p. 18.

42. *Ibid.*

43. *Ibid.*

44. Gerbner, Gross, Morgan, and Signorielli, p. 30.

45. *Ibid.,* p. 30.

8
ADVERTISING
AND REGULATION

This chapter will deal with the question: What forces should be allowed to regulate the institution of advertising? Should it be regulated by natural market forces, organized market forces (consumerism), self-regulatory forces, governmental forces, or media forces? (See Figure 8-1.) Are these mutually exclusive approaches or synergistic when operating simultaneously?

NATURAL MARKET FORCES

As discussed in Chapter 2, the market is presumed, in the best of worlds, to be entirely self-regulating. Consumers will always seek out the lowest prices for products or services. If consumers find some advertising to be inadequate, they will turn away from it and seek other competitive advertising sources that will satisfy their information needs.

Advertisers will promote their products or services in their own self-interest, and this advertising will be successful only if it is in agreement with the self-interest of potential buyers. If advertisers find their messages are deficient in this regard, they will alter their practices or lose their competitive advantage.

It is the simple yet complex world of Adam Smith. There may be some short-term aberrations; but in the long run, the market will make appropriate adjustments if allowed to run its own course. Or could it be that the long run does not matter, as significant damage could be done in the short run?

ORGANIZED MARKET FORCES (CONSUMERISM)

"Consumerism" is a word that can be defined in many different ways. Betty Furness has described it as follows: "Consumerism is an effort to put the buyer on an equal footing with the seller. Consumers want to know what

140

FIGURE 8-1

The Forces of Regulation

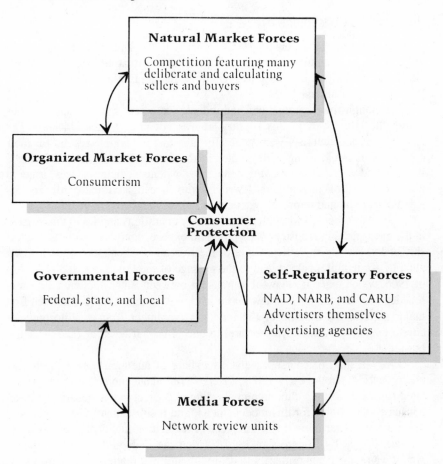

Source: Adapted from Jagdish N. Sheth and Nicholas Mammana, "Why Consumer Protection Efforts Are Likely to Fail," Faculty Working Paper, No. 104 (Urbana-Champaign: University of Illinois, College of Commerce and Business Administration, April 11, 1985).

they're buying. What they're eating. How long a product will last. What it will and will not do. Whether it will be safe for them and/or the environment."[1]

A somewhat broader view is offered by Aaker: "Consumerism is an evolving set of activities of government, business, independent organizations, and concerned consumers that are designed to protect the rights of consumers. It is an evolving, dynamic movement with an enlarging scope and changing spokesmen and issues. It is action oriented and, therefore, more than an analysis of problems."[2]

History of the Consumer Movement

Is consumerism a new idea? Certainly not. Consumers were attempting to cooperate in a number of ways to improve their situation as early as 1844. For it was in this year that poor weavers in Rochdale, England, formed the first "co-op" of consumers.[3]

Although many groups and individuals were active in consumer issues during the late 1800s in this country, it was not until Upton Sinclair's *The Jungle*[4] that consumerists were generally able to see tangible results for their efforts. This book, along with articles in the *Ladies Home Journal, Collier's Weekly,* and *Good Housekeeping* concerning patent-medicine abuses, ushered in the era of the "muckrakers," writers who investigated and publicized alleged corruption and improper practices in industry and government.[5]

Sinclair's book dealt with the unsanitary conditions and fraud that existed in the meat-packing industry. This powerful expose, combined with the leadership of Dr. Harvey W. Wiley, Chief of the Bureau of Chemistry in the Department of Agriculture, helped lead to the passage of the Pure Food and Drug Act of 1906, which made it unlawful to transmit between states adulterated or misbranded food or drugs. This law was a landmark in that it represented the first major shift in the attitude of the federal government from a philosophy of *caveat emptor* (Let the buyer beware) to one of *caveat venditor* (Let the seller beware).[6]

Advertising, of course, received its share of attention during the muckrakers' period. In the early 1900s, *Printer's Ink* magazine established a set of legal standards to help eliminate misleading and deceptive advertising. Many consumerists lobbied for this model statute, and it subsequently became law in many states. A far more important piece of legislation that dealt with advertising was passed by Congress in 1914. Titled the Federal Trade Commission Act, it was established primarily to deal with antitrust matters and unfair methods of competition. The newly formed commission quickly interpreted the act as a weapon against deceptive interstate advertising practices.[7]

Certainly, this is not a complete picture of what happened during this tumultuous era. It can be said, however, that for the first time large numbers of consumers were made aware of the potentially dangerous consequences of consumption. The edifice of the market had begun to show signs of strain.

The thrust of the consumer movement was reduced by the period of affluence that followed in the 1920s. Many of the heated issues were set aside or forgotten, and many of the existing laws were not adequately enforced, owing in part to key court decisions. For example, in *FTC v. Raladam Co.,*[8] the court held that the Federal Trade Commission must find that not only consumers but also competitors were injured by the misrepresentation. This was a situation (the competitor's injury) which was extremely difficult to prove in court.

With publication of *Your Money's Worth* by Stuart Chase and Frederick J. Schlink in 1927, the "movement" again came alive. The book became a best-seller because of such comments as: Bar soap for women is made with "a little creosol, a common and cheap disinfectant recommended by the government for disinfecting cars, barns, and chicken yards."[9] Over the next decade, this book seemed to spawn a series of others that criticized advertising and indicated that the consumer was being deceived. They included *Skin Deep*[10] and *Eat, Drink, and Be Wary.*[11]

Of the attacks made on advertising, many were bitter and far-reaching. These challenges were different from previous ones in that critics struck at the very existence of advertising rather than merely its excesses or the products that advertising promoted.

Thus, the spotlight turned once again to the imperfect marketplace. Spurred by the devastating effects of the Great Depression, consumers and governmental bodies were again ready to take action. More consumer-oriented legislation was passed than ever before, including the Securities Act of 1933 (which provided potential investors with protection against deceptions concerning new issues of corporate securities), the Federal Food, Drug, and Cosmetic Act of 1938 (which strengthened the Pure Food and Drug Act of 1906), and the Wheeler-Lea amendments to the Federal Trade Commission Act of 1914 (which extended "unfair methods of competition" to include deceptive acts or practices).[12] The Wheeler-Lea amendments eliminated the problems of the *Raladam* decision for the FTC.

Consumer Research and Consumers' Union were born; Sears, Roebuck and Macy's began testing products before selling them; *Good Housekeeping* checked products to ensure that advertising claims were accurate; the American Medical Association tested proprietary drugs; and the National Bureau of Standards tested products before government purchase.[13]

But the movement, which had lasted almost two decades, faltered again. The postwar recovery and the increasing affluence of the 1950s moved the consumer into a period of complacency.

The most recent consumer movement had its beginnings in the 1960s. An influential book again served as a trigger mechanism; *The Hidden Persuaders*[14] by Vance Packard argued that the consumer was being manipulated unconsciously by advertising. Other best-sellers during this time frame included John Kenneth Galbraith's *The Affluent Society,*[15] Rachel Carson's *Silent Spring,*[16] and Ralph Nader's *Unsafe at Any Speed.*[17]

For some, President John F. Kennedy's watershed message to Congress on March 15, 1962 began the "new consumerism cycle." In that speech, he enumerated four basic consumer rights:[18]

1. the right to safety
2. the right to be informed
3. the right to choose
4. the right to be heard (redress)

The above mentioned books, Kennedy's address, and a number of other underlying currents including: (1) technology which produced products that were considerably less than 100 percent reliable; (2) a series of revelations about the ingredients used in frankfurters and hamburgers; (3) the condition of our fisheries and water supplies; (4) reports about corruption of public officials on an unprecedented scale; (5) soaring medical and dental costs; and (6) special tax privileges for the few, all combined to generate and nurture the "new consumerism."[19]

New consumer laws included the Fair Packaging and Labeling Act of 1965 (to regulate the packaging and labeling of consumer goods), the Child Safety Act of 1966 (to strengthen the Hazardous Substance Labeling Act of 1960 by preventing the marketing of potentially harmful toys), the Consumer Credit Protection Act of 1968 (to require disclosure of annual interest rates and their finance charges on consumer loans and credit buying, including revolving charge accounts), the Federal Boat Safety Act of 1971 (to provide for a coordinated national boating safety program),[20] and the Magnuson-Moss Warranty-Federal Trade Commission Improvement Act of 1975 (to improve warranties and warranty information for consumers and allow the FTC to order restitution for consumers).[21]

The post of Special Assistant for Consumer Affairs was established under President Johnson, while new bureaucracies were created including the Consumer Product Safety Commission, the Environmental Protection Agency, and the Occupational Safety and Health Administration. Ralph Nader became institutionalized by establishing far-flung organizations throughout the country to deal with consumer matters. Some housewives boycotted stores to protest high meat prices, while other housewives formed Action for Children's Advertising, a potent lobbying group that is still attempting to correct abuses in advertising to children.

The Outlook for Consumerism

As we move through the 1980s and 1990s, how will consumerism fare? There is great divergence on this issue. Some negative views include a 1982 Harris poll which found a greater mistrust of consumer activists than in the 1970s. In 1977, 22 percent of the respondents had agreed with the statement that activists such as Ralph Nader were out of touch with consumer interests.[22] In the 1982 poll, the percentage in agreement had more than doubled, to 45 percent. This later Harris poll also found that respondents believed the consumerists "do not consider the cost of what they are asking for."[23]

There is little doubt that the policy of consumerism has diminished in the 1980s. As one writer observed: "The return swing of the pendulum . . . was just as rapid and unexpected. Specific industries—insurance, breakfast cereals, advertising, tobacco, medicine, began to spend serious money on candidates. Consumerists, having attached to so broad a front, unified their enemies. Umbrella trade associations like the Chamber of Commerce and the Business

Roundtable were able to exploit wider misgivings about too much government. . . . Things got so silly that Representative Marty Russo of Illinois could claim with a straight face that the funeral cost-disclosure rule would reduce productivity.''[24]

Assael believes a major flaw in the consumer movement of the 1960s and 1970s was its failure to leave behind some sort of national consumer organization. Lacking such an organization, consumers have not been able to establish a major countervailing force to big business.[25] The implication of this statement may be that the consumer movement, as we have discussed it, cannot continue to leap from one issue to the next without losing some of its momentum. Only with an established infrastructure, like a national consumer organization, can the movement continue to move forward and prosper.

Bloom and Greyser have a somewhat different perspective:

> Although it is in the mature stage of its life cycle, consumerism is not, we believe, in a declining or faltering stage. We reached this conclusion after considering the results of several recent public opinion surveys which point to continuing strong, though latent, public demand for actions that help consumers obtain a better deal. We also believe that certain aspects of consumerism—redress assistance, education, cooperative buying, and deregulation—are still well accepted, although some older offerings (such as consumer protection legislation) have fallen on hard times.
>
> In sum, we foresee a quieter but still active consumer movement during the 1980s. We think the public will shift from its past role as largely cheering spectators to one of active participants. We envision participative consumerism a major characteristic of the marketplace.
>
> The daily behavior of many people will be influenced by consumerist issues; we expect consumerism to entail a great deal of activity by people on their own—like consumer education, consumer information, redress assistance, cooperative buying, and homegrown products. On the other hand, we anticipate much less activity propelled by national organizations and their leaders.[26]

A recent Lewis Harris and Associates study confirmed some of Bloom and Greyser's speculations. The study found that the public is even more concerned today than previously about such issues as interest rates, low product quality, and deficient after-sale service, but respondents also indicated that few wanted to take any kind of activist role.[27]

Returning to our original question—How will consumerism fare?—it appears that there is no definite prognosis. The consumer movement is a myriad of ideas and organizations. It ranges from national organizations to highly specialized local groups. Some elements of the movement view the consumer as the ''economic man'' discussed in earlier chapters, while other elements call for protection in the broadest sense. Some see the need for legislation, while others call for more "individual consumerism" through education. Some areas will prosper, while others will not; but the heyday of the movement is over for the moment.

SELF-REGULATORY FORCES

Self-regulation is not new to the institution of advertising. During the last two decades of the 1800s, the *Ladies Home Journal* and *Good Housekeeping* developed advertising acceptance policies. In the early 1900s, the *Printers' Ink Model Statute* was developed and later became the model for many state advertising laws. During the 1920s, Better Business Bureaus were established to help deal with such practices as false comparisons, misleading statements, false claims as to quality, and "bait and switch" advertising.

Is self-regulation an admission that natural market forces are insufficient to regulate the marketplace, or is it simply a reaction to increased concern on the part of consumerists and governmental agencies? Zanot provides a perspective:

> Apparently self-regulation has been a response and a reply to forces impinging upon the trade from the outside. Self-regulation can be considered a reaction by the trade to downturns in the economy, criticism from the public or, especially, the threat of legislation. Although the altruistic motive of protecting consumers undoubtedly enters to some degree, the primary motive behind self-regulation is thought to be enlightened self-interest. Although this analysis does not permit tight cause-and-effect statements, it appears that the trade has used self-regulation to not only eradicate false and deceptive advertising but also to dampen public criticism and forestall government legislation.[28]

The National Advertising Division and the National Advertising Review Board

Whatever the reason for the establishment of self-regulatory mechanisms, it is still important to review the major ones and discuss their effectiveness. In 1971, the American Association of Advertising Agencies, the American Advertising Federation, the Association of National Advertisers, and the Council of Better Business Bureaus (CBBB) established the National Advertising Review Council (NARC), which in turn established two operating arms, the National Advertising Division (NAD) of the Council of Better Business Bureaus and the National Advertising Review Board (NARB).

"The NAD/NARB system focuses on truth and accuracy in advertising; it deals almost exclusively with cases of false and misleading advertisements (print) and commercials (broadcast). Complaints related to unfairness, social responsibility, taste and morality are not handled by the NAB, although the NARB has issued a few papers about such issues as safety and women in advertising."[29]

The NAD/NARB does not have codes or guidelines of its own but instead relies heavily upon those of the Council of Better Business Bureaus and the Federal Trade Commission. The exception to this statement is childrens' advertising.[30]

The NAD is the investigative arm of the NARC. It operates on a full-time basis and is staffed by people with backgrounds in advertising. It essentially receives complaints or questions about the truthfulness of national advertising from a variety of sources including competitors, consumers, and local Better Business Bureaus. The NAD also has its own monitoring system.

The NAD's own monitoring, together with competitor challenges, provide roughly 75 percent of the 98 to 150 cases investigated each year. Direct consumer complaints represent only about 10 percent of the case load.[31]

When a complaint is received, the NAD may contact the advertiser in question and request material to substantiate the claims made in the advertisement. If it finds the substantiation inadequate, it urges the advertiser to modify or withdraw the advertising. If a satisfactory resolution cannot be found by either the advertiser or the NAD, the case is referred to the NARB.

The NARB is composed of fifty national advertisers, agency personnel, and public members; each serving a two-year term. This last component of the NARB group membership marks the first time in the history of self-regulation that non-industry individuals have been included.

When a case is referred to the NARB, five members are assigned (one public) to the case. If the final decision of these five members is not accepted by the advertiser (assuming it is a negative one from the advertiser's point of view) the NARB will refer the matter to the Federal Trade Commission. In addition to referring the case to more traditional legal channels, the board will make public the facts of the disputed case along with any statement the advertiser might wish to make. Tables 8-1 and 8-2 (pages 148 and 149) present data on the activity of the NAD and the NARB since their establishment in 1971.

Between 1971 and 1987, the NAD found 969 or 43 percent of contested advertising claims to be substantiated. During the same period, the NAD negotiated a modification or discontinuance of an ad in 1244 cases, or 55.7 percent; eight tenths of a percent, or 19 claims, were appealed to the NARB.[32]

Is the self-regulatory process performing adequately? That may be dependent upon an adequate regulatory process. As Howard and Hulbert stated: "We wish to make two points on the rule of self-regulation: first, The National Advertising Review Board is likely to have a major impact only insofar as there is a strong (FTC) Commission policy operating. Second, as the procedures now provide, the extreme cases will have to come to the attention of the Commission."[33]   The power of self-regulation derives from government

TABLE 8-1

Source of Complaints Handled by the NAD, 1971–1987 (in Percentages)

Source of Complaint[a]	1971	1972	1973	1974	1975	1976	1977	1978	1979	1980	1981	1982	1983	1984	1985	1986	1987
NAD monitoring	10	10	51	40	35	52	56	48	34	45	43	39	37	31	37	27	30
Competitor challenges	2	6	8	11	27	25	21	36	39	37	35	39	42	45	41	43	40
Local BBBs[b]	53	20	15	22	16	10	11	12	9	12	12	10	11	10	10	15	13
Consumer complaints	9	25	14	13	15	10	9	2	16	6	8	9	5	9	11	12	13
Other[c]	26	39	12	14	7	3	3	2	2	—	2	3	5	5	1	3	4
	100%	100%	100%	100%	100%	100%	100%	100%	100%	100%	100%	100%	100%	100%	100%	100%	100%

[a] Based on incoming cases; year 1982 forward based on published reports.
[b] Half of all BBB referrals are estimated to be consumer initiated.
[c] Includes organized consumer groups, professional or trade associations, federal and state regulatory agencies.

Source: National Advertising Division, 1985, 1986, 1987, 1988.

TABLE 8-2

Cases Closed by the NAD, 1971-1987

Disposition of Case	Mid-1971 Through 1973	1974	1975	1976	1977	1978	1979	1980	1981	1982	1983	1984	1985	1986	1987
Substantiated	191	75	72	67	94	64	63	57	68	61	46	22	31	26	32
Modified/discontinued	126	65	101	95	60	99	99	78	80	79	64	83	70	80	65
Referred to NARB	9	2	—	1	1	—	1	—	1	—	—	—	2	1	1
Suspended pending FTC litigation	—	—	—	—	—	—	—	—	1	—	—	—	—	—	—
Total	326	142	173	163	155	163	163	135	150	140	110	105	103	107	98

Source: National Advertising Division: 1985, 1986, 1987, 1988.

prodding and the threat of further regulation or from stronger enforcement of existing laws.[34]

The Children's Advertising Review Unit

In 1974, the NAD created the Children's Advertising Review Unit (CARU), which is funded by major children's advertisers. The CARU attempts to review advertising through the eyes of children, taking into account that they may lack the sophistication and understanding of adult audiences. The CARU tries to ensure that children's advertising is fair, with the word *fair* encompassing such issues as social values, product presentation, pressure of purchase, endorsements, safety, and premiums.[35]

Ads are evaluated against the CARU guidelines which were revised in 1983. The staff makes subjective judgments about ads, sometimes with the advice of the CBBB's legal staff. In addition, seven academic advisers are occasionally consulted on matters relating to particular cases.

Armstrong made a rather complete review of the CARU activities from 1974 to 1982 and has drawn some interesting conclusions:

1. The case load is small by any standard (an average of about 15 cases per year, and falling, as compared to 175 cases per year for NAD). Though casework may provide input for the development and testing of the Unit's guidelines, this volume of cases is probably too small to enforce the guidelines effectively or to set meaningful precedents for improvement of advertising to children.
2. CARU casework appears to be largely inner-directed, even more so than NAD casework. Most is generated from internal monitoring. CARU has even less consumer input than NAD (14% vs. NAD's 22%) and is used much less by advertisers to resolve complaints against competition (3% vs. NAD's 38% in recent years).
3. The level of case activity appears to fluctuate substantially with external pressures in children's advertising. For example, efforts peaked in 1978-79 when the industry was threatened by the FTC trade regulation rule on children's advertising. When the threat had passed, the case load decreased considerably.
4. The development of a set of specific guidelines appears to have aided CARU in its casework. Comparison with NAD (which has no such guidelines) shows that CARU had higher proportions of initial "unacceptable" decisions (71% vs. NAD's 16%) and fewer requests to substantiate (22% vs. NAD's 82%). The Unit resolved more cases in its favor (37% vs. 31% for NAD) and received more "previously discontinued" responses (38% vs. 17%). These and other facts imply that the guidelines have resulted in better CARU case selection and proportionally greater effectiveness in removing potentially abusive ads.[36]

Armstrong feels that the CARU is "little more than a token effort by the advertising industry. It is an organization with sweeping and impressive mandate to assure truth, accuracy, and fairness and to develop precedents and advisories for the improvement of child-directed advertising but with paltry resources with which to accomplish the mission. Given the extent of its mandate, CARU is seriously undermanned and under-funded."[37]

Armstrong's conclusions may be a bit harsh, but he does raise serious concerns about this attempt at self-regulation within the advertising industry. Given the seriousness of the children's issue, it is important that this form of advertising be monitored vigorously.

GOVERNMENTAL FORCES

Our focus in this discussion of government forces will be the federal level. Although all states and some local jurisdictions attempt to deal with advertising, their approaches are often so varied that it is impossible to arrive at a common position regarding their efforts.

Before we begin a discussion of the formal regulatory process, it is necessary to stress the importance of the "mood" of Washington in legislation and enforcement. The philosophy of the White House during any given administration strongly influences what legislation will be passed and what areas of enforcement the Justice Department and the Federal Trade Commission will concentrate on.

The mood of Washington under the Reagan administration was best summarized in the president's 1982 economic report: "While regulation is necessary to protect such vital areas as food, health, and safety, too much unnecessary regulation simply adds to the costs of businesses and consumers alike without commensurate benefits."[38] The Reagan administration had made clear its position that government regulation is justifiable only if it (1) produces benefits that outweigh the costs, and (2) is the least expensive solution to the problem.[39]

As a result, regulatory agencies are being required to justify their actions with some type of cost-benefit analysis indicating the value of the proposed regulation. As Assael has pointed out, this puts the burden of proof on the agencies, "whereas in the 1970s the burden of proof was on industry to ensure consumer protections."[40]

The 1980s have also meant cutbacks in most consumer agencies. Concerning the agency we are most interested in, the Federal Trade Commission (FTC), the following has occurred:

1. Elimination of a proposed rule to ban food advertising to children.[41]
2. Elimination of industrywide guidelines for advertising claims in the over-the-counter drug market.

3. Elimination of rules that would have required manufacturers to disclose nutritional information.

4. Elimination of a rule that would have added to advertising warnings now required on labels of antacid products.

5. Elimination of rules requiring disclosures within food ads making health and nutrition claims.[42]

6. Elimination of its ten-year-old case against the three leading cereal manufacturers in which the FTC claimed that the companies' advertising and marketing practices constitute "shared monopoly" resulting in higher prices.[43]

In addition, Congress passed the Federal Trade Improvement Act of 1980, which revised the manner in which the FTC could improve trade rules and regulations, provided for congressional review of the commission's actions, and removed "unfairness" as the basis for trade rules dealing with advertising.[44] Now deception had to be present to justify a new industrywide trade rule or court litigation.

The 1980s have also led the Federal Trade Commission to institute major policy changes within the organization, many of which were suggested by James C. Miller III, a former chairman.[45] The most important of these changes revolve around the key concept of deception.

The commission has recently adopted "new" standards for this term. The FTC will now find deception if there is a representation, omission, or practice that is likely to mislead the consumer acting reasonably in the circumstances and to the consumer's detriment.[46]

According to a court of appeals, this new standard of deception imposes a greater burden of proof on the FTC to show a violation of Section 5 than the old standard. First, the FTC must show probable, not possible, deception ("likely to mislead," not only a "tendency and capacity to mislead"). Second, the FTC must show potential deception of consumers acting reasonably in the circumstances, not just any consumers. Third, in determining consumer detriment, the new standard considers as material only deceptions that are likely to cause injury to reasonable consumers who relied on them. The old standard reached deceptions that consumers might have considered important whether or not there was proof of reliance on the deceptions.[47]

Yet, important tools adopted in the 1970s remain "on the books" as regulatory options for the Federal Trade Commission. Some continue to be used, while others are in need of refinement. Some of the most important ones are:

1. ADVERTISING SUBSTANTIATION. This policy states that it is illegal to advertise an affirmative claim for a product without having a reasonable basis. Claims must be substantiated if they relate to a product's

safety, performance, quality, or price.[48] The commission continues to actively enforce this policy.

2. CORRECTIVE ADVERTISING. This FTC strategy would require advertisers who have made deceptive or unfair claims to spend a certain amount of future advertising dollars to make statements to correct the deception. Listerine was required to spend $10 million to communicate the message, "Listerine will not help prevent colds or sore throats or lessen their severity." The effectiveness of this remedy in the present form has been questioned by some researchers, although several excellent modifications for this remedy have been suggested.[49]

3. REDRESS OF CONSUMER INJURY. The Magnuson-Moss Act authorizes the FTC to bring civil actions to redress consumer injury. This could include the rescission of contracts, refund of money, return of property, and payment of damages. The FTC can only bring such actions if there has been a violation of a trade regulation or if there is a violation of a cease-and-desist order.[50]

The commission has also developed a policy to notify consumers of redress situations. In a recent case, the Commission had charged that Ford was repairing autos that were inadequately lubricated by quietly fixing the problem for only those who complained. Ford was ordered to run ads in several consumer magazines to deal with the problem.[51]

4. AFFIRMATIVE DISCLOSURE. This policy would require marketers and advertisers to inform potential customers of certain facts about the product or service offered. These disclosures would deal with the deficiencies or limitations of the product or service as well as any positive characteristics. The most widespread use of this policy is for cigarette advertising and labeling.

5. UNIQUENESS CLAIMS. Even substantiated claims may not be used if (unsupported) uniqueness is implied in an advertisement. Wonder Bread advertised that it "helps build strong bodies twelve ways." While technically true, every bread appears to contribute to growth in much the same way.[52]

Although most current federal government policies continue to point towards deregulation, this "back to basics" regulatory philosophy may well change with the Bush administration. Whether the regulatory pendulum continues to move in the direction of "back to basics" or moves towards "tightening the control mechanisms" remains to be seen. What we do know is that the pendulum will always continue to move.

CURRENT COMPLIMENTARY NATURES OF THE FTC AND NAD/NARB

Boddewyn indicates several similarities between the forces of self-regulation and governmental forces:[53]

1. limited outside participation
2. emphasis on "hard issues and criteria"
3. choice of cases to handle
4. shared standards

Concerning limited outside participation, the FTC is primarily composed of civil servants, although the commission has occasionally utilized outside expert witness and advisers. The NAD does not use outsiders, except as expert advisers and the one in five member of panels to review advertising complaints. Both of these organizational structures appear to allow little room for outside participation in the fundamental processes of either organization.

Both the FTC and NAD/NARB tend to focus on hard cases and refuse to handle soft issues, such as taste, social responsibility, and morality. The NARB currently has a policy to consider the content of messages for reasons other than truth and accuracy. The NAD/NARB, however, has generally declined to handle such cases because "there is no government agency to which such cases could be referred."[54]

Both bodies also tend to select similar types of cases; each tries to choose cases that set precedents and send important signals to businesses. "Both emphasize cases of poorly substantiated and misleading advertisements, . . . and they both use a case-by-case approach now that the FTC has largely abandoned the pursuit of broad trade regulation rules and industrywide rounds."[55]

Finally, concerning the issue of shared standards, the NAD/NARB has repeatedly acknowledged that FTC and FDA rules and rulings constitute many of its own main standards. FTC Commissioner Patricia Bailey referred to the NAD/NARB self-regulatory program as "now grounded in FTC precedent and policy."[56]

MEDIA FORCES

In 1979, a civil antitrust suit was brought against the National Association of Broadcasters (NAB) charging that its television-code rules that regulate television advertising were anticompetitive and in restraint of trade. In 1982, a consent decree was signed by all parties which basically eliminated the NAB code. There are now no formal standards concerning:

1. The number of commercial minutes per hour.
2. The number of commercials per hour.
3. The number of consecutive commercials at each commercial interruption.
4. The number of products that can be promoted in a commercial lasting less than 60 seconds.
5. The purchase of network time for liquor ads.
6. The actual consumption of beer or wine on television.[57]

Although there are no longer any specific prohibitions in the areas maintained above, some are still being enforced by individual networks, such as time for liquor ads and consumption of beer or wine on television. All the networks have maintained also their guidelines for deceptive advertising. Advertisements will not be broadcast by networks unless they meet standards of truth, fairness, and adequate substantiation.[58]

However, guidelines concerning the number of commercials per hour, per minute, and the number of products that can be promoted in commercials lasting 60 seconds are not being upheld. There are now more advertising messages in a given hour, and the 15-second commercial spot is an acceptable industry practice.

Some critics also believe that many cable stations are adhering to even less rigid standards for what is considered deceptive advertising. For example, some toy manufacturers have complained that toy ads on independent cable networks often violate basic network standards.

It would appear that self-regulation on the media's part is in some disarray. The removal of the NAB code and the factionalization of media outlets present continuing problems.

SUMMARY

Returning to the question at the beginning of the chapter—What forces should be allowed to regulate the institution of advertising?—it is clear that there will always be some combination of forces involved in regulation. The exact mix of these forces is dependent on the tenor of the times. Since shifts in sociopolitical attitudes change the mix from decade to decade, one probably should not expect to find a consistent stream and heritage of regulation. A certain amount of instability in the marketplace is inevitable for both advertisers and consumers.

The swing of the sociopolitical pendulum toward deregulation has allowed natural market forces to dominate. Consumers are now viewed as more capable of looking out for themselves than the government has given them credit for. The market is viewed as a capable regulator, enabling sellers and buyers at different levels of market sophistication to interact well.

Will this feeling about the marketplace spill over to the self-regulatory mechanisms currently in place? Will the quieter, more individualistic consumerism of the 1980s find little need for concern about the changes in the legal and self-regulatory environments of the 1990s? How will the consumer fare in this environment? As discussed in Chapter 3, depending on the sets of assumptions the reader makes about such fundamental matters as human nature, the proper role of the market, and the presence of government, the resultant feeling may be one of optimism or pessimism.

ENDNOTES

1. William T. Kelley, ed., *New Consumerism: Selected Readings* (Columbus, OH: Grid, Inc., 1973), p. vi.
2. *Ibid.*, p. iv.
3. Eugene R. Beem, "The Beginnings of the Consumer Movement," in *New Consumerism: Selected Readings,* William T. Kelly, ed. (Columbus, OH: Grid, Inc., 1973), p. 13.
4. Upton Sinclair, *The Jungle* (New York: Viking Press, 1946); originally published in 1906.
5. Beem, pp. 17-18.
6. *Ibid.*, pp. 18-19.
7. Francis J. Charlton and William A. Fawcett, "The FTC and False Advertising," *Kansas Law Review,* vol. 17 (1969), p. 606.
8. *FTC v. Raladam Co.,* 283 U.S. 643.
9. Stuart Chase and Frederick J. Schlink, *Your Money's Worth* (New York: Macmillan, 1927), p. 254.
10. Mary C. Phillips, *Skin Deep* (New York: Vanguard Press, 1934).
11. Frederick J. Schlink, *Eat, Drink, and Be Wary* (New York: Covici-Friede Co., 1935).
12. Marshall C. Howard, *Legal Aspects of Marketing* (New York: McGraw-Hill Book Co., 1974), pp. 10-11.
13. Beem, *op. cit.,* p. 28.
14. Vance Packard, *Hidden Persuaders* (New York: McKay, 1957).
15. John Kenneth Galbraith, *The Affluent Society* (Boston: Houghton Mifflin, 1958).
16. Rachel Carson, *Silent Spring* (Boston: Houghton Mifflin, 1962).
17. Ralph Nader, *Unsafe at Any Speed* (New York: Grossman, 1965).
18. James F. Engel, Roger D. Blackwell, and Paul W. Minard, *Consumer Behavior* (New York: The Dryden Press, 1986), p. 583.
19. "MIN's Historical Perspective on Consumerism" *Media Industry News Letter,* May 11, 1972, p. 7.
20. Ralph M. Gaedeke and Warren W. Etcheson, *Consumerism Viewpoints from Business, Government, and the Public Interest* (San Francisco: Canfield Press, 1972), pp. 374-375.
21. Dorothy Cohen, *Advertising* (Glenview, IL: Scott, Foresman and Company, 1988), p. 600.
22. "New Harris Consumer Study Causes Few Shocks in Adland," *Advertising Age,* May 30, 1977, p. 2.
23. *New York Times,* February 17, 1983, p. A-16.
24. "Is Consumerism Dead?" Editorial Notebook, *New York Times,* November 22, 1982.
25. Henry Assael, *Consumer Behavior and Marketing Action* (Boston: Kent Publishing Co., 1983), p. 622.

26. Paul N. Bloom and Stephen A. Greyser, ''The Maturing of Consumerism,'' *Harvard Business Review,* November-December 1981, p. 131.

27. Lewis Harris and Associates, Inc., ''Consumerism in the Eighties,'' (Study Number 822 047, 1983).

28. Eric J. Zanot, ''The National Advertising Review Board: Precedents, Premises, and Performance,'' doctoral dissertation, University of Illinois, College of Communication, 1977, pp. 62-63. Also see G. E. Miracle and T. R. Nevett, *Voluntary Regulation of Advertising: A Comparative Analysis of the United Kingdom and the United States* (Lexington, MA: Heath/Lexington, 1987).

29. J. J. Boddewyn, *Advertising Self-Regulation and Outside Participation: A Multinational Comparison* (New York: Quorum Books, 1988), p. 296.

30. *Ibid.*

31. *Ibid.*

32. *NAD Case Report* (New York: National Advertising Division, Council of Better Business Bureaus, Inc., January 1985, 1986, 1987), p. 1.

33. J. A. Howard and James Hulbert, *Advertising and the Public Interest: A Staff Report to the Federal Trade Commission* (Chicago: Crain Communications, 1973), pp. 93-94.

34. J. J. Boddewyn, p. 310.

35. Gary M. Armstrong, ''An Evaluation of the Children's Advertising Review Unit,'' *Journal of Public Policy & Marketing* 3 (1984), p. 39.

36. *Ibid.,* pp. 51-52.

37. *Ibid.,* p. 53.

38. *New York Times,* January 21, 1983, p. A-16.

39. ''Deregulation, A Fast Start for the Reagan Strategy,'' *Business Week,* March 9, 1981, p. 62.

40. Assael, p. 628.

41. Stanford L. Grossbart and Lawrence A. Crosby, ''Understanding the Basis of Parental Concern and Reaction to Children's Food Advertising,'' *Journal of Marketing* 48 (Summer 1984), pp. 79-92.

42. ''Despite Antiregulatory Sentiment, Advertisers Still Must Battle Washington 'Policy Shapers,''' *Marketing News,* April 30, 1982, p. 1.

43. C. H. Sandage, Vernon Fryburger, and Kim Rotzoll, *Advertising Theory and Practice* (Homewood, IL: Richard D. Irwin, Inc., 1983), p. 483.

44. William H. Bolen, *Advertising* (New York: John Wiley & Sons, 1984), p. 59.

45. Sandage, p. 438.

46. *Southwest Sunsites, Inc., Green Valley Acres, Inc., Green Valley Acres, Inc., II, Sidney Gross, and Edwin Kritzler v. Federal Trade Commission,* CCH # 67,021 (Ca-9, April 1986; BNA ATRR No. 1260, April 10, 1986), 633, in ''Legal Developments in Marketing,'' *Journal of Marketing,* vol. 51, no. 1 (January 1987), pp. 114-115. Also see Letter from the Federal

Trade Commission to the U. S. Senate Committee on Commerce, Science and Transportation, dated October 14, 1983.

47. *Southwest Sunsites, Inc., Green Valley Acres, Inc., Green Valley Acres, Inc., II, Sidney Gross, and Edwin Kritzeler v. Federal Trade Commission, op. cit.,* pp. 114-115.

48. Cohen, p. 604.

49. William L. Wilkie, Dennis McNeill, and Michael B. Mazis, "Marketing's Scarlet Letter: the Theory and Practice of Corrective Advertising," *Journal of Marketing,* vol. 48 (Spring 1984).

50. Cohen, p. 608.

51. "Ford to Run FTC-Ordered Ads in 1981," *Advertising Age* (October 27, 1980), p. 28.

52. *ITT, Continental Baking Co., et al.* (1971), 3, *Trade Req. Rep.,* par. 19, 539.

53. Boddewyn, p. 298. The in-depth discussion of these issues is also taken from Boddewyn.

54. *Ibid.,* p. 299.

55. *Ibid.,* p. 300.

56. Patricia F. Bailey, "When Is an Ad Deceptive? The Regulation of Advertising at the FTC," *New Trends in Advertising,* Presentation at the American Advertising Federation's 1983-1984 Law and Public Policy Conferences (Washington, DC: American Advertising Federation, 1984), p. 14.

57. Bolen, p. 76. Also see T. Barton Carter, March A. Franklin, and Jay B. Wright, *The First Amendment and the Fifth Estate* (Mineola, NY: The Foundation Press, Inc., 1986), p. 291.

58. See Eric Zanot, "Unseen But Effective Advertising Regulation: The Clearance Process," *Journal of Advertising,* 14:4, 1985, pp 44-51.

9
ADVERTISING
AND ITS ETHICAL
DIMENSIONS

Over the years there have been a great many nasty things said about advertising and advertising people. A sampling:

◆ After reviewing a number of novels about the advertising business published in the post-World War II period, historian Stephen Fox concluded:

From these dozen novels came a remarkably consistent picture of the advertising world: false in tone, tense in pace, vacant and self-hating, overheated and oversexed.[1]

The picture is no less flattering in the decades before or since, in spite of relatively benign contemporary treatments in films such as *Nothing in Common* and television shows such as *thirtysomething*.

◆ In 1976, economist Robert Heilbroner called advertising "the single most value-destroying activity of business civilization." Reviewing his remarks more than ten years later, he found no reason to recant.[2]

◆ Richard Pollay, whose article we examined in Chapter 4, summarized the evaluation of advertising by significant humanities and social sciences scholars:

They see advertising as reinforcing materialism, cynicism, irrationality, selfishness, anxiety, social competitiveness, powerlessness and/or loss of self-respect.[3]

◆ Or consider these thoughts by the late Howard Gossage, a member of the Advertising Copywriters Hall of Fame, and one of advertising's most penetrating gadflies: "To explain responsibility to advertising people is like trying to convince an eight-year-old that sexual intercourse is more fun than a chocolate ice-cream cone."[4]

◆ The most recent Gallup poll on the subject we've seen lists a category called "Advertisers" third from the bottom of 25 occupations on ''honesty and ethical standards.'' They were listed below labor union leaders, but above insurance salesmen and car salesmen.[5]

THE LARGER ETHICAL CLIMATE

Now, it could be contended with considerable force that advertising is hardly alone in the ethics jungle:

- A seven-page article titled ''A Nation of Liars?'' appeared in *U. S. News & World Report* in early 1987.[6]
- A *Time* cover story asked, ''What Ever Happened to Ethics?'' later in the same year.[7]
- In early 1988, Professor David Rankin, editorializing in *Newsweek* under the title ''A State of Incivility,'' offered these thoughts:

  We have come to accept as normal broken contracts and broken dates; public display of pornography and profanity and, I fear, even theft.[8]

- In a column commenting on the host of ethical confrontations in drought-stricken mid-1988 involving politicians, TV evangelists, inside traders, Pentagon officials, defense contractors, and even West Point cadets, columnist Cal Thomas observed, ''the water table for ethical behavior is sinking faster than the Mississippi river.''[9]
- Then there are the volatile concerns of right-to-life, right-to-choose, right-to-death, the homeless, gene splicing, etc., etc.

So advertising can be categorized as being in good (or bad) company on the larger societal ethical scale. This is not a new perspective. In 1927, advertising pioneer Bruce Barton observed:

If advertising persuades some men to live beyond their means, so does matrimony. If advertising speaks to a thousand in order to influence one, so does the church. If advertising is often garrulous and redundant and tiresome, so is the United States Senate.[10]

THE BUSINESS PERCEIVES ITSELF

Rather than taking Barton's we're-no-worse-than-the-other-guy position, the trade organizations that represent the advertising business frequently emphasize what they perceive as advertising's societal contributions. Apart from the now familiar litany of serving the sovereign consumers and lubricating the economy, they point to:

''Enforced'' social responsibility through:

◆ Codes of advertisers, media, agencies, and trade organizations.

◆ A much respected National Advertising Review Board.

◆ A Federal Trade Commission that is still a presence in spite of its relative inactivity during the Reagan years.

◆ A more combative Food and Drug Administration that has become quite active as advertisers move closer to health claims with assertions about "natural" ingredients, fiber content, and the like.

◆ A downright feisty group of State Attorneys General who have already attempted to establish national guidelines for the advertising of airlines and rental cars in addition to their often robust activities within individual states.

"Voluntary" social responsibility through:

◆ The Advertising Council and its $1 billion efforts on behalf of such causes as crime prevention, arresting high-blood pressure, the Negro college fund, and AIDS education, among hundreds of others.

◆ The "Partnership for a Drug Free America" with its $1.5 billion in donated space and time over a three-year period.

◆ The American Association of Advertising Agencies' $25 million effort to combat functional illiteracy.

◆ Virtually, daily goodwill efforts on the part of advertisers, agencies, and media for a host of state, regional, and local concerns. (The Leo Burnett agency reported that in 1987 it devoted 6,639 hours to *pro bono* projects for 46 organizations).[11]

The Ethical Battlefield

In their provocative work, *Social Communication in Advertising,* William Leiss and associates observe:

Because it stands at the intersection of industry, communications, and group interactions, advertising can come under attack from anyone who is upset about any feature of these three domains.[12]

"Industry" (marketing practices), "communications" (the mass media), and "group interactions" (stereotyping) represent fertile fields for ethical encounter, and we shall turn to these, and others, after a few preliminary observations about ethics in general.

Ethics is the liberal arts discipline that appraises voluntary human conduct insofar as it can be judged right or wrong in reference to determinative principles.[13]

First, then, in order to come to understand advertising in relation to ethics, we must confront principles of ethical behavior which involve critical thinking about moral questions and serve as the channel for values.

Pursuing this thinking, it follows that a workable ethical system involves *deliberation, careful distinctions,* and *extended discussions.* Clearly these are not conditions that are easily found in the business world, with its priorities of competitiveness and quick response. This conflict in mind-sets may in part explain why earnest attempts of the advertising business to deal with critical ethical salvos have often fallen short of achievement.

SEVEN AREAS OF INHERENT ETHICAL CONFLICT IN ONGOING ADVERTISING PRACTICE

Inevitably, we believe, the individual involved in advertising practice will encounter areas of practice that seem fraught with moral controversy. Thus the ensuing decisions on the part of the advertising practitioner can be "judged right or wrong in reference to determinative principles," and advertising can be found wanting or vindicated accordingly.

1. *The advertising business is rationalized predominately by classical liberal assumptions.*

Recall the basic assumptions of self-interest, the individual as a competent decision maker, and the virtue of competition leading ultimately to the good of all concerned through a "natural harmony of self-interests" that are central to the classical liberal idea system and the ensuing ideology of the market system.

Now, if one *accepts* these positions (as practitioners generally do) there will also be an acceptance of:

◆   Consumer sovereignty.
◆   Advertising as a mirror, a socially passive force.

But if one *questions* these positions (as critics generally do) there will generally be an acceptance of:

◆   The advertiser as sovereign, with the consumer open to manipulation.
◆   Advertising as a sharper/selective reinforcer, a socially influential force.

Thus, at the most fundamental ideological levels, we have the ongoing reality of different perceptions of advertising performance, with predictable ethical judgments.

2. *The advertising message is one-sided communication, with the inherent potential of deception by omission.*

In his important work, *The Making of Modern Advertising,* Historian Daniel Pope addressed the issue of the bias of the advertising message:

> For advertising to play a large part in market strategy, consumers
> had to be willing to accept this kind of self interested persuasion as

a tolerable substitute or compliment to more objective product information.[14]

Thus, advertising is seen as a trade-off, sacrificing value-free information for a form strong on convenience but laced with persuasion. The ethical mine fields seem apparent.

For example, do we (or should we) learn from advertisements that:

◆ Jell-O has been assessed as 82.4% sugar?[15]
◆ That a consumer test using disguised samples indicated that all major hair shampoos would do a fine job cleaning hair, including a liquid dishwasher detergent which was thrown into the test for comparison?[16]
◆ That Acme white tuna was rated tops in taste and nutrition?[17]
◆ That Prudential Property and Casualty Insurance was recently rated dead last in an evaluation of insurance policies, and that such heavily advertised brands as Fireman's Fund, Aetna, and Liberty Mutual were near the bottom?[18]
◆ That it's estimated a family can conserve $2500 a year at the supermarket, without sacrificing nutrition, largely by buying store brands rather than their heavily advertised national counterparts?[19]

Is this and other information potentially useful to the consumer? Arguably, yes. Yet, a consumer seeking information such as this would be far more likely to find it in publications such as *Consumer Reports* or, perhaps, reliable word-of-mouth, rather than advertising.

Now, advertisers would argue that their advertising is a nakedly transparent form of self-interested communication, accepted as such by the public, and that other sources of market information should pursue their own agendas while advertisers pursue theirs. The consumer, they would contend, is well served in such a climate of market communication *pluralism.* Yet, others will argue that advertisers take their responsibilities as reliable communication sources too lightly.

After reviewing three recent books by prominent advertising figures, Roger Draper of the *New York Times* concluded that these practitioners apparently believe that consumers should settle for advertising providing "some of the truth."

By this they mean not the amount of truth that can reasonably be compressed into a reasonable amount of space, but the product of efforts to suppress an important fact: the similarity among competing brands. If "some of the truth" in this sense is an acceptable alternative to all of it, the value of truth itself becomes puzzling.[20]

Advertising is a form of "interested" communication, and the ethical underbrush is tangled indeed.

3. *The purpose of all advertising is to cause us to think or act in accordance with the advertiser's intent, whether it be noble or venal.*

At the *societal* level:

◆ Legendary advertising practitioner Theodore MacManus (creator of the much honored "Penalty of Leadership" ad) was an eyewitness to what several historians consider the beginnings of the "culture of consumption" in the 1920s. His 1928 thoughts on advertising's role are insightful:

> The cigarette has become almost a health food—certainly a weight reducer. The humble cake of soap has risen far above its modest mission of cleansing, and confers the precious bloom of beauty upon whomsoever shall faithfully wash. We are all glowing, and sparkling, and snapping, and tingling with health, by way of the toothbrush, and the razor, and the shaving cream, and the face lotion, and the deodorant, and a dozen other brightly packaged gifts of the gods. Advertising has gone amuck in that it has mistaken the surface silliness for the sane solid substance of an averagely decent human nature.[21]

Here, advertising sets the consumption agenda. In Chapter 4, we had explored similar themes from Potter, Schudson, and Pollay, not only in terms of setting priorities for goods and services high in the individual's agenda, but also, as we had previously noted through Leiss and colleagues, suggesting interpretations about:

> . . . interpersonal and family relations, the sense of happiness and contentment, sex roles and stereotyping, the uses of affluence, the fading of older cultural traditions, influences of younger generations, the role of business in society, personal autonomy and persuasion, and many others.[22]

(Need we be reminded that one brewer has decided to co-op nothing less than half of our day—"The Night Belongs to Michelob." One wonders where we go to seek permission to use it.)

There are, of course, more *specific* areas of concern about advertising's persuasive power as well. Among them:

Beer. The August 8, 1988 issue of *Sports Illustrated* devoted its cover story to a lengthy exploration of the relationship between sports and beer. They noted:

> It is the cause of some ugly social problems, which leads some to wonder just what kind of cultural hypocrisy is going on when Americans relentlessly insist on immersing sport—our most wholesome, most admired, even (sometimes) most heroic institution—in a sea of intoxicating drink.[23]

Not surprisingly, advertising figures prominently in the ensuing discussion, as does television, with reference to the eye-catching statement that

American children between the ages of 2 and 18 see some 10,000 commercials for beer.[24] (It is interesting to note that the same issue of *SI* contained a full-page Budweiser ad. *Sports Illustrated's* readers between the ages of 18-24 are estimated to be 25.5% of their total audience. Doubtless many of those are below the legal drinking age of 21 in many states.)

As we have noted previously, Senator Strom Thurmond took issue with the lack of "responsibility" of the brewing industry while holding aloft a Spuds MacKenzie doll on the floor of the U.S. Senate.

Cigarettes.   Many consider it unprincipled that over $2 billion is spent advertising and promoting a product that has been called "the only legally available product that is *harmful when used as intended.*"

Nor are critics comforted to learn through *Advertising Age* that "R. J. Reynolds Aims New Ads at Young Smokers." The company decided to modernize their camel symbol ("Old Joe") by turning him into a "smooth character," shown in such settings as Hollywood, in an attempt to appeal to the ever popular 18-24 year olds, currently drawn to the macho symbolism of Marlboro.[25]

Then there are concerns about persuasive activities on behalf of:

◆   Birth-control products.
◆   Political candidates. (Virtually a chapter unto itself.)
◆   Legal services.
◆   Doctors, dentists, hospitals, etc.

So it seems inevitable that since advertising has a persuasive agenda—like preaching, politics, and numerous other activities of our civilization—it will be accused inevitably of unethical practice by those who (a) disagree with the *ends promoted,* and/or (b) advertising as the *means.*

4.   *Frequently, advertising seeks out the individual rather than individual seeking it.*

Except for catalogs, classifieds, directories, the food ads in the mid-week newspaper, and the like, we are frequently the sought rather than the seeker. Not surprisingly, this raises a host of questions with ethical dimensions in areas such as timing, privacy, and frequency to mention only the most obvious. For example:

◆   An *Advertising Age* survey of 1,000 adults concerning the most disliked television commercials showed a clear winner (or loser)—women's personal hygiene products. Many regarded the information in the ads as potentially useful, but found the context—a television viewing room, often in mixed company—totally unacceptable.[26]
◆   In the recent America's Cup race, viewers were treated for the first time to a corporate logo on the sail of the American entry.

◆   It is now commonplace to find advertising in and about college football
    stadiums, where only a decade or less ago such a presence would have
    been considered unseemly.

◆   Cinema advertising (the appearance of brand advertising before the main
    feature in theaters) continues to be a growing presence. It is, we believe,
    the only major form of advertising not requiring even a grudging consent
    on the part of the potential viewer.

◆   Another emerging presence is the appearance of advertising messages be-
    fore the feature films on videotapes. *Advertising Age* columnist Bob
    Garfield lamented the presence of a Jeep ad before the award-winning
    movie *Platoon*. The message, he said, was "War is hell. Buy Chrys-
    ler."[27]

The reader is invited to add his or her own examples of advertising's apparently ravenous appetite to "get at us."

Now, it can be contended that some of this potential conflict will subside
as market and media fragmentation continue apace. That is, we are more likely
to find advertising for golf clubs compatible as a reader of *Golf* magazine, and
messages about low-cost insurance policies may be welcomed by the readers of
Modern Maturity. Indeed, even television, clearly the lightning rod in this and
other areas of advertising/ethical encounters, may find it easier to match viewer
interests with appropriate advertising as cable watching becomes even more
routine, with appropriate selectivity in program content.

Yet, advertisers will be seeking us perhaps more relentlessly than ever
before through the mass media, as well as through increasingly untraditional
forms. The ethical signal flags are apparent.

5. *Advertising continues to be a controversial third party with the mass media.*

From the mid-to-late 19th century with newspapers, from the early 20th
century with magazines, shortly after the earliest days of radio, and from the
outset of the American television system, advertising has been a third party
with the traditional publisher/reader and broadcaster/audience relationship.
The ensuing trade-offs are the ongoing stuff of pride (advertising helps the media to be available less expensively without possible dependence on government subsidy), as well as controversy. Herewith, some of the more common
ethical charges:

That advertising can change the subject of the media coverage itself.
The most obvious case is television, where the availability of advertising dollars for some kinds of programming in some particular time slots has proven a
seductive lure. How common it is, for example, for college football and bas-
ketball teams to reschedule their starting times for games, almost oblivious to
the wishes of the spectators, to accommodate network time preferences. In another area, several midwestern writers have lamented the arrival of night base-
ball at Chicago's historic Wrigley Field, a move dictated by the quest for a
larger share of the television pie. Simply, the selection of television subjects

and subsequent timing is frequently determined by the explicit or implicit preferences of advertisers.

That advertising can alter the content of the media coverage. A study by the American Council on Science and Health indicated that cigarette and health issues received relatively poor coverage in magazines with heavy cigarette advertising—e.g., *Time, Newsweek, Mademoiselle, Ladies Home Journal, MS, Redbook,* and *Cosmopolitan.*[28]

In the last years of the 1980s, all three major television networks have downscaled their commercial clearance departments (comprised of those individuals who screen advertisements before they're accepted for broadcast). Further, NBC recently announced that its department would become more involved with attempting to make programs commercially profitable, including exploring possible product tie-ins. (These actions resulted in a protest from leading advertising trade organizations, urging that the networks keep their acceptance standards high.)

That advertising can affect the type of available media. Media follow markets, so it seems self-evident that we are more likely to see advertising supported magazines with titles such as *Self-Indulgent Jogger* and *Young and Possessive* than *Ghetto Life, Migrant Worker,* or *Old and Poor.*

Again, there seems a sign of hope in the increasing specialization of the media, albeit to pursue advertisers' markets more efficiently. Thus, specialized magazines, zoned editions of newspapers, CATV, and the like seem destined to arrive at a more satisfactory medium/advertiser/reader-viewer relationship than the more heterogeneous couplings. (One presumes a world record in customized media was set with the May, 1985 issue of *Farm Journal* claiming 8896 separate advertising/editorial mixes in that single issue.[29])

There is, however, an offsetting concern with the growing "clutter" in *all* advertising media. Again, however, the focus falls on television, with the acceptance of the 15-second time slot as a standard advertising buy. Advertising practitioner Stan Freberg reflected on his experience watching one commercial "island" in a made-for-television movie on NBC:

> There were only a few 15s. But melding one into the other were a montage of images for: Volkswagen, Visine, Kellogg's Raisin Squares, Fab, a movie promo, Reunité, an NBC promo, an "NBC News Digest," Salad Bar pasta, Miller Lite, Toyota, a Phil Donahue promo, and the NBC logo. Quickly now! The second commercial you saw was . . . what?[30]

6. *The advertising agency commission system continues to reward agencies for what they buy (media space and/or time) rather than what they produce (ads).*

Historically, the advertising agency receives a commission (usually 15% or less) on the cost of the advertising space and/or time it buys with the advertiser's money. This venerable system is now somewhat in decline as a form of compensation as compared with fee and other arrangements, but it still represents a significant force in the process. Former practitioner Howard Gossage says:

> You show me a business where one's income is dependent on the amount of money spent rather than the amount of money that comes in and I will show you a business that is doomed, even with the very best of intentions, to mutual distrust and enormous psychological barriers.[31]

It is, for example, hard to imagine an agency recommending that an advertiser *cut* his or her advertising budget and devote the savings to some other aspect of marketing activity—say, beefing up the sales force. In addition, some claim that the value of the advertisement itself is diminished because the best ad and the worst have equal (media) value; however, the counter-argument would assert the "good" ad is likely to be repeated more often, thus benefiting the agency.

Ethical concerns in and about such a compensation arrangement are apparent and, judging by the ongoing agency mega-mergers and subsequent squabbling from advertisers about what constitutes "fair value" for advertising service, still quite real.

7. *Finally, the underlying uncertainty regarding the outcome of the advertising process leaves it wide open for differing interpretations of the same event.*

We will not tax the reader with needless repetition here, but encourage the rereading of Principle 3 in Chapter 1. As long-time advertising observer Edward Buxton noted:

> The advertising business is rife . . . with baffling intangibles. Nobody knows for sure how it works in many cases. The ad-making process itself is highly subjective, opinionated—and largely unprovable as to what is a good ad and what is not. Such pervasive uncertainties are breeding grounds for disquietude.[32]

And these pervasive uncertainties are breeding grounds for ethical ferment as well. For, given the ambiguity of the process, critics and supporters will "see" different advertising realities as individuals "see" different shapes in the classic inkblot test.

If, for example, a critic and a supporter assess such topics as *advertising to children* and *advertising of cigarettes* the following may result: In *one* "reality" these activities can be seen as a highly principled meshing of the self-interests of sellers and buyers in a strictly voluntary relationship; while in *another,* they can be seen as the unprincipled actions of manipulation and exploitation involving a crafty communicator and a hapless, if not helpless, audience.

PERSPECTIVES ON THE ETHICAL DIMENSIONS OF ADVERTISING PRACTICE

At this point some observations seem in order:

1. These seven areas of ethical confrontation are likely to be an ongoing presence for advertising practitioners and critics for the foreseeable future.

2. Some of these areas of concern are simply not high on advertising's ethical agenda. For example, studies by Rotzoll and Christians as well as Hunt and Chonko[33] have revealed that practitioners' primary areas of concern are: (a) agency/client/vendor relations, and (b) the advertising message.

   At the very least, these don't touch such sensitive areas as advertising as a third party with the media, and advertising as the seeker rather than the sought.

3. Therefore, critics will tend to regard advertising practice as *unprincipled* to the extent that (a) they regard advertising practice in any of these areas as *not* being based on ethical principles and/or (b) that the ethical principles that the practitioners *do* choose to invoke to support their decisions are different than those the critics would deem appropriate.

   Now, what principles *do* practitioners bring into play? Based on observation and the findings of research, they would seem to be:

(I) The *personal* criteria of individuals—advertisers, agency people, media personnel—that frequently involve some standards of *fairness,* often based on variations of the "Golden Rule," the "Golden Mean," and so on, as well as such *prima facie* (deontological) ideals as "Don't lie," etc.

   Following this reasoning, it is obvious to contend that the advertising business contains many principled *people;* yet, there is no assurance that these highly individualistic criteria will have an impact on the overall ethical standards and performance of the business, nor that they have been well thought-out by these individuals in terms of the arabesques of "real world" application.

(II) The level of *formal* principles embodied in a host of codes, guidelines, federal, state, and local regulations. Some examples:

◆ The American Advertising Federation and its predecessor have offered a set of principles from the early 1900s, with the most recent revision in 1984. The American Association of Advertising Agencies has provided similar standards.

◆ The guidelines and codes of dozens of trade associations, ranging from the American Wine Association through the National Swimming Pool Institute.

◆   The gatekeeping activities of the various media, including the standards of individual magazines, newspapers, television and radio stations, as well as the now somewhat less vigorous activities of the networks' commercial clearance offices.

◆   The National Advertising Review Board, without question the business's most serious self-regulatory effort, offers some normative guidelines in areas such as children and women, but generally operates *post hoc.*

Ethical thinking at this level of formal standards seems largely deontological, involving the assumption of basic truths that should be applied to all—do this, don't do that, etc.—some very general, some quite specific.

Several observations in this critical area:

1.   Historically, advertising business efforts at self-regulation have only been spurred by the threat of government regulation, which in turn tends to wax and wane with the political winds, and, therefore, provides an unstable platform for ongoing ethical standards. Currently, for example, there is a relative lull in regulatory activity at the federal level. The resulting vacuum is being filled in part by vigorous state activity.

2.   The NARB represents a serious and now institutionalized effort, but it is limited as an ethical force by its predominately *post hoc* functions as well as lack of exposure to the general public.

There are several *assets* to the use of these relatively formal standards for ethical decision making:

◆   They do provide touchstones for practice, if utilized.

◆   They provide the business with showpieces to promote their good works and to ward off potential regulation.

◆   There is likely to be some thoughtful discussion of ethical principles and their application to everyday practice in the developing of the principles, codes, etc.

The *limitations*, however, are equally apparent:

◆   The stipulations of the codes are sometimes too general (e.g., "advertising shall tell the truth, and shall reveal significant facts, the omission of which would mislead the public"[34]) to be readily transferred to moment-to-moment decision making.

◆   No matter how well-intentioned, they are often not part of the mind-set of the working practitioner where ethical decision making is most critical. (At a recent meeting of a chapter of the Public Relations Society of America, for example, one of the authors asked the practitioners if any could cite any of the principles of the thoughtful PRSA Code of Professional Standards. None could.)

(III) The level of *inherent business ethics.*

This is the ''world taken for granted'' level that is part of the enculturation process of those in the business. It is learned from watching the actions of others, hearing them explain decisions, and hearing and reading pronouncements from the trade organizations.

In advertising the ethical system is often expressed in terms of ''market forces,'' based on classical liberal thinking and rationalized in the ethical sphere by the concept of *utilitarianism,* the greatest good for the greatest number based on some notion of cost/benefit analysis. One common variation is that pursuing self-interest will result in the good of the whole—''as if by an invisible hand,'' to return to Adam Smith's well-traveled phrase. Thus, the system is assumed to be self-corrective, and ''If they don't like the advertising we do, they won't buy the product, and we'll be punished at the cash register.'' A representative statement is found in the American Association of Advertising Agency's response to a government inquiry regarding the question of whether limits should be imposed on the number of commercials in children's programming.

> The AAAA's position is that advertising self-regulation provides adequate safeguards against advertising abuses; that advertising does not harm children and that, therefore, there is no need to protect them from it; and that if a program has ''too many'' commercials, children will stop watching it. In sum, market forces will serve the interest of children by naturally regulating what is broadcast to them.[35]

The classical liberal heritage is clear—''market forces'' will regulate—''naturally.''

Thus, the primary asset of the use of utilitarianism as the working ethic for the advertising business is its use to rationalize the entire market system of which advertising is a part. And it is, of course, a system that can be quite appropriate as an ethical touchstone when the ''greatest good for the greatest number'' can be estimated.

But therein, we believe, lies the central flaw of the system for much day-do-day advertising practice centered on ethical issues dealing with the business's crucial product—the advertisement. For, given the difficulty in determining the advertising outcome that has been discussed so frequently through this book, there are serious problems in predicting the outcome in most advertising situations.

Thus the central irony, with advertising's predominate ethical system (utilitarianism) often being incompatible with its primary product (ads).

A NORMATIVE PERSPECTIVE ON ADVERTISING'S ETHICAL MILIEU

We again return to the premise that advertising will continue to be criticized in the ethical arena for either being unprincipled or by utilizing principles seen as inadequate for the task. As we have suggested, deontological principles (no concern over effects—absolute standards) and utilitarianism (concern with effects) are all found in the business to varying degrees, with utilitarianism dominant as a rationale for ongoing practice and deontological principles used as the primary critical weapons. As Donald Robin and R. Eric Reidenbach observe:

> Of the two dominant ethical traditions, deontology is favored by many moral philosophers today. Further, deontological reasoning offers many people who are critical of marketing an approach for justifying their attacks. Utilitarianism, the other major tradition, has been attacked by moral philosophers because it seems to suggest certain untenable outcomes when applied to particular hypothetical situations. Utilitarian arguments are used historically to provide much of the ethical justification for the modern economic systems of capitalistic democracies.[36]

Now, considering what we have learned, we offer several observations for the student's consideration:

1. Deontological thinking, with a dash of fairness, seems perfectly adequate for agency/client/vendor encounters—e.g., don't lie to suppliers, honor contracts, deal with others as you would like to have them deal with you, etc.
2. But to deal adequately with the full range of ethical quandaries outlined in the previous pages, there can be seen to be a need to:

◆   Not rely on the *randomness* of individual ethical systems.
◆   Not rely on the *formalities* of codes or the *verities* of the regulatory and self-regulatory winds, which are often not part of the mind-set of individuals in day-to-day decision making.
◆   Not become overly comfortable with *utilitarianism,* to the degree that it is often uncritically assumed in day-to-day practice.

At a normative level, then, one could suggest that a serious attempt be made to modify the current ethical climate at the *individual firm* level with a more systematic injection of principles of *fairness* into the system, to compensate for the abstractness and lack of flexibility in many codes and guidelines, and the lack of certainty in predicting utilitarian outcomes.

This would, of course, be a long-term effort and would only become a force if there were enough advertisers, agencies, and media who:

◆   Recognize advertising's ethical performance as a problem.
◆   See it on the larger scale of areas of inherent ethical encounter described in this chapter.
◆   Want to do something about it.

Perhaps, however, the ethical reexamination that seems to have been under way in this country since the late Reagan years may provide an appropriate seedbed for such an initiative.

One option could be the establishment of an *ethical ombudsman* within interested firms, who could essentially represent the consumer in the advertising transaction, introducing the arguably missing dimension of fairness in some persistent way.

Why might a firm take such action? Certainly, many would not, but:

◆ The resulting actions and publicity could prove good business in an increasingly skeptical marketplace.

◆ Such an action would lend itself to effective public relations among employees, stockholders, government officials, consumer organizations, etc.

◆ Such a principled action could appeal to a high company official with compatible individual ethics.

There could be at least three principle benefits:

1. Such an action would at least assure a raising of ethical issues that are not currently assumed under the easy and frequently unexamined assumptions of market utilitarianism.

2. There would seem likely gains through a raising of consciousness on the part of individuals within the firm with, potentially, greater sensitivity to virtually all the likely areas of ethical confrontation.

3. The ongoing presence of the ethical ombudsman would assure that the enculturation process of the firm includes ethical thinking. The firm would be saying, to existing and new employees, ''We take ethics seriously here.''

SUMMARY

Advertising is frequently assailed as being unprincipled in an ethical sense by critics and undervalued by the public in various polls. Yet practitioners point to their enforced social responsibility through codes, guidelines, government regulations, as well as their various voluntary good works through the Advertising Council, special task forces to deal with social issues, and so forth. Advertising, it is contended, will continue to confront ethical issues because:

1. The advertising business is rationalized primarily by a classical liberal ethic.

2. The advertising message is one-sided communication, with the inherent potential of deception by omission.
3. The purpose of all advertising is to cause us to think or act in accordance with the advertiser's intent.
4. Frequently, advertising seeks out individuals rather than we seeking it.
5. Advertising continues to be a controversial third party with the media.
6. The agency commission system continues to reward agencies for what they buy rather than what they produce.
7. That underlying uncertainty of the advertising process leaves it open to differing interpretations of the same event.

Advertising practitioners seem to operate on the ethical level of (a) individual criteria, (b) the level of formal principles embodied in codes, and (c) the workday ethic of utilitarianism. It was proposed that a presence of fairness was needed to overcome the limitations inherent in each of the present levels.

ENDNOTES

1. Stephen Fox, *The Mirror Makers* (New York: Vintage Books, 1985), p. 206.
2. Robert L. Heilbroner, "Advertising as Agitprop," *Harpers,* January 1986, p. 71.
3. Richard W. Pollay, "The Distorted Mirror," *Journal of Marketing,* April 1986, p. 18.
4. Howard Luck Gossage, *Is There Any Hope for Advertising?* (Champaign, IL: University of Illinois Press, 1987).
5. "Gallup Poll," Champaign-Urbana *News-Gazette,* August 15, 1985, p. 5.
6. *U. S. News & World Report,* February 23, 1987.
7. *Time,* May 25, 1987.
8. David Rankin, "A State of Incivility," *Newsweek,* February 8, 1988, p. 10.
9. Cal Thomas, "Lack of Moral Values 'Trickling Up,'" Champaign-Urbana *News-Gazette,* June 23, 1988, p. A-4.
10. Fox, p. 108.
11. "Burnett's *Pro Bono* Through the Years," *The Burnettwork,* May/June 1988, p. 5.
12. See William Leiss, Stephen Kline and Sut Ghally, *Social Communication in Advertising* (New York: Methuen, 1986), chap. 12.
13. Clifford G. Christians, Kim B. Rotzoll and Mark Fackler, *Media Ethics* (New York: Longman, 1987), p. xviii.
14. Daniel Pope, *The Making of Modern Advertising* (New York: Basic Books, 1983).
15. "Too Much Sugar?" *Consumer Reports,* March 1978, p. 139.
16. "Shampoos," *Consumer Reports,* September 1984, p. 192

17. *Consumer Reports* promotion piece, "We Have Two Free Buyer's Guides. . . . ," n.d.
18. *Ibid.*
19. "How to Save $2500 a Year in the Supermarket," *Consumer Reports,* March 1988, pp. 156-163.
20. Roger Draper, "The Faithless Shepherd," *New York Review,* June 26, 1986, p. 18.
21. Fox, p. 117.
22. Leiss, *et al.,* p. 3.
23. "Beer. How It Influences the Games We Play and Watch," *Sports Illustrated,* August 8, 1988, p. 70.
24. *Ibid.,* p. 78.
25. Judann Dagnoli, "RJR Aims New Ads at Young Smokers," *Advertising Age,* July 18, 1988, p. 3.
26. Scott Hume, "'Most Hated' Ads: Feminine Hygiene," *Advertising Age,* July 18, 1988, p. 3.
27. Bob Garfield, "Ad Review," *Advertising Age,* October 19, 1987, p. 32.
28. *ACSH News & Views,* May/June 1986, pp. 1, 8-10.
29. "Data Bank Driven Binding," *Marketing Communications* (March 1985), reprint by R. R. Donnelly & Sons Company, n.d.
30. Stan Freberg, "Irtnog Revisited," *Advertising Age,* August 1, 1988, p. 32.
31. Gossage, *op cit.*
32. Ed Buxton, "Fear & Loathing on Agency Row," *Adweek,* September 5, 1983, p. 34.
33. Kim B. Rotzoll and Clifford G. Christians, "Advertising Agency Practitioners' Perceptions of Ethical Decisions," *Journalism Quarterly,* August 1980, pp. 425-431; and Shelby D. Hunt and Lawrence B. Chonko, "Ethical Problems of Advertising Agency Executives," *Journal of Advertising,* vol. 16, no. 4, 1987, pp. 16-24.
34. American Advertising Federation, "Advertising Principles of American Business," reprinted in Christians *et al.,* p. 221.
35. Patty Siebert, "AAAA Files Kid-Vid Comments with FCC," *The 4As Washington Newsletter,* January 1988, p. 2.
36. Donald P. Robin and Eric Reidenbach, "Social Responsibility, Ethics, and Marketing Strategy: Closing the Gap Between Concept and Application," *Journal of Marketing,* January 1987, p. 46.

AFTERWORD

In 1958, a perfectly wonderful book was published called *Madison Avenue, U.S.A.* Among his hundreds of interviews with the leading lights of advertising practice, journalist Martin Mayer held a session with J. Walter Thompson's legendary James Webb Young. Mayer recounts:

> Early in 1956, *Fortune* magazine sent a girl researcher up to see Jim Young at the Thompson company. . . . "She wanted to know about all the changes in the advertising business in the last twenty-five years," Young says. "When I told her there hadn't been any, she nearly fell off her chair. But it's true."[1]

This is a useful perspective to begin this tentative exploration of advertising's future with which we close the book. For, as we have argued elsewhere,[2] it can be contended that advertising's basic institutional forms were in place prior to 1915—i.e., the relationships between advertisers, agencies, and media; the agency commission system; the dependency of the media on advertising revenue; criticism and reform. Thus, it is not surprising to find that two recent crystal-ball treatments of advertising by prominent practitioners give the distinct impression that the advertising of the future will be much like the advertising of the present—only more so.[3]

Specifically, the dominant word is *specialization*. There is agreement that increasingly "narrow" media forms—e.g., cable television, specialized magazines, various forms of direct marketing—will enable marketers to direct their advertising to individuals who are most likely to be interested in the products or services (some estimate 75 percent of the consumer sector will be dominated by the latter). This trend has at least the potential of lowering advertising's irritation factor, caused predominately by involuntary exposure to the advertising of personally irrelevant products and services. But there is agreement also that there will be *more* advertising, perhaps twice as much, caused primarily by shorter television commercials, but also by expansion to other media forms—e.g., motion picture theaters, prerecorded videotapes.

176

Thus, although the irritation level may be lowered due to greater efficiency in the advertiser/prospect/medium mix, it may be raised by relentless, frequently involuntary, exposure to special pleading in all media.

It is clear that advertising, to one degree or another, reflects changes in its culture. (This is not to dismiss the argument that advertising may be a shaper of some of those changes, but advertising, as any enduring institution of a society, must remain linked to the central ideas—i.e., Hamilton's "common sense"—shared by the constituencies to which it relates.) Thus formulated, some forces *outside* the direct control of business, with the potential to shape future advertising thought and practice, include:

Population factors. By the turn of the century the much discussed "baby boomers" will be between their mid-30s and early 50s, with predictable effects upon institutions. This is a group much sought after by marketers due to their sheer numbers and overall affluence, and they will clearly continue to influence the subjects and tone of advertising messages.

The growth of the Hispanic and non-white sectors of the population will continue, with more advertising attention directed toward their consumption potentials. A related factor is the presence of so-called functional illiteracy. Aside from the ominous strains on the social fabric, this will clearly influence such advertising-related factors as media selection.

It has been estimated that in the relatively near future 75 percent of women may be in the work force, possibly reinforcing the trend toward smaller households and accentuating advertisers' attempts to reach an increasingly elusive population segment.

Finally, it is reasonable to expect the average life span to lengthen, through medical advances, better nutritional and exercise habits, and the diffusion of Health Maintenance Organizations (HMOs) promoting preventative medicine and health-care practices.

Technological changes. Inventions, of course, do not arrive at fixed intervals. Even when potential is present, a host of economic, political, or cultural factors may keep an innovation from being fully developed. (If much of the futurist literature of the 1940s was to be believed, we should all be commuting by personal autogyros and living in fully robotized homes.)

What seems safe at this juncture is to project a twenty-first century strongly infused with microcircuitry, thus facilitating communication and reformulating the workplace of home and factory. For better or for worse, this will presumably enable more personalized persuasion appeals. Also, the potential liberation from some of the rigors of the workplace will provide opportunities for an even more significant emphasis on the utilization and marketing of the leisure industries.

Regulatory climate. As we have seen, there have been three relatively clearly defined periods of intense regulatory activity in relation to advertising: the first two decades of the century; the 1930s; late 1960s through the mid-1970s. As the regulatory hand is lightened, excesses eventually emerge, thus leading to a new cycle of confinement. Certainly, the Reagan administration's *laissez-faire* economic philosophies have supported deregulatory practices. Yet, as history would indicate, there is every reason to expect a future tightening of the reins. At the moment, this seems particularly likely in the areas of special audiences (particularly children) and the potential for abuse with unregulated cable systems. The potential problems in ever more personalized direct marketing efforts are also apparent.

Global imperatives.   The notion of Spaceship Earth is not as fashionable now as it was 20 years ago. Yet, as we will shortly detail in another context, the specters of overpopulation, poverty, hunger, and pollution are present for all wishing to look. These landscapes can give pause to individuals pondering the allocation of planetary resources by market mechanisms that at times seem deadened to the imbalances of the haves and have-nots. The advertising business is not insensitive to these issues, and there is much good work done at the advertiser, agency, and media levels. Yet, these offerings are minuscule in relation to the priorities of consumption. One may pause to realize that there is now more than $2 billion spent advertising and promoting cigarettes in this country, and speculate what good might ensue if the same amount was spent to encourage programs meant to lead to *healthy* ends.

"Worldview."   Certainly, as Idea Systems——>Institutions, it is clear that advertising enjoys full flower as an institution under idea systems encompassing such assumptions about "human nature" as the positive values of self-interest, competition, and the belief that the private pursuit of profit will ultimately lead to societal gain. Should we change these ideas, the expectations and tolerations of advertising will change apace. Recent history would suggest an eventual swing of the pendulum back toward ideas more compatible with the modern liberal agenda and its philosophical thrust of social responsibility. In this case, advertising would adapt, albeit in a somewhat more regulated state. Yet, there is the possibility that what we witnessed in the Reagan years was a true watershed—a reaffirmation of conservative, classical liberal, free enterprise, individualistic values that may serve as the idea model for years to come, as the New Deal did for forty years and more. In either case, advertising seems destined to flourish, as both systems still rely heavily on our continuing ethic of private consumption.

In many ways, the heart of this issue hinges on the individual as a decision maker. For, as we have seen, advertising flourishes in economic systems that allow considerable latitude for individuals to make their own decisions. Thus, although advertising can be logically associated with the market and capitalism, it can also exist in various mixed economies (such as those of Europe, the Middle East, and, now, even the People's Republic of China and the Soviet Union) as long as individual decision making is encouraged, or at least tolerated.

The broadest question, then, is likely to be to what extent can societies through the last decade of this century and beyond continue to allow individual decision making instead of some type of government direction? Matters such as these will put this fundamental ideological question to a test:

ENERGY. The world has finite energy resources of a natural variety. And there is an enormous gap between the use of those limited resources in the "have" versus the "have-not" countries. Can we allow individuals to continue to call their own energy shots through their purchases, or will elimination, or at least curtailment, of opportunities be necessary?

ECOLOGY. Can we survive as a living planet? What price of individual and corporate freedom are we willing to pay to attempt to restore clean seas and waterways, healthy air, drinkable water, non-toxic environments? Again, can we continue to allow individual consumption, even though the end result may be a depletion of our precious ecosystem?

POVERTY/HUNGER. A relatively small percentage of this planet's population is well-off, while the remainder teeters at or near the brink of life. Can we continue to live with this staggering inequality? If not, what can be done, and how might market systems—based on individual self-interest—be affected?

In a very fundamental sense, then, the answers to these and related questions will determine the *presence* of advertising in the remaining years of this century and beyond.

As for its *impact,* that, of course, will continue to be the stuff of debate, due in no small part to differing assumptions about rationality, competition, the proper dimensions of self-interest, the state of the economy, and the proper role of regulation, as developed in Chapter 3.

> Increasingly regulated on one side and increasingly scorned or ignored by consumers on the other, advertising has been shooting smaller weapons at a more garrisoned target. Along with most other contemporary institutions, advertising now has trouble finding anybody to believe it.[4]

So concluded historian Stephen Fox in assessing advertising's modern relationship to society, which, he contends, reached its peak of influence in the 1920s. Of course we can refer back to Schudson's perspective of capitalist realism (Chapter 4) and its understanding that advertising does not *need* to be believed in order to selectively reinforce parts of our value system.

On reflection, then, a realistic assessment of advertising in society, now, or in at least the foreseeable future, should require at least the following questions:

◆   What, *precisely,* is the advertising issue under discussion, given due consideration for the tendency to generalize from very specific pieces of the advertising experience?

◆   What are the essential assumptions about human nature, the relationship between the individual and society, etc., that are held by the contending parties?

◆   Which set of assumptions, or which combination, do *you* find most compatible?

For a host of reasons that we hope we've made clear, advertising seems destined to remain ambiguous, structured in many cases by its own internal complexities and by the interests and passions of those observing it.

Daniel Boorstin once observed, ''If we consider democracy as a set of institutions which aim to make everything available to anybody, it would not be an overstatement to describe advertising as the characteristic rhetoric of democracy.''[5] It is our hope that these chapters have provided you with some perspectives, and an array of analytical tools, to come to a clearer understanding of this fascinating rhetoric.

ENDNOTES

1. Martin Mayer, *Madison Avenue, U.S.A.* (New York: Harper & Brothers, 1958), p. 21.

2. Charles H. Sandage, Vernon Fryburger, and Kim B. Rotzoll, *Advertising Theory and Practice* (New York: Longman, 1989), chap. 2.

3. ''Advertising in the Year 2000,'' *AAAA Newsletter* (New York: American Association of Advertising Agencies, December, 1984). The general thrust of this thinking is also found in Kim B. Rotzoll, ''The Now and Future Advertising Education,'' *Journalism Educator,* Fall 1985.

4. Stephen Fox, *The Mirror Makers* (New York: William Morrow and Co., 1984), p. 380.

5. Daniel G. Boorstin, ''Advertising and American Civilization,'' in *Advertising and Society,* Yale Brozen, ed. (New York: New York University Press, 1974), pps. 11-12.

INDEX